SONS
OF HARVARD

By Toby Marotta

SONS OF HARVARD
THE POLITICS OF HOMOSEXUALITY

SONS
OF HARVARD

Gay Men from
the Class of 1967

TOBY MAROTTA

QUILL

New York   1983

The lines from Roger McGough's "At Lunchtime a Story of Love" copyright
© 1967 by Roger McGough from *The Mersey Sound*, Penguin 1967. Used
by permission.

Library of Congress Cataloging in Publication Data

Marotta, Toby.
 Sons of Harvard.

 Originally published: New York : Morrow, 1982.
 1. Homosexuals, Male—United States—Biography.
2. Harvard University. Class of 1967. I. Title.
HQ75.7.M37 1983   306.7′662′0922   83-3000
ISBN 0-688-01020-2
ISBN 0-688-01907-2 (pbk.)

Printed in the United States of America

First Quill Edition

1 2 3 4 5 6 7 8 9 10

For Mother Harvard—
And My Own Mother

Harvard College

Class of 1967

10th Anniversary Report

CAMBRIDGE

Printed for the Class

1977

(TOBY) ROBERT PAYNE MAROTTA. *Home,* 934 Carleton St., Berkeley, Calif. 94710

Rusty Kothavala and I worked together on a number of student-faculty committees when I was in college, and our collegial relationship grew closer when I went on to graduate school at Harvard. Both of us were greatly affected by the challenge to traditional values posed by the counterculture and the New Left in the late 1960s, and as the counterculture gave birth to the gay and women's liberation movements at the turn of the decade, each of us was moved to acknowledge the importance of our homosexuality and to make it an integral part of a moral and fulfilling life-style. First as lovers, then as partners hopeful of a life together, we inched away from our previous professional preoccupations. While I taught sections in government, social policy, and education, Rusty turned his interest in mineralogy, adventure, and India into a business, Crystals of India, importer of mineral specimens for museums and collectors. Once the business was established, I stopped my dissertation on the politics of school desegregation and began a thesis on the politics of homosexuality. Last year we moved to California and now Rusty is extending his expertise to gems while I'm revising my thesis into a book on gay political activity and working at the Center for Homosexual Education, Evaluation and Research at San Francisco State University on a study of the effects of decriminalizing sodomy. We love living in the west and enjoy letting Crystals of India take us periodically to Europe and India.

Foreword

I wrote about my life with great candor for the class report because I was a very political homosexual. I had spent years studying gay politics. At the beginning, I'm sure, my political fervor stemmed more than anything else from the difficulty I had accepting my own homosexuality. Then I began to see that I could make a contribution to society and earn some money by helping people understand how homosexuals of my generation are transforming gay life.

I don't know whether my own process of coming to terms with homosexuality has been more or less difficult than most people's, but I do know that it is unusual in that it has been heavily influenced by a new conception of politics. There have always been people who have been able to repress and to divert their homosexual feelings. There have also been individuals who have developed covert but not necessarily unhealthy or unethical ways of accommodating their homosexual desires. But most with strong homosexual feelings have suffered to some extent because of ignorance and prejudice about homosexuality. Older generations of homosexuals have tended to adjust to the world without making a big fuss about the problems they've encountered. What sets my generation apart is our belief that we can make things easier for ourselves, other homosexuals, and everyone else by being very open and very honest about our homosexuality. Indeed, having been taught to take Freudian premises as implicit assumptions, we believe that everyone would be better off—more comfortable and fulfilled as individuals and more successful in their relationships—if people were more informed, open, and honest about all of their feelings.

The more politically-minded of us think that airing matters traditionally considered private is political, both because that will influence the power dynamics in human relationships and hence the civility of day-to-day existence, and because it will affect the public opinion responsible for the way social and political issues emerge and are dealt with in American society. Hence, ours is a new genre of political activity, one best called liberationist politics. Where members of previous generations have given the country leadership as it has traditionally been understood, endowing it with unprecedentedly high levels of technical expertise, military might, and material living standards, we have focused our attention on the nature of personal growth, relationships, and cultural evolution, believing that we can contribute most by improving the quality of modern life. By making everyone more knowledgeable about sexuality and more sophisticated about human variations in intimacy, we hope to reduce if not eliminate unnecessary suffering, mental illness, personal and social irresponsibility, prejudice, inappropriate laws, social conflict, violence, and injustice. Our aim is to make contemporary living more courteous, neighborly, equitable, and fulfilling.

In outlook, if not always age, we are children of the sixties. We're homosexual members of that generation whose sensibility was shaped by the decade that began with the dash and hope of the Kennedys and ended with the challenges and withdrawal of the hippies. If nothing else, the sheer speed of this change in zeitgeist stirred us to rethink conventional assumptions about how people should live. So we sought out adults who would pay attention to us and tried to learn from them. We lionized older people who seemed to have worked out life-styles that permitted them all the good things while accommodating their self-expression. We let our eyes be opened by beats, beatniks, hippies, and Yippies. We strove to understand the cultural critiques of Charles

Reich, Philip Slater, Robert Theobald, Theodore Roszak, Alvin Toffler, and Carlos Castaneda. We read existential philosophy and explored avant-garde therapies. We grew romantic with the Beatles and sexy with the Stones. And because we came to believe it less important to abide by convention than openly to enjoy dimensions of our selves and our relationships that society said we should ignore, repress, restrain, downplay, and keep private—sex, the senses, our psyches and emotions—we called ourselves, and were called, countercultural.

Those of us in the counterculture who were most political called ourselves liberationists and made it our goal to enlighten mainstream culture. We saw that many common prejudices were nothing but myths, really. We realized that people were often unhappy because they had internalized popular misconceptions about individuals who had unusual backgrounds, looked odd, expressed themselves in noncomforming ways, or enjoyed unconventional pursuits. We were especially concerned about those who suffered because of the emphasis placed on certain kinds of achievement, which seemed not only to make us and many others overly obsessive and competitive in our work, but also to produce big, seemingly unnecessary, walls between people. What we wanted in society was more "human interaction"—more empathy, intimacy, honesty, candor, and passion.

During the late sixties and early seventies, the war in Vietnam loomed so large in our lives that many of us turned our major attention to that. But those of us who came to believe that working to live in more natural and humane ways was as important, and political, as being involved with public issues, became ever more deeply involved in personal matters. This included a lot of us with strong homosexual feelings that we had difficulty integrating into our lives, politics, and pictures of the future. While most of our contemporaries, often after brief periods of experimentation with life as singles, sex before marriage, open relationships, living together, marijuana, hallucinogenic drugs, and therapy, turned their attention to more traditional paths (training for the professions, making money, building careers, establishing security, getting married, raising children, contributing to community affairs, exercising influence, acquiring status, and enjoying friends, family members, neighbors, and colleagues), we worked to reorder our lives—and the world around us—so that we would experience minimum discomfort on account of our homosexuality. Indeed, so that we could truly enjoy it.

Hence, in my own life I saw the story of a new generation of homosexuals, those I wrote about at length in *The Politics of Homosexuality.* The counterculture gave us the idea that it was good to express ourselves fully and freely and important to respect others who did the same. The New Left led us to believe that we could protect and promote these ideals by joining together. Working for sexual, sex-role, and indeed human liberation alongside feminists and cultural radicals of every kind, we called ourselves gay liberationists. Unlike our gay political forebears, who styled themselves homophile leaders and took their cues from the civil rights movement, we strove not to persuade the public that homosexuals were just like heterosexuals (though we felt that, basically, they were) but to define, embolden, and organize "gay people," not least so that others would be able to *see* just what it meant to be gay.

Liberationist gay political activity required us to devote an extraordinary amount of attention to our sexuality. Realizing that one is homosexual, which is often only a matter of accepting that term for feelings one has deep down inside, is only a first step in the process of coming to terms with and revealing one's homosexuality, known in gay life as "coming out." Involving oneself with other homosexuals—which is necessary whether or not one believes in liberationist politics if one wants to have kindred spirits when it comes to one's deepest longings—is often a much more intimidating task. For those of us who approached that task with the idealism so characteristic of the counterculture, it was especially challenging, for when we looked for other homosexuals we had a hard time finding them. What most of us saw was only a shadowy and illicit homosexual underworld—a world of eccentric bachelors and effeminate characters, of unsavory public sex scenes and dingy bars and steam baths, of secretive homosexuals and upset relationships, of indirection and inhibition, confusion and conflict, discomfort, trauma, and tragedy.

The term "gay community" was our creation. We wanted to replace what seemed like an almost invisible and often unhealthy subculture with something that would be as much a symbol and a haven for homosexuals as "Black community" was for "Negroes." Indeed, we wanted to make it possible for all people with strong homosexual feelings to embrace their homosexuality and to relate to other homosexuals with our own countercultural appreciation of openness and honesty, intimacy and solidarity, attention to personal growth and respect for social diversity, intelligent living and equality of good feeling. Homosexuals with countercultural values we called "liberated," meaning freed from traditional ways of thinking about and dealing with homosexual desires.

This job of gay-community building turned out to be much more difficult than most of us had anticipated. For one thing, we discovered that traditional gay life was so multifaceted that, at a minimum, we had to distinguish between very different lesbian and gay male subcultures as bases for community. The existing gay male subculture revolved heavily around sex, and since this was a realm that prudish parents, socially conservative educational institutions, and personal hang-ups had left most of us rather naïve about, we found, of all things, that we had to become liberated sexually in order to build socially and politically. Dealing with other male homosexuals involved handling attractions that had traditionally been expressed only, or at least mainly, sexually. And to have credibility with those enamored of existing gay male mores, we had not only to talk about sexual promiscuity sensibly, but to demonstrate that we were comfortable with it personally.

In organizing male homosexuals, we worked to reinvigorate traditional gay male patterns. As the gay male subculture diverged from mainstream culture most dramatically in the place it made for recreational sex and in its infrastructure of sex-related customs, pastimes, and institutions, so we made enlightened promiscuity an ideal of liberated gay male community. Indeed, we made skill at enjoying sexual variety, both as singles and in the context of sustained relationships, the measure of liberated gay men. Individuals willing to promote the idea that people should adopt countercultural perspectives on homosexuality and gay life we called gay liberationists. Radical gay liberationists we saw as fighters for sexual freedom for everybody.

I couldn't even have conceived of being a liberated, liberationist-minded gay man back in the mid-sixties when I was a Harvard undergraduate. I was terribly conflicted about my homosexuality throughout high school and college. Because I couldn't admit that I was homosexual, I was neither comfortable with myself nor mature in my dealings with others. I saw effeminacy, indeed idiosyncratic behavior of every kind, as somehow queer. I was afraid to let anyone—even my secret sexual partners—think that I knew what homosexuality was. I avoided any male whose looks or actions struck me as suspicious.

The first person to open my eyes in a way that made me more accepting of my homosexuality was Rusty. He was so at ease with his homosexual feelings and so judicious in the ways he expressed them that I didn't even know what his sexual preferences were until after we had become fast friends. Through Rusty I saw that a man could be gay and yet also manly, self-assured, professional, popular, idealistic, shrewd, and tough. It was our friendship that enabled me to be honest with myself, and then with him, and then with others. It was our relationship that permitted me to refocus my graduate studies on the politics of homosexuality, and then to involve myself in gay politics and gay professionalism, and then to work out my conflicts about homosexuality and gay life.

All that I learned from Rusty was reinforced by what I found in the gay leaders I studied. To portray them accurately, I thought it important not only to find out about their philosophical outlooks and political activities, but to understand them well enough to draw conclusions about the health and morality of the ways in which they lived. They impressed me so much that even before my research was written up, I declared myself one of them, albeit one with a special mission: I wanted to make myself not only a historian and interpreter of gay political activity, but a chronicler and assessor of the changes in gay life that were coming about as more and more homosexuals became liberated.

Only two of the gay leaders I got to know during the course of my field research had gone to Harvard, and that, plus the absence of fellow liberationist-minded gays I encountered in the University, led me to believe that homosexual Harvard men were probably a good deal less countercultural and political than homosexuals elsewhere. I speculated that this was because they attached more importance to social approval and professional success and were reluctant to forgo or to risk losing these by associating themselves in any way publicly with something so disreputable as homosexuality. This had been true of me until Rusty and I began to question traditional views and values and to experiment with countercultural living. Then I meshed new personal and political ideals with Harvard-cherished social and professional ambition by working to make myself an authority on gay life. But for a long time I was certain that this set me apart from other Harvard homosexuals, and certainly from my college classmates.

Those fellow members of the class of 1967 were important to me in a way that perhaps only those who have attended Harvard College can truly appreciate. Because Harvard undergraduates who at all imbibe the ethos of the University and the Establishment are led to believe that the members of their college class are the cream of those who graduated from high school the year they did. Even graduates who come to see a lot of snobbishness and provincialism in this sense of Harvard people being "the best and the brightest," if they retain or recapture any sense of conventional ambition, find it difficult not to view the accomplishments of old classmates as standards against which to measure their own. Even as a countercultural and political homosexual, I couldn't completely shake the ghosts of my Harvard College classmates.

The University encourages this class and college chauvinism. Five years after graduation and every five years thereafter, the Alumni Office arranges for classmates to submit autobiographical updates for a report that is published and sent to every member of the class and to University officials interested in Harvard's "old-boy network." After the color of their covers, these reports are often referred to as "redbooks." For those who receive them over the years, they resemble nothing so much as a running *Who's Who* of the members of one's class.

In the spring of 1977, when I received a form asking for my contribution to the tenth-anniversary report of the Harvard College class of 1967, I had very mixed feelings. Though Rusty and I had moved from Cambridge to Berkeley, I was still enrolled in the University's Graduate School of Arts and Sciences, paying tuition to write up *in absentia* my research on gay politics. I felt that I had grown a lot personally but was far from having blossomed professionally. And I wasn't at all sure that Harvard people would approve of, let alone appreciate, how I was using my education.

My ambivalence was greater than it might have been for others in my situation because I had so loved and respected the University previously. As an undergraduate, I had all but moved to Cambridge from my home in nearby Medford because I found the Harvard community so exciting. I had immersed myself in undergraduate activities of every sort, gotten involved in the Greater Boston alumni network, been active in student government and elected a class marshal, and gone on to graduate programs at the Kennedy School of Government, then the Graduate School of Education, then Arts and Sciences. Because I was such a familiar figure on campus and such an ardent booster of the University, I was appointed permanent secretary of my class, the official link between it and the Alumni Office. I was the member of the class of '67 who solicited entries and wrote the preface for the fifth-anniversary report. Yet only five years later, because I was so unsure about what Harvard people would think of what I was doing and so disillusioned by the University's imperviousness to the issues being raised by outspoken homosexuals, I was ready to ignore the request for information issued by my successor as secretary . . . and yet not quite able to.

What most kept me from tossing the whole thing aside was an almost devilish impulse to show old classmates that the best and the brightest could also be the gayest. And my itch to "tell it like it was" was only quickened when I ran into Nick Bollman '67 shortly before Rusty and I moved west. Nick had been every bit the politico I was in college. He'd presented the same All-American persona and set out on the same paths into the Establishment. And he too had ended up a very liberated, liberationist-minded gay man.

Discovering that Nick's postcollegiate evolution had very much paralleled my own also made me suspect that there were other classmates whose lives had changed as ours had. I wondered if these included any of the really attractive ones. I was curious to see if I could ferret out anyone I had known and admired. I considered it political to try to bring homosexuals together. I didn't know what Nick was going to write for the class report, but I wanted my own entry to be both a wave and a prod to fellow travelers and a jolt to classmates with stereotypical biases about homosexuals. I submitted my squib, as I did most everything in those days, in the spirit of liberationist politics.

The results were surprisingly affirming. Shortly after the report was circulated, with my entry the only one to mention homosexuality, I began to hear from classmates eager to congratulate me for what I had done, most of them people I had known only casually back in college. During the next year and a half, thirteen classmates got in touch. Two who sent notes on Christmas cards and one who came to visit were heterosexual. Three who made contact said they were bisexual. The rest presented themselves as fellow gay men. Though each of these last was less public and political about his homosexuality than Nick and I were, all were liberated in that they were enjoying substantially homosexual lives in relatively open, healthy, and ethical ways.

Like a good gay liberationist, I explored the politics of the homosexual classmates who engaged me in correspondence and came to visit, and in every case tried to make them more political. I say "more political" because all of them were political in the sense that they believed that homosexuals were ignorantly stereotyped, and that institutions shouldn't discriminate against individuals on the basis of their sexual orientations, and that gay political activity was worthy of support. What they lacked or were less clear about was my own liberationist conviction that endeavors conventionally minded people thought purely personal, social, and educational were, in fact, very political.

Before long, I was proposing to make my next book one in which my classmates could do their political bit. I envisioned *Sons of Harvard* as a book of interviews that would complement *The Politics of Homosexuality* by showing how the social and political movements I had analyzed academically were manifested in the lives of real individuals. I wanted to illustrate not only how individuals with strong homosexual feelings, and those involved with them, were made to suffer unnecessarily because of popular ignorance and prejudice, but also how life had improved for homosexuals, their intimates, and everyone else as a result of the gay liberation movement. For all the diversity I found in the men who had gotten in touch, I saw in their lives the patterns of our generation.

Six of these classmates agreed to let me interview them. Four others were unwilling to talk for the record, but all but one of them encouraged me to proceed with the book and two offered to be of help behind the scenes. Yet these were all classmates who had seen my entry in the class report, and I wanted, in the name of our political venture, to extend a hand to peers who might have passed it by. Using the addresses listed in the redbook, I sent a letter describing my efforts and asking for volunteers to the 1,180 other living members of the class of '67 (ten had died). This group included one classmate with whom I had had a romantic affair in the early seventies and four others who I had heard were homosexual. In response I got four more interview subjects, none classmates I had known about previously.

In May of 1979, to tape interviews with the classmates who had volunteered to talk with me, I set out on a trip across the country. I saw myself not as a social scientist out to conduct research according to the accepted canons of my profession, but as a politically minded gay scholar ready to enhance, by some personal exploration, understanding gained from previous and ongoing research.

By the time I arrived back in Cambridge to conduct my final two interviews, I felt that the experiences I had had meeting, getting to know, and taping classmates revealed as much about our lives and times as did the conversations I had recorded. This, plus my feeling that interview transcripts introduced in the course of narrative would be more accessible to the general reader—and more eye-opening than a book of conventionally analyzed case studies to the intellectual one—led me to develop an unusual format for presenting my findings. I weave transcribed portions of my taped interviews into a personal chronicle, sometimes analytical, sometimes descriptive, but always intended mainly to help others understand how liberated gay men of my generation really think, actually relate, truly live.

Most of the dialogue in my chronicle is based on conversations with classmates recorded during my trip. The rest of the narrative, to the extent that it attempts to recapture scenes and shared experiences, is based on notes taken during my visits, recollections, and my judgment about how most usefully and appropriately to portray the personalities and life-styles of the men I profile. In most cases I have changed details to conceal their identities. Nick Bollman is the only classmate willing to join me in using real names, but the others have asked only that I disguise them enough to prevent dear ones who might be hurt from suffering embarrassment and to deter others from threatening them personally or professionally for being gay, or for being so honest about what that means. All of us believe that society has a lot to learn about homosexual lives such as ours, and from them.

The indented sections of text woven into the chronicle, each set apart from the narrative by small shields, have been transcribed verbatim from tape-recorded interviews and edited to eliminate repetition and to facilitate reading. Copies of letters and other written material have also been edited. Each of the ten classmates I feature has reviewed, amended, approved, and released his letter and transcript material. None has seen or taken any responsibility for the narrative. It is by me alone that readers are assured that this supplement to the tenth-anniversary report of the Harvard College class of 1967 is, as best I can present it, University-revered truth—*Veritas.*

Contents

Foreword 9

KEN RYAN 23

BEN MILLER 37

WILLKIE SCHOPENHAUER 68

MARTY BRENNER 85

SANDY ANDERSON 107

DAVID FREDRICK 148

NICK BOLLMAN 184

PETER FORRESTER 213

COTTIE ADAMS 228

PAUL DETROIT 250

Afterword 280

Acknowledgments 287

1

KEN RYAN

My plane to Los Angeles was late, but I didn't mind because I was feeling very good. I was off to see my old friend Ben Miller. I felt I had just made an old friend of Ken Ryan. Our interview had been an intimate experience.

Nothing at San Francisco International Airport dampened my euphoria. In fact, the airport was filled with dapper young men who reminded me of Ken, and I was sure that many of them would find much to identify with in his story. Every homosexual's life, like every human being's life, is unique in its specifics. Yet in almost every active American homosexual's life one finds common themes—patterns of ignorance, fear, struggle, and adaptation that most with strong homosexual desires experience as they come out.

Ken's coming-out story was very different from mine. Though we had both grown up in rather similar working-class suburbs of Boston, he had found it much more difficult to act upon his homosexual feelings. Yet once he had actually begun to have sex, he had had a much easier time making himself at home in gay bars and taking advantage of gay bathhouses. On the other hand, he'd been much later in arranging his professional life so that he could be open about his homosexuality even on the job. Thus far he'd worked only in large corporations, building a career in personnel management he cared very much about. In fact, he'd given up the good position he had in Boston only after becoming convinced that in San Francisco he would have the opportunity to be all that he wanted to be personally and socially, as well as all that he aspired to be professionally.

It is probably easier for homosexuals to feel completely fulfilled in San Francisco than in any other city in the world, for gay people constitute such a sizable percentage of the local population that they have an incomparable degree of social, economic, and political influence and hence a good measure of acceptance. In San Francisco, for example, a man can be single, have a rich gay social life, and still feel perfectly comfortable attending functions of the local Harvard Club. Other members might suspect that a bachelor is gay, but, like most San Franciscans, they will probably have been sufficiently exposed to homosexuals to know that most of them are perfectly civilized. Many, in fact, are as genteel and professional as Ken, who joined the Harvard Club of San Francisco soon after relocating. One might almost say that Ken came to San Francisco so that he could be a gay "Harvard man."

He had told me as much the very first time we got together, meeting for lunch at the Olympic Club during his second vacation in San Francisco, several months after he had seen my entry in the class report. From that point on, I knew that Ken's gay niche in San Francisco was going to be very different from my own. I had hooked up mainly with other politically minded gay men—members of the local chapter of the Gay Academic Union, homosexual students and others who went to rap groups at the Pacific Center for Human Growth in Berkeley (one of the first gay community centers), and gays from the East Bay whom I met at the White Horse, a funky bar located just down Telegraph Avenue from the Berkeley campus of the University of California. So that we could put all of our resources into our professional endeavors, Rusty and I had chosen to live thriftily in a small cottage in the Berkeley flats. More than anything else at that point, I was a very rebellious, very political graduate student working on the book that would explain my politics and my people to my professors. Outside the mineral business, which was a network scattered all over the country, the friends Rusty and I most enjoyed were other male homosexuals who shared our aspiration to build a community of earthy and entrepreneurial gay souls.

The gay set that attracted Ken was very different. Upon making his own move to the Bay Area, he arranged to share a large Victorian house in San Francisco's fancy Pacific Heights district with a gay man the same age who owned not only the house but several successful businesses "catering to the gay community." When he wanted to socialize, he went to the "piss elegant" gay bars near Union Street. When he wanted sex, he went to the "hot" baths at Eighth and Howard. The life Ken settled into was that of San Francisco's gay gentry.

To the extent that he was unhappy in this life, it was in the realm of love. Ken had never had a lover, something he confided during our first intimate conversation, and he had moved to San Francisco partly in hopes of finding "Mr. Right," whom he fantasized as being "just like one of the guys from college, only gay." I flinched whenever he used the term "Mr. Right," for it made me fear that he was one of those gay men who have great difficulty settling into sustained relationships, if only because—thanks to general social pressures and antihomosexual prejudice—they are kept for so long from having lovers, forced for so long to limit their homosexual yearnings to fantasy, that they have a hard time being realistic when becoming part of a same-sex couple finally seems feasible. Long years of fantasizing do little to prepare individuals for the negotiations and accommodations required of sustained relationships.

Partly because he was so intrigued with my own sustained relationship, Ken became friends with Rusty as well as with me. More than most of my political friends, he was fascinated with Rusty's tales of business and travel and impressed with his success as a mineral dealer. In addition, he felt right at home with Rusty's taste for fine living, his conservative views about individual responsibility and the economy, and his native gentility. With me, the root of continued contact was the Harvard connection. More than any of the other gay classmates who had responded to my redbook item, Ken was taken with my idea of forming a gay Harvard alumni group—if only because he could think of no better place to find Mr. Right.

Though he was always enthusiastic when I talked to him about helping me organize that group, he was frequently out of town when I turned to him for help. Ken's job required a good deal of traveling. He was in and out of San Francisco International Airport several times a month. Periodically in the course of our interview he had spoken wistfully of getting the promotion that would permit him to put down roots. As it was, Ken remained one of the many gay San Franciscans for whom the airport was a cherished landmark, the doorway to the city that they turned to and returned to for that very special sense of home.

It all began, I think, when I was fourteen or fifteen. A friend of mine spent the night. We were playing around taking pictures, and I took a picture of him flexing his muscles with just his pajama bottoms on. After I got the pictures back, I found that one and, looking at it, got aroused. From then on I started being aware of muscular bodies—at school in the locker room, in pictures in magazines or movies.

I knew that I wasn't supposed to have those feelings. I knew that they were sexual, but I had no idea how to express them behaviorally. I just wanted to touch the arms or the chest of the man I found attractive, that's all. But I got aroused sexually thinking about it. I knew these weren't the feelings you were supposed to have, but I kept thinking that they'd go away.

I used to go to mass and, before communion, pray that that act of communion would take away all my homosexual feelings. I used to pray to God and go to communion and then the mass would be over and I'd realize with a pang that the feelings were still there.

The first person I described them to was a priest in confession. He told me that I'd just have to work at not thinking about them. He said that this was my cross and that I'd just have to bear it, that I'd just have to live with it.

Before that I'd had all the confidence in the world in myself. I had the best grades in school. I was very good in tennis. I had lots of friends. I enjoyed being me, enjoyed being alive. But dealing with the homosexuality took a lot of that away. I was always having to hide something about myself because I thought that if people knew the truth, I would be ridiculed and ostracized. I began to feel that I just wasn't as good as everybody else. That continued even after I got into Harvard.

*   *   *

I was depressed constantly. I couldn't conceive of any of our classmates being homosexual. Even though I didn't, I thought that anyone who was homosexual would act in certain stereotypical ways. There was one guy in our class who had horn-rimmed glasses and was pale, thin, and effeminate. That's what I thought homosexuals were like. So I spent a lot of time fantasizing about this guy on the swimming team or that guy on the basketball team, but I didn't think they could possibly have homosexual feelings. I felt very alone.

I did not seek help until after an incident in my junior year. My roommates and I all used to horse around and wrestle together a lot. One night Jim, who was very tall and muscular, was brushing his teeth. He was wearing only pajama bottoms and his chest was bare. Well, I went into the bathroom and started horsing around with him the way we did, tickling him, grabbing him. He got so pissed off that he pushed me back against the wall, and put his legs up on the sink, and pressed me against the wall as hard as he could. It was such a turn-on to be so close to him that I climaxed. Before I had only done that in wet dreams. Jim didn't notice what had happened, but I got really scared. And that made me think that I had to do something.

So I went to a psychiatrist and told him that I wanted all my sexual feelings for men to be gone and sexual feelings for women to be there instead. If he'd told me, "Hey, listen, you know that can't be; this is the way you are and I'll help you adjust and cope with it," I would have said, "No thanks, that's not what I want." I don't know whether I'd have committed suicide, but I do know that there was no way that I could have accepted my homosexuality.

I found the name of that psychiatrist in the Yellow Pages. I didn't go to the Health Services because I didn't want anyone at Harvard to know. I didn't want this to get on my records.

I went to that shrink for a few months at the end of my junior year, then stopped over the summer. When I came back, I put off going to see him because I had fallen behind in my payments for past visits and was having trouble putting the money together for more. When I finally called his office, I found that he'd had a heart attack and died. I was referred to a psychiatrist on Beacon Street, and I saw him most of my senior year.

I worked in the library, and I used to work at the Harvard Coop in the Square. But I just couldn't make enough money to pay for a psychiatrist.

My parents separated when I was five, and I saw very little of my father until I was in college. He was living in Georgia, but he had business near Boston, and when he was in town he'd call me and we'd see each other. I told him why I wanted to go to the shrink because I needed money. And I asked him not to tell my brother, Terry. Well, he didn't give me any money, but he did tell Terry.

I still needed money, so I told my mother. I hadn't wanted to do that, because to me this was a shameful thing and I didn't want her to be ashamed of me. I told her only to get the money I needed to try to get cured. Sure enough, she said she was terribly ashamed.

For a while she helped me financially, and then she stopped. She said she was sure that I had a hormone problem, or that I was going through a phase, or that I was just dwelling on something that I shouldn't be thinking about anyway. She said she didn't believe in psychotherapy.

When I went home for Christmas vacation, my brother was there, and he was really nasty to me. All of them were angry at me, but none of them wanted to help pay for my psychotherapy. At least not then.

As part of the Army ROTC program, I was supposed to go into the service when we graduated. But during my senior year, my psychiatrist told me that I could not go into the Army and continue psychotherapy. He said that I would either have to stop therapy for four years, which was the minimum commitment I'd made to the Army, or would have to tell the Army that I was seeing a psychiatrist about my homosexuality.

Since the doctor said that if I stopped therapy for four years it would be even more difficult to get cured, I told the Army. I went to the commanding officer and explained the situation to him. He went to Dean Munro, and they had me see Dana Farnsworth, the head of the Health Services. It was arranged for me to take a three-year leave of absence from the Army. I was supposed to finish psychotherapy, become straight, and ready myself for military service. I thought that was wonderful.

When we graduated, my father and my brother were living in Georgia, and they asked me to come live with them so that they could help me. By that time they'd decided it was all my mother's fault. They were convinced that once I was away from her evil influence, I'd be cured.

My father is an alcoholic who'd been in AA for years, and he figured that he could cure me better than any psychiatrist. And my brother was going to help by getting me dates. They were sure I'd be okay if they could just get me in bed with a good woman. I had a few narrow escapes.

Soon I discovered that my brother believed that he was responsible for my being homosexual. He was only a year and a half older, but after my parents had divorced, he assumed that he was supposed to be some model of manhood. Instead he beat me up a lot. And he didn't include me in his friends' activities. Once he learned that I was homosexual, he began to feel guilty. That's why he was so hot to get me cured.

For the first ten months I was in Georgia I lived with my brother, my father and his second wife, and their four children. It was a crazy house. My father and I were having a lot of problems. I got myself another psychiatrist, and it got to the point that half of what I was saying in therapy was about my father. When I'd come home from therapy, he'd ask me to report on everything that was said, and that made it really difficult.

He and his wife were also having problems. There were lots of fights, and under the barrage of my father's verbal attacks, my stepmother would sometimes become hysterical. I remember one time she became so upset that she just kept screaming, "You're crazy, you're crazy." So he called the police to have himself taken away. And here I was in this household, working two jobs to pay for my psychiatrist and trying to deal with all of that. But every Sunday, regardless of what had happened the night before, we had to be up at quarter to seven in order to be at eight o'clock mass.

My brother could see that this was not good for me, and

he finally asked me if I wanted to get an apartment with him. When we told our father what we were going to do, he went berserk. He said we were rats deserting the ship.

My father was working at a defense facility, and when it became apparent that everything was going down the tubes there, he managed to get himself transferred to Seattle. He asked me to go with him so he could continue to help me. By this time I had figured out that he was more unbalanced than I was—that was a big step forward for me. I said that it wouldn't be good for me to leave therapy, since I'd built up rapport with my doctor and gotten into a therapy group. My father responded by calling my boss and telling him I was homosexual, figuring that if I got fired I would have to go with him.

My boss called me in and told me what my father had said. I told him that it wasn't exactly true—that I was in psychotherapy because I was unsure of myself when it came to relationships with women and had these attractions to men. He didn't fire me. He had seven sons, and he said that he wouldn't have wanted one of his sons treated as I had been.

The psychiatrist I had in Georgia never said very much. He just listened to what I said and every now and then would say, "What do you think about that?" He'd draw correlations between situations, but he'd never tell me what I should do or what I shouldn't do. I think that was a good thing. I began to feel that what I really needed to be listening to was my own feelings instead of the psychiatrist. After about a year in therapy, that's what I started to do.

Through a theater group I met a gay man who lived with his lover. He and I got to be good friends. I was living by myself by then, and pretty often he'd stop by and visit for a half an hour or an hour. When he left, he'd always touch me. It started out just as a friendly gesture, a touch on the shoulder or on the back. But each time he'd hold it a little longer, and then one night he put his hand on my shoulder and just didn't take it off. I put my arms around him and we started kissing.

We were going to visit some people that night along with his lover, so we arranged it so that I wouldn't have my car and he'd have to take me home, which he did. When we were back at my place, he went into the bathroom, and I took off my shirt and sat and waited for him on the couch. When he came back, I took off his shirt, and we hugged and kissed each other.

At that point, even at the age of twenty-three, I didn't know what men did together sexually. I had never thought about contact with another man other than touching his chest and arms and legs. So after we stopped kissing and it seemed like he should leave, I stood up. He reached over and unzipped my pants, going for my penis. I didn't know what he was doing, and so I zipped my pants back up. I didn't dare be naked with him. Just lying down with him and feeling his body and squeezing him close was enough to make me come.

By now my psychiatrist had moved his practice to Atlanta, and instead of an hour and a half of group therapy once a week, he had the whole group drive four hours down to Atlanta for an all-day marathon session one Saturday a month. When the session was over, I didn't get into my car and drive back home. I'd stay there and look for gay spots.

That's where I discovered the baths, which is where I began to have homosexual experiences I enjoyed. But I never wanted them to get personal. I felt so guilty about my homosexuality that once I came I would want to get away from the person I was with as soon as I could. It's funny how much I've changed. Now I feel it's really important to spend the night with someone I've had sex with.

When I'd started seeing the doctor, he'd had a sign out in front of his office that said "Dr. Charles Beauchamps." Somewhere along the line, after he'd moved to Atlanta, that sign was replaced with one which said "Christian Mental Health Society, Inc." My therapy took a religious tack. I was told that what I needed to do to solve my problem was to let go of my feelings for men and trust in God. I was told that if I had faith in God, God would put feelings for women in me. I said to myself, well I've asked God to put those feelings in me for a long time and nothing has happened. Why should it be any different now? Finally I wrote the doctor a letter saying that I wasn't coming back.

It was around this time, I think, that I realized that as much money as I had spent and as much time and effort as I'd put into trying to change, I wasn't going to change. I still wasn't very happy about it. I still felt inferior to other people. I still felt I had to hide my homosexual feelings. But I admitted to myself that I was homosexual and that this wasn't so horrible that I had to kill myself.

This was about five years after I'd first told my family that I had these homosexual feelings. They kept asking me about my therapy. They were waiting for me to report that I was finally cured. To get them off my back I just told them I was cured. I said that I'd finished therapy and was okay. That was the beginning of another five years of making up stories about girl friends and plans to get married and all that. But things were progressing, and my self-image got better as I began to meet more gays and to find out that I had things in common with them. Of course, the big change didn't come until I came out to San Francisco for the first time.

I dated a woman in Georgia for about a year and a half. She was from Boston, grew up in Brighton, and she was down there teaching emotionally disturbed children. I met her at dinner one night at a mutual friend's house; we hit it off instantly. I enjoyed the times that we spent together, and we spent a lot of time together. But I had to force myself to be intimate with her sexually. I wasn't sure what I was supposed to do.

After a year our relationship was at a point where everyone expected us to get married. I said that I just wasn't ready. What that meant was that I didn't think I could make it work. As much as I felt for her, I knew I couldn't ignore these feelings I had for men.

We continued to see each other for another six months, but by this time I was going out to the bars and going home with guys—always one-night stands followed by terrible bouts of guilt. Our relationship deteriorated, and after a year and a half she said, "I don't see any point in our continuing this." We broke it off. I just couldn't fake it.

Then, in 1977, I got a job in Boston and moved back there. I was feeling better about being homosexual; I felt comfortable about having sex with guys, but I didn't yet dare have a sustained relationship with a man. So I started dating Anne. I was seeing Anne 'cause I liked her and also so that I'd have somebody to go with to business parties and things like that. We broke up about four months before the tenth reunion.

I went to the reunion because I was curious to see some of the guys I hadn't seen for years. I think the thing that struck me most was that they didn't look that different. All the guys who lost their hair or got fat must have stayed at home 'cause there were very few bald heads or fat bellies. I realized that for all that had happened, ten years wasn't a very long time.

On Sunday night, after the reunion was over, I had dinner with one of my old roommates, Frank, and his wife, Ellen. Big Jim was in town that night on business and so it was the four of us. During dinner, some mention was made of how we used to horse around and wrestle. Ellen made the comment, "Yeah, isn't it funny. That's the way you guys showed affection for each other, because back then it was so difficult for guys to be openly affectionate with one another." It was a very astute comment for her to make, and I wondered if she was trying to set the stage for me to make an announcement. I didn't rise to the occasion. I wasn't ready then.

During that whole reunion weekend I didn't tell anyone that I was gay and I didn't see any sign that anyone else was. The only other single there was a priest. It wasn't that I missed other gay people exactly. It was just that I felt a little out of place.

You can never tell what's going to happen. I never dreamed that one of the most important women in my life would be Betty, the sister of a straight friend of mine whom I met for an hour and a half in Boston once. I had heard what the gay scene was like in San Francisco, and I wanted to see it. I knew two people who lived there: this straight woman—Betty—and this gay guy who had moved out from Boston. So I wrote them both letters saying that I was coming and that it would be fun to get together for a drink. I was hoping that the guy would write back and say, "I'm glad to hear you're coming. If you need a place to stay, you can stay with me." Well, that's the kind of letter I got from her. From him I got a letter saying how happy he was that I was coming and that he'd be happy to help me make hotel reservations.

I almost canceled the trip the day before I was to leave. I just couldn't figure out how I was going to get away from this woman to see the part of San Francisco I was interested in. But I came after all, and she and I hit it off fantastically well. We went out Friday night and had dinner and went disco dancing at 2001 down on Union Street. Then on Saturday we went all over the place, from Muir Woods to Ghirardelli Square. And that night we saw *Beach Blanket Babylon.* We really had a ball, talking the whole time, getting to know each other. And every time there'd be a lull in the conversation she'd say "So . . ." That meant, "Tell me something else about yourself."

Well, along about Saturday afternoon I was running out of responses to her "so's." I kept going but was feeling more and more distant. Then after the theater we were standing on the street waiting for the cable car and she said "So . . ."

And I said, "Betty, there's only one more *so,* and I'm not sure that you want to hear it." I knew I had to tell her. I couldn't spend another night in her apartment and not have sex with her unless I did.

She said, "What is it?"

And I said, "I'm gay."

And she said, "So?"

Then she put her arms around me and hugged me. It gave me the most wonderful feeling. That was the first time I felt totally accepted by a straight person. And not only was it a straight person, it was a straight woman who had wanted to go to bed with me. That did more for my self-esteem than any other one thing. I went back to Boston and decided that it was time to tell my brother and his wife that I was gay. About six months later I told my mother. It's not something they're crazy about, but we've all become much closer. I'm glad I told them.

I had seen in our tenth-year report that Doug Sanders, one of my old roommates, was practicing law in San Jose. He'd moved into our room junior year. I enjoyed spending time with him because of his sense of humor, his outlook on life, his values. He's a very good and honest person. Senior year he kind of took up with another group of guys and drifted away. But when I decided to visit San Francisco, I called him and suggested we get together.

He was coming up to San Francisco to do some business on Saturday, and so he arranged to come by Betty's apartment and pick me up. He was going to drive me around and show me the sights. Well, five minutes after we were in the car, I said, "Doug, if this reunion is going to mean anything at all, I've got to tell you right now that I'm gay."

His reaction was, "No kidding. When did you come out?"

I was surprised. That's something most straights wouldn't say. So I told him a little bit of my story.

Then he told me his. He said that during senior year he'd been smoking grass one night with this guy, and the guy began to get really physical and affectionate with him. He'd thought a lot about having a homosexual experience and so he said to himself, "Why not let it happen now?" He liked it.

Soon after that he started going to the gay bars in Boston —the Punch Bowl, Sporter's, all the old bars. It's funny. I thought that he was drifting away because he didn't like us anymore or because his mind was going off in some other direction. Well, I guess it was. I wish I had known. It might have made it easier for me to accept the direction mine was going in.

So he explored his homosexuality much earlier than I did, but he also had his problems accepting it. After coming out he'd led an exclusively gay life for a few years, and then he'd had a bad breakup with a lover. It affected him so strongly that for a few years he was completely asexual. Then he started having relationships with both men and women. When we met, he thought of himself as bisexual. He was roommates with a straight man who had no idea that he was gay, and he went to the baths when he wanted to have sex.

I had joined the Harvard Club when I moved up to Boston, and one of the things I did for them was to interview high-school seniors who were applying to Harvard. So I'd occasionally be in the Admissions Office. The assistant director of Admissions was Bill Fitzsimmons, who's in our class. When I was chatting with him on one of my visits, we got to talking about the tenth-anniversary report. He asked me if I'd read what Toby Marotta wrote. I said I hadn't. All he said was, "You've got to read it. You won't believe it." My guess was that you had written that you were something more spectacular than anybody else: that you had become president of some huge corporation, made a lot of money, married the most beautiful woman in the world, or something. . . .

I went home and it slipped my mind for about a week. Then, the next time I thought about it, I looked you up in the book. I couldn't believe it. Fitzsimmons was right.

You had come out totally, to the rest of the class and to whoever else might pick up the book. I started calling you that night. When I couldn't get you, I wrote a letter. But I kept calling you. I just had to tell you how happy I was that you wrote that—and that I was gay too. I knew then that I was going back to San Francisco for my next vacation.

2

BEN MILLER

If my leave-taking was reminiscent of Ken, my arrival in Los Angeles was characteristically Ben. He had said he would meet me at the airport but was nowhere to be found at the arrival gate or the baggage claim. I was sure he had quarreled with Mario and been delayed, until I burst through the door to the street and found him grinning at me through the open window of his old Dodge. "Get in," he said, macho staccato, soft voice. As usual, he was wearing a white T-shirt and looking like a rumpled Tab Hunter.

Ben was the first classmate to visit me after word of my homosexuality appeared in the class report, and he and Ken were the classmates I had gotten to know best. They were as different as Harvard graduates can be. Ken was formal, polished, and aspiring; Ben was casual, unpretentious, and "laid back." Ken was committed professionally and in search of Mr. Right; Ben worked only when he had to in order to support his song-writing and next to that was most enamored of recreational sex. My friendship with Ken grew through a chain of reciprocated social invitations and a common interest in making contact with other gay "alums"; my relationship with Ben was an earthier and more intimate voyage of mutual discovery. At that point, Ben's love of gay "low life" intrigued me more than Ken's emergence in San Francisco's gay establishment.

I had decided to make Ben the first out-of-towner I visited, because I wanted to buy a good portable tape recorder to carry with me and he had volunteered to help me select one. Never one to waste a minute, he drove us right from the airport to his favorite stereo supply shop and then back to the small ranch-style house that was supposed to have been his and Mario's honeymoon cottage. Along the way he confided that Mario had still not moved in.

That I could see from the way the house was furnished. But for Ben's big electronic organ, walls lined with makeshift bookcases bearing boxes of tapes, records, microphones, recording equipment, notebooks, and song sheets, and bare floors cluttered with newspapers and magazines, the front room was empty.

Ben offered me a cup of coffee and then said he was ready to begin taping. What he meant was that he wanted to fiddle with my new machine. It seemed to me that he wanted to hear how each of the "one-two-threes" he spoke into the microphone sounded with every combination of switches switched and buttons pressed. I sensed that this was partly defensive. Ben was very shy, and he really didn't like the idea of being "interviewed." When I finally insisted we begin, he became silly, wooden, and tongue-tied. Soon he was protesting, "You already know most of what there is to know about my life. What else can I tell you?"

I said that I wanted ours to be my practice interview—that I wanted him to answer all of the questions I was planning to ask each of the classmates I was going to visit. The point of my questions was to get him to recount how he had discovered he was homosexual, how he had handled his homosexuality at Harvard, how his life had evolved after graduation, and what he thought and how he lived as a gay man today. I said it would be especially interesting if, as on so many of our outings, he would describe the various gay sex scenes he enjoyed and explain why he found them satisfying, why he believed them so harmless and legitimate: "Most people find promiscuity pretty sick and sex in public places irresponsible." While I lectured him, he wrinkled his nose. "You might be able to help others understand why so many gay men think otherwise."

Ben had certainly done a lot to change my own mind about sexual pastimes I had once been very uneasy with, patterns and institutions my research revealed were staples of the traditional gay male subculture. Indeed, there were times when I felt I was learning more about gay life from Ben than from all the books by and about homosexuals I read and all the interviews about gay politics I conducted and all of the conversations and observations I was undertaking in San Francisco's Tenderloin, where I had begun to do research on life in what I believed was a prototypical inner-city red-light district. Ben was a homosexual whose counter-cultural perspective permitted him to enjoy gay life in healthy and moral ways and whose education permitted him not only to understand but to articulate about what he did and why.

From my point of view, all Ben lacked was the political perspective that would have inclined him to try to reorient and reinvigorate traditional gay male ways in the name of gay community. Among other things, this meant that he and I disagreed about whether his locales for sexual liaisons were always appropriate. I tended to think that contacts made at the baths and in other institutions licensed to house recreational sex were perfectly legitimate, but not sex in public places—the low life—at least not in any but those clearly identified as gay spots by custom and usage or by virtue of their dense homosexual populations. I also argued that homosexuals interested in promoting liberation should enjoy sexual promiscuity in ways that were morally exemplary and politically strategic. But about the spirit in which Ben involved himself in gay low life, his mental health, and his character, integrity, and sense of personal and social responsibility generally, I had no question—at least not by the time I was ready to interview him. At first I had been more skeptical.

I knew from dozens of past conversations that Ben could talk about his sex life intelligently. But when I asked him to do so with my tape recorder on, he acted like a newly apprehended murder suspect under questioning. Despite all my urging that he speak at length so that I could include substantial pieces of his monologue in my chronicle of our friendship, he would only answer the questions I put to him and engage me in debate. For all that we knew, loved, and trusted each other, interviewing Ben was like pulling teeth.

You generally have a favorable view of traditional gay sex scenes, don't you? Don't you ever find gay low life tawdry or frightening?

Well, yes, but there's a line from a Woody Allen movie that sums up my feelings about that. The psychiatrist asks Woody Allen if he thinks sex is dirty. He answers, "It is if you do it right."

Meaning the tawdriness and riskiness are part of what you enjoy?

Meaning that's part of the fun. Having things a little tawdry and risky, as you say, doesn't necessarily take away from the pleasure of the sexual escapade. Sometimes it even adds something.

Are there any gay sex scenes that turn you off?

Sure. There are things I'm not into, like fistfucking. That I'm just not inclined to do. But somebody else probably could enjoy it and not be turned off at all. Obviously there are people who do.

Aren't there any aspects of the scenes you encounter in public places that turn you off?

Yeah. I don't like crowds. I don't like it when there are a lot of people hanging around looking like they're ready to pounce. I like there to be circulation. I never hang around in one place for very long. I come and go, maybe several times, so that there isn't an intimidating atmosphere for everybody to walk into.

So you think that those scenes would work better if people were more sensitive to one another?

Yeah, I think everything would work better if people were more sensitive to one another. Sex is about being sensitive. I mean, not only to other people, but to life, to what it's possible to do out there.

Well, just what is it possible to do in a public rest room? Are homosexuals really sensitive to one another in locales like that?

Yeah. I remember thinking that that was one thing I was never going to do. But then I decided that I wouldn't know what it was all about until I tried it. So I did, and it was lots of fun. Most of the people you see are really nice. The uptight ones are the only ones who create problems.

You've tried all the different alternatives?

Sure. The rest rooms, the parks, the porno arcades, the theaters, the back-room bars, the beaches. The variety of locales is endless. I wouldn't know what they were about if I hadn't tried them.

You prefer those institutions to gay bars?

Yeah. I don't like drinking that much, and besides, bars aren't as exciting or as efficient.

Efficient?

Sure. In the places I go you get to have sex without going through any social rigmarole. I mean, I like people, and I like getting to know them, but sometimes that isn't what I want. And it's phony to go through all that when that isn't what you really want—when what you really want is just sex.

I smile whenever I think of my early meetings with Ben. He'd seemed like such an angel. He'd turned out to be such a devil.

I'd heard from him first about three months after the class report was circulated. In a small, halting voice, he'd introduced himself over the phone as someone who'd met me once at Harvard and been reminded of that by my piece in the redbook. Since he sounded uncomfortable, I thanked him for getting in touch and asked him when we'd met. He mumbled that he'd been friendly with Ted Somes, one of my freshman roommates, and that it had been in Ted's room. He went on to say that he was living in Palo Alto and working in a computer outfit there. I invited him to come up to Berkeley for dinner just as soon as Rusty and I returned from Tucson, where Crystals of India was in the big gem and mineral show.

About six weeks later, three weeks after we'd returned from Tucson, Ben called again, this time sounding even more abashed than before. Feeling embarrassed about having let my invitation slide, I invited him to dinner on Friday night. Even before he consented, I was telling him how to reach our cottage in the Berkeley flats.

That Friday night when the bell rang, I was frying spices for curried chicken, so Rusty answered the door and led Ben into the kitchen. Wearing a loose gray sweat shirt, a white undershirt, dungarees, and sneakers, he looked like one of the guys I had gone to Medford High School with.

It was no surprise to learn that Ben was also from the Boston area originally, if only because his style of dress was so familiar. I had worn that uniform upon arriving at Harvard, before realizing that the prep school look was what most people expected of Ivy Leaguers. Then, slowly but surely, I had replaced my sweat shirts, undershirts, dungarees, and sneakers with pastel-colored broadcloth shirts, chinos, and Topsiders, then added tweed jackets, silk ties, gray flannel slacks, and Weejuns (Ken's wardrobe still!). Ben still dressed like a "townie," what the preppy set called those of us who were obviously from local public high schools. I wondered if he was one of those local boys who had gone to Harvard and been unable to fit in, or one who had been unaffected by social pressure, or one, like me, who had striven for a time to look like an Ivy Leaguer and then embraced the more natural, work-ingman's look that was popular first in the counterculture and then in the gay male subculture—jogging tops, T-shirts, jeans, and Adidas.

For the first hour or so of our visit, I was sure that Ben was a

townie who had failed to fit in. He remained stationed by his glass
of milk at the kitchen table while I went about stewing and serv-
ing my chicken. He only picked at his curry, remarking that he
"didn't much like spicy food," and left the gizzard. His conversation was riddled with those dirty little jokes that had been the
mainstays of socializing among the guys at Medford High. He
blushed when I asked him how long he'd been gay, then said he
wasn't sure he was "all" gay.

That surprised me. I'd been assuming that Ben had made contact out of some sense of gay social or political spirit, the type of
thing that would presuppose his thinking himself gay. But when I
asked him if that were the case, he said no, he didn't think so, he
just thought it would be nice to get together—he was curious to
know what I looked like now. Ben was so matter-of-fact it
killed me.

He didn't perk up that night until I mentioned that I had had a
lover in the class ahead of me all through high school. Then, his
blue eyes brightening, he said that he had had a high-school lover
too. The big difference, we found, was that I was actually having
sex with my lover, while he was making love to his in vivid mas-
turbatory fantasies only.

Tom lived up the street. He'd sometimes come down to the
house to leave a list of things his dad wanted from my
father's store, and I'd see him. I thought he was attractive,
but for a long time I didn't like him because he seemed so
arrogant. He had this really annoying habit of turning everything into a dirty joke. He couldn't say a single sentence
without making some kind of corny, obscene joke of it. He
knew it was stupid, but he wouldn't stop doing it because he
was so stubborn. I thought the only way I could show him
how ridiculous it was, was to do it back at him. So I started
cracking the same sorts of dumb jokes, and of course, it got to
be fun. We both liked it, and it sort of brought us together.
Pretty soon we started making up dirty lyrics to all the popular songs. That's probably how I started writing songs.

When I'd been younger, I used to play with the guys, and
we'd pull down our pants and look at each other's cocks. But
Tom was too old for that. He was uptight already. And he
was pretty heterosexual. Even though I really fell in love

with him, there was never any kind of sex between us. But we stayed best friends all through college, and even after I moved to California.

As Ben and I continued to compare notes, it became clear that there were dramatic differences in the ways we'd handled our homosexuality as teenagers. He hadn't had sex with a male until after he'd graduated and gone into the Navy, but he'd decided he was homosexual in high school. ("I saw the word in my mother's sex manual and looked it up in the dictionary.") I'd had sex with so many of my male friends in junior high and high school that I assumed that every boy did that until it was time to get married, but I'd neither seen nor used the word *homosexual*. Ben had never been able to get his friend Tom to respond to him sexually, but he'd continued to love him and eventually became friends as well with his wife. I'd promised eternal devotion to my own first love, yet when he'd told me he no longer wanted to have sex with me, I'd worked to rid myself of all feeling for him and refused to attend his wedding a few years later.

I wondered if Ben and I treated those we had loved in high school differently because we had responded in such different ways to Harvard. For me, who at sixteen had lost my father to cancer and been abandoned by his large Italian clan, who had been elected captain of the soccer team, senior class president, and valedictorian at Medford High but seen little of the world beyond, Harvard appeared as one big opportunity after another. Once I moved into Harvard Yard, I studied all the time, acquired a résuméful of student activities, tried hard to impress college officials, and made as many friends as I could—especially among classmates who wore stylish tweed jackets, gray flannels, and Weejuns. No longer did I have time for those back in Medford. Over holidays and for vacations, I went home with befriended preppies to Williamstown, Manhattan's East Side, and Washington, D.C. On weekends I drove off with wealthy roommates to mixers at Wellesley and dances at Belmont Country Day. I got summer jobs in the Harvard Admissions Office so that I could stay around Cambridge and join my friends for sojourns on Mount Desert Island and Naushon. Even graduate school I viewed mainly as an opportunity to remain part of the worlds I was exposed to, thanks to my Harvard College classmates.

For Ben, on the other hand, "the College" was one big disappointment after another. In high school, thanks to the wife of the prominent Harvard dean who lived nearby, he had believed that being admitted to Harvard was "like dying and going to heaven —the ultimate reward through which you would be granted absolute knowledge." But what he found when he moved to Cambridge was "a shockingly inadequate level of instruction," "a disillusioningly high degree of competition," and "a huge bureaucracy which seemed mainly interested in reinforcing its own assumptions." Most weekends Ben went home to see Tom: "He always went out with his future wife on Saturday nights, but otherwise we'd spend the whole weekend together, watching TV, making up dirty songs, palling around."

Yet for all that life as he experienced it at Harvard, and the boy back home, kept Ben away from Cambridge, as an upperclassman he fashioned a living situation in which he felt completely comfortable. While I was busy collecting classmates who could introduce me to exciting new worlds, he was building friendships in which he could be himself. I ended up with fifteen roommates who knew nothing about how I ticked; he ended up with a roommate who was the first person to know he was gay.

I wasn't especially attracted to Alex physically, but I found him honest. We were both pretty open with each other from the start. We were Ayn Rand fans and got into an Ayn Rand group. That really brought us together. We'd talk about what was going on there and laugh about how fucked up some of the people in the group were. Of course, we let each other know that we weren't so perfect either. We were pretty open about talking with each other about our lives and our feelings.

And we were both pretty down-to-earth. When we lived in Leverett House, he'd have to come through my room to get to the bathroom. Most every morning he'd come bouncing through my room, stark naked, then bend over and shoot me this open-faced moon, usually with a fart for fanfare. He told me all about the first time he jacked off. And I told him all about my homosexual feelings.

He was pretty comfortable with what I said. I think he had homosexual feelings too, but they weren't that strong. He was pretty secure with where his sexual fantasies were. So he could understand and accept my feelings.

I knew that there must be other homosexuals, I guess, but I didn't know how to meet them or what I would do if I did. I felt very awkward about the whole thing. You know the old joke about people not being able to imagine what homosexuals do in bed; well, it applied very literally to me.

When I asked him if he was currently in touch with any old classmates, Ben said that he still saw Alex, who was now married and living near Palo Alto. He also told me that he had decided to move to California back in college, after seeing a feature in *Life* that said that San Francisco and Los Angeles were meccas for homosexuals. That was the only information about gay life he could find.

The moment he said this, I jumped up from the dinner table, ducked into my office, and returned with the issue of *Life* he had mentioned. I had begun collecting copies of almost all the first published articles about homosexuality when I discovered, upon starting my thesis research, that there were no gay archives or study collections.

Looking amused and pleased, Ben thumbed through the pages until he found his article, which was headlined the "Secret World [of] Homosexuality in America." Then, chuckling at the close of each recitation, he read the captions beneath the photographs aloud:

A homosexual sits on a rail in Los Angeles' Pershing Square, where homosexuals new in town make contacts. A few who frequent it are male prostitutes, but most just seek company.

When Hollywood police closed "gay" haunts near his Santa Monica Blvd. bar, Barney Anthony put up a sign warning homosexuals "Fagots (sic)—Stay Out." "I don't like 'em," he said. "They'll approach any nice-looking guy. Anybody does any recruiting, I say shoot him. Who cares?"

A San Francisco bar run for and by homosexuals is crowded with patrons who wear leather jackets, make a show of masculinity, and scorn effeminate members of their world.

Two fluffy-sweatered young men stroll in San Francisco's Tenderloin, ignoring the stare of a "straight" couple. Flagrant homosexuals are unabashed by reactions of shock, perplexity, disgust.

Concluding this performance, Ben looked up and said, "I came out to California and found all of these places—thanks to *Life.*"

"Times have changed, haven't they?" I replied, hoping he might respond by telling me more about his personal life. "I mean, there are many more gay neighborhoods and much more attractive places for gay people to meet and lots more gay couples."

Ben flipped the magazine shut. He was ignoring my bait. He said, "Yeah." I knew he was going to change the subject. "Hey, now it's my turn to play show and tell. I want you and Rusty to hear some of my songs."

Asked what he meant, Ben explained that he only did computer programming to make money and that his real love was writing music. He composed popular songs, "sort of pop fifties stuff," and he liked to sing his own songs while accompanying himself on his organ. Withdrawing a cassette from a pocket in his jeans, he asked if we wanted to hear some of his work. Informed that we didn't have a tape recorder, he suggested we go out and use the machine in his car.

So Ben, Rusty, and I ended our first evening together by trooping out to the '65 Dodge parked on the darkened street in front of our cottage and crowding into the front seat. Ben popped the cassette into the machine. There was a burst of organ music. A happy voice chimed forth. It was loud, simple, sing-along music, and I asked Ben why he hadn't arranged for a bouncing ball to lead us all in song. He responded by starting to sing along himself, putting one of his arms through mine. I put my free arm through Rusty's and pulled first toward Ben and then toward Rusty, until the three of us, arms linked, were swaying back and forth in time with the beat. That was my idea of gay community, at least then. I didn't know if it was Ben's.

From that point on, Ben and his music became a regular feature in our lives. Almost every Friday evening the telephone would ring, and sounding a continent away, Ben would say, "Doin' anything tonight?" While he was driving up to Berkeley, Rusty or I would cook up some exotic Indian dish and call around to see if any of our friends wanted to join us for a relaxed evening. Inevitably, as the night wore on, we would pile into Ben's Dodge and sing and sway our way up to the White Horse, the gay bar on Telegraph Avenue.

"Some day we'll find Ben's songs on the juke box," Rusty joshed.

"Only if he'll write songs with gay themes," I jibed. I had decided that Ben needed to be much more of a gay liberationist.

I especially loved Ben's Friday night visits when Rusty was off traveling and I'd come home from work in the Tenderloin to an empty house. The first time he came up when Rusty was away, we ate the same curry, digested on the same sing-along ride to the White Horse, and did the same laughing and joking about Ben's future pop-stardom and the gay angle that would assure it. As the night wore on and my exuberance reached a peak, I talked about how he could be a great hit on the gay show-bar circuit if he would only write some gay songs and sing them while accompanying himself. Suddenly seeing him as a young Tab Hunter—he had the same golden hair, the same slightly freckled fair complexion, the same boy-next-door look—I introduced him to the guy standing next to us at the bar as the next great gay pop hero. "And this is my manager," Ben said softly. "It's all *his* idea!"

Before long it was closing time, and I asked Ben whether he wanted to spend the night at our cottage instead of driving all the way back down to Palo Alto. When he threw his arm around my shoulder and said, "Great," I was suddenly anxious to make sure he realized that I wasn't inviting him to have sex. Although Rusty and I had by this time worked for almost five years to maintain a relationship in which each of us was free to have sex with others, we were usually careful not to become involved separately with men we wanted to have as common friends. I was just about to explain this when Ben added that he loved sleeping with his friends because it reminded him of the nights he used to spend with Tom and Alex.

But I just couldn't decide whether Ben was incredibly innocent or extraordinarily liberated—he was just so natural when it came to sex. On the one hand, he was still in love with his best friend from high school, he wrote saccharine love songs, and he unfailingly blushed and put me off when I asked him specific questions about his sex life. On the other, he was extremely comfortable with gay men and at home in gay bars; he wasn't the slightest bit fazed when I expounded on the virtues of open relationships; and he seemed almost smug, if silent, when I told him about the healthy promiscuity I was discovering in the gay male subculture.

I got my first evidence that Ben was more worldly than I had originally assumed when, about four or five months after his initial visit, he opened up enough to tell me about his earliest homosexual experience. This had taken place when he was in the Navy, which he had joined shortly after we graduated because he didn't want to be drafted and yet couldn't honestly report that he had engaged in homosexual activity. As things turned out, he did that first with another sailor.

There was a movie on TV I wanted to watch, but the TV set in the day room was broken. I remembered that Louis Palansky, who lived downstairs, had a set in his room, so I went down, knocked on his door, and asked if he was interested in watching that film. "Oh sure," he said, "come on in." We started watching the movie and talking.

I don't know exactly how or why, but it soon became very clear that I could broach the subject of my sexual feelings and not get a bad response. I said something like, "I like boys a lot more than girls." And he said something like, "I do too," or "I have those feelings too." We ended up leaving the base that night and going off to a motel. It was so easy. I didn't have to *explain* about my feelings.

We did that for two or three nights in a row. Then he took up with another sailor. The other one was married, but his wife wasn't with him on base. So the two of them would go off, saying they were going to look for girls, and stay out all night. One time the other guy sidled up and propositioned me, but I didn't take him up on it. I didn't know him well enough to feel comfortable.

Ben was stationed in Monterey, and once he actually had sex with another man, he was determined to have more. On weekend leaves he would drive up to San Francisco and look for the spots he had read about in *Life*. During his first expedition he found a bar in the Tenderloin that looked exactly like one he had seen pictured. After getting drunk for the first time, he had gotten himself picked up. And though he never really enjoyed the bar scene, if only because he didn't like to drink, this was the only way he knew of to meet other homosexuals until he left the Navy and went to work in Palo Alto. There he learned from one of his coworkers that not too far away there was a nude beach "filled with queers."

Probably the biggest leap forward for my gay sex life was discovering San Gregorio Beach. There's a big public beach right off the Coast Highway, and a little ways up the shoreline from this regular beach there's an area where people swim and sunbathe in the nude. Over the years, the nude part of San Gregorio has become more and more gay. You can walk to it from the regular beach, or you can park in a lot up on top of the cliffs and climb down directly.

I've had my most satisfying sex there. It's outdoors. It's beautiful. You're in this great expanse of beach surrounded by high rocky cliffs. And you can see a lot of nice-looking people lying in the sun naked. They're pretty friendly and relaxed, and you can get it on with them right there on the beach or you can go up into the trestle and have sex there. It's really paradise.

As I was discovering that Ben was very much involved in traditional gay male sex scenes, he was realizing that I talked a good deal about the gay male subculture but knew relatively little first-hand about its earthier dimensions. There followed a period in which the dynamic of our relationship was what I called mutual consciousness-raising and he called adventure. I would tell Ben what I was learning from my interviews and observations in the Tenderloin; he would take me to his favorite gay rendezvous and show me how they worked in practice.

It was a bright day in May of 1978 when Rusty and I headed down the Coast Highway in our truck to meet Ben at his favorite outdoor recreation area. At a small cardboard sign that read *Parking,* about three hundred yards up from the public entrance to San Gregorio Beach, we took a rough little road into the private parking area. A grizzled attendant came up to the window as we pulled into a slip and said, "This beach is nude, you know." I wondered whether he knew it was gay as well as nude until, having walked about twenty yards to the top of the coastside cliff, I looked down and saw a few naked women and a trail of bronzed male bodies stretching from the sweep of sand directly beneath us to a large outcropping of brown rock that brought the beach to an end about a mile and a half to the right. Even from this vantage point I could see that there was more than sunbathing going on.

As we picked our way down a steep dirt path, I saw that not everyone on the beach was completely bare: Here and there was a woman wearing a bikini bottom or a man in shorts. But most of the beach crowd was completely unclothed. Dogs and naked toddlers romped playfully among the others. And all of the grownups were playing with the dogs and the kids, or sitting or lying in the sun, or strolling along the shore without a trace of self-consciousness. Rusty pulled off his jeans as soon as we reached the sand. I felt a clutch in my throat and remarked that I planned to keep my cutoffs on.

There were fewer and fewer women and children and almost no men in shorts as we made our way down the beach toward what Ben had described as the gay section. Most of the men here were sitting or lying in little pens constructed of driftwood.

About halfway down this line of encampments there was a cleft in the cliff wall that opened onto a mass of green foliage. Jutting out from the greenery was a giant lattice-work of huge timber beams, the weathered remains of a railroad trestle that had fallen into the canyon long ago. A naked watchman, berry-brown, stood at attention in front of the tall bushes at the bottom of the trestle. Other naked men were positioned at various points in the wooden wreckage or picking their way among the beams. Every so often two or three would disappear behind a particularly dense cluster of beams or beneath overhanging branches and have sex.

I watched as we walked until Rusty pulled at my arm. We turned in, walked till the canyon seemed to disappear into the cliff, and then stepped gingerly among several walled enclaves of nude cohorts until we reached the one containing Ben. Rusty leaped over the driftwood wall, plopped himself down on the sand, and gave Ben a hug. I looked around to see if anyone else was wearing shorts.

"What's the matter?" Ben drawled. "Afraid you'll get a hard-on if you take off your pants?"

Stepping carefully into the compound, I admitted that I did feel a little out of place. Ben's response was almost gleeful. "That's the trestle," he said, pointing in the direction we had just come from. "And a lot of the guys are having sex right in their shelters. Wanna walk around and watch?"

I didn't. I felt fine about endorsing healthy sexual promiscuity in the name of gay community, but the thought of actually watching others have sex still made me uncomfortable. And this *was* a public place. Everyone around seemed perfectly at ease with what was going on, and I had seen some men and women stroking each other sensuously as we had walked up the beach. But I didn't know that all the children were as unfazed as they had seemed, and I didn't want to get involved in anything I couldn't justify morally and politically. To regain control of the situation and put myself back at ease, I remained intellectual. "Until I moved out here, the very idea of a beach where people openly had sex would have made me uneasy. What happened to your inhibitions?"

Acting almost as if he wanted to reward me for venturing into his terrain, Ben took my question seriously. And there as we sat in the sun, me in my shorts and him in the nude, he for the first time told me how he had gotten involved in some of the more controversial sexual pastimes enjoyed by many gay men.

One night somebody I met in a bar took me to Dave's Baths, down in North Beach, at about three in the morning. I remember I didn't do anything at the time, but I got used to being with all those naked bodies in the steam room and in the sauna and just watching TV. So later on, when I moved up to San Francisco, I wasn't freaked out by the idea of going to the baths.

Did you stop going to bars altogether?

No, but I'd usually get most of my sex elsewhere. I'd go to the baths whenever I felt frustrated, because I knew I could always have sex with somebody there. People are less inclined to play hard-to-get games at the baths. But I also liked Land's End and Buena Vista Park and of course San Gregorio Beach. I guess I like outdoor sex.

How did you, being so shy and inhibited ...

I wasn't so shy and inhibited once I got into it. You don't have to be some kind of pro to get it on outdoors. There are usually lots of bushes. So you walk around looking, and if you look at somebody and they look back, you go into the bushes and they follow you, or they do and you follow them. If I found somebody attractive, I'd go after them and just undo their pants and start in.

What do people actually do?

It's usually sucking. That's the easiest thing to do under the circumstances.

How often did you go in for this type of sex?

Well, that depends on the time in my life. The year I lived in San Francisco I wasn't working, so I'd spend some time almost every day in the park or at the baths.

Did you ever have any bad or frightening experiences?

You mean in the parks? Well no, not really. Some times were better than others. But I can't think of anything that was ever really bad. I've never been hurt or even threatened. I've seen the police hassle people in the park a few times, but I was never directly involved.

How about the public? Do you think it's right for homosexuals to carry on in places where members of the public might run into them and be offended?

What's really done in public is the cruising, which is so subtle that people who aren't attuned to it rarely realize what's going on. As for actual sex in public view, that rarely happens. People usually go off and have sex in the bushes or somewhere else out of sight.

Though there's a certain excitement that comes from the feeling that one might be stumbled upon, there's nothing that douses erotic arousal faster than actually being interrupted by someone who's shocked and upset by what's going on. People willing to risk having sex in public are usually very sensitive to their surroundings. Though they have sex in locales that are officially public, they take great care to stay out of view, or at least not to freak out those who might be offended.

Was all this sex totally impersonal, or did you meet people sometimes and develop relationships?

Sometimes I saw people I met at the baths or in the parks several times afterwards, though none of those relationships carried on after I moved back to Palo Alto in '73. After my year of debauchery, I had to go back to work again and earn some money. But even those relationships that were one time affairs weren't totally impersonal. I mean, I usually talked with the people I was having sex with, if only to make sure that they were finding the experience satisfactory. Sometimes I liked them, sometimes I didn't.

I was never really searching for a lover. I was happy with things the way they were. When I went up to San Francisco, I moved in with a guy named Skippy whom I'd tricked with at San Gregorio. We didn't call ourselves lovers, but we lived together for a while. Then, after three or four months, an apartment opened up in the same building and I moved down there. Neither of us was very clear about what we wanted out of that relationship, and there weren't any hard feelings when we broke up. I found life as a gay bachelor fully satisfying after that.

It was a telephone call I received almost five months after Ben's first call that led to a dramatic change in his gay life-style and to a marked attenuation of our unusual colleagueship. This call could not have been more unlike Ben's first call: The voice of the caller was loud, flowing, and expressive; his words were mellifluous. The man on the other end of the line was Mario Montano, another from the class of '67, and he told me that he had seen my name on a friend's Gay Academic Union membership list and then looked me up in the class report. "Congratulations for your courage," he cooed. "And your piece was so-o-o well written."

I remembered that Mario had said something about being a successful playwright in his own squib and remarked on that. He sounded pleased. And when he told me that he was working in

Los Angeles but planning to be in San Francisco for a month beginning next weekend, I invited him to come for curry on Friday night. "Ben Miller will probably be here," I added. When he asked who Ben was, I teased him. "Oh, just another of our exotic classmates."

The suave Mario who showed up for dinner looked nothing like the chubby Italian boy I, identifying with my WASP mother rather than my Neapolitan father, had found so unattractively foreign back in college. Now Mario was trim, his clothes tailored, his hair long, prematurely or artificially silvered, and wavy on the sides. "How much you've changed," I said when I greeted him, sure from his apparent prosperity that he had made it big in writing. "This is Ben," I continued, pulling Ben up from his post at the kitchen table. "He's a songwriter. Why don't you take him back to Hollywood and make him a star." I was in a good mood, a joshing mood, and I joked about Ben's star potential until Rusty groused at me.

Rusty and I wanted to go to a dance at the gay community center in San Francisco that evening, and we asked Ben and Mario to go with us. When they both agreed to, I suggested we all go in Ben's car so that Mario could hear the music.

Well, before we were halfway across the Bay Bridge, Mario was as caught up in the singing and swaying as the rest of us. Before we even got to the dance, he was proposing that he and Ben collaborate on a musical comedy. "Go ahead, Ben," I hooted from the back seat. "You two can be the Rodgers and Hammerstein of the class of '67!"

Inside, Mario dazzled Ben with his smooth cha cha, Ben grinned and blushed like a courted schoolboy, and the two were necking in a corner before the evening was out. So much for Ben's pronouncements about the virtues of gay bachelorhood, I thought; I should have guessed from his sentimental songs that he was a sucker for romance.

From that point on, Ben was no longer available on Friday nights. He was always going to a play with Mario or meeting one of Mario's contacts or spending time with one of Mario's colleagues. Now Rusty and I saw the happy couple with some regularity on Saturday afternoons. They called us their godparents and said they never would have met if it hadn't been for me and my "goddamned gay liberation."

The "goddamned" was always in there because they didn't share my passion for gay politics. Ben had long since told me he thought me some kind of political fanatic when he first came up to visit; it was only when I showed him I was willing to weigh my theories against his practice that he began to get a kick out of all my enthusiasm for things gay. Mario had also made it clear he believed I made too much of being gay. That very first time he came for dinner, when I introduced the subject of a gay alumni group, he broke into a long harangue: "Gay, gay, gay. Is that all you ever think about? I don't believe in labeling people on the basis of their sexual preferences. The important thing to empha-size is humanness."

Familiar with this line of argument, I responded didactically. "Labels are necessary to help members of minority groups develop pride in their distinctive characteristics. Aren't you sensi-tive to that as an Italian? To feel equal, people have to be proud of the ways in which they differ from others as well as of the ways in which we're all human."

Mario huffed and looked away. But a few minutes later he allowed that perhaps he was unjustifiably provoked by all the importance I gave things gay because he had come out so late—and so painfully—himself. I saw Mario as another candidate for consciousness-raising.

But by the end of the month, when he flew back to L.A., I had learned nothing more about Mario's homosexuality and been given no opportunity to try to make him feel better about it. And a few weeks later, when Ben announced he was going to move to Los Angeles and live with Mario, I felt that an important new friend was being lured right out from under me. "Mario really likes my music," Ben assured me when I asked him if he was really going to uproot. "Don't worry. I'm not gonna go for six months. And I'll stay in touch when I do."

It was during that summer, the summer of '78, that I first began to talk about writing *Sons of Harvard*. When I mentioned the book to Ben, he only looked at me quizzically and shrugged. When I asked him if he'd be one of my "sons," he said, "Mmm," and then, "Yeah, but I won't use my real name 'cuz I don't want to embarass my parents."

Partly to keep him interested, I kept Ben posted on each devel-opment in the book's generation: When I had called to tell Nick

Bollman about my plans, his lover had assured me that Nick was now heavily involved in gay politics and would be happy to participate. From David Fredrick, the classmate with whom I was engaged in very unusual correspondence, I'd received a typically strange letter of support. Ken Ryan was excited about using the project to attract others interested in a gay alumni group. I had made contact with a literary agent who thought the idea had commercial potential, and he was also interested in my thesis. "If *Sons of Harvard* is a big popular success," I kidded Ben, "you can do the music for the movie. I'll outbid Mario for your services."

There was a snideness in my tone that was not without roots in competitiveness. The one thing that had become clear from my visits with Mario was that he was still struggling to make it professionally—as I was. I knew he didn't think much of my politics. I sensed he viewed me as something of a rival for Ben's affections. I didn't expect him to be very excited about my newest writing project. Still, in order to do the right thing by Ben, and to be thorough in preparing the unusual class report I expected the book to be, I felt I had to ask Mario if he wanted to be one of my interviewees.

I was prepared for him to refuse. In fact, regardless of what he did, I knew I could conceal his identity and write about our interaction to illustrate why many homosexuals shy away from the self-revelation I considered so political and to show how rivalry as well as affection can color relationships between old Harvard classmates. But I really wanted Ben to be in the book, not only because we'd developed such an interesting relationship, but also because I didn't know if I would encounter other classmates who could and would talk candidly about gay low life. So I spoke about my plans regularly with Ben, who resumed his Friday night visits once Mario had returned to Los Angeles, but decided not to approach Mario until my plans were firmer and I had time to write him a long letter.

That time came in the fall of 1978 when, after signing a contract to publish both a revised version of my thesis and *Sons of Harvard,* I went off to India with Rusty. From there I wrote Mario a long letter describing the book I envisioned, noting how happy I was that Ben and five other classmates had agreed to be interview subjects, and saying that I would be happy if he would join the group but understanding if he chose not to.

I had no idea what kind of response I was going to get, but I figured it would come in January, when we'd be back in Berkeley and he, according to one of Ben's letters, would be spending another month in San Francisco. It came, in fact, on one of those warm winter afternoons, a Saturday, that always make me so happy to be in California rather than Cambridge. Rusty and I were sunning ourselves on our back porch. The phone rang. Rusty answered it and reported that Ben and Mario were on their way over.

I let Rusty answer the doorbell, knowing that he would begin to chat with Ben and that Mario would be free to come out to the porch and say something about my letter. I just sat there and waited, my back to the door, my eyes trained on the fig tree next to the fence. Soon there were the expected footsteps, then a firm hand on each of my shoulders. "I got your letter . . . and I won't have anything to do with your project."

I turned and looked up into Mario's dark brown eyes, smiling to show him that there was no offense. "I thought that might be the case." Then, to assure him that I was neither surprised nor wounded by his response, I changed the subject. "How's your own writing coming?"

Mario said that everything was fine, but when I went on to ask about the new musical, he snapped, "But to get back to the subject. I can't be in the book for two reasons. First, being associated with anything gay would automatically sink me professionally. My career is just about to take off. You can't believe how uptight everyone in Hollywood is. And second, *my* life is *my* material. I just can't let you use it."

Before I had a chance to reply, Ben was in the doorway. "Here's Rodgers," I joshed. "How are Rodgers and Hammerstein doing?"

Ben said that he had composed two songs for the new musical while I was in India and that Mario's agent was talking with several producers who seemed interested. Mario looked away as Ben spoke, then excused himself, saying he had some work to do but would join us later for dinner. "Ben's decided to move to L.A. in March," he threw over his shoulder as he stalked out. "Isn't that wonderful?"

Ben smiled and explained that Mario had lined up a house for them to live in and that he was sure he could get some kind of programming job to support himself while he composed. "That's nice," I said. "Then I'll have a place to stay when I fly down to interview you." I wanted to see if Mario's reaction to my invitation had in any way affected Ben.

"Yeah," he replied. "You can come for a long weekend."

But even loving, loyal Ben looked aghast when later, after dinner, Mario turned to me and fumed, "I just can't go on without saying this. That letter of yours made me so mad. How dare you ask me to talk about my sex life publicly. And all that bit about your motives being political. Personally, I think you're just exploiting Harvard to get yourself published. And I don't want any part of it."

Mario's outburst took me by surprise. As usual, my defense was to remain intellectual. "I haven't asked you to do anything, Mario. All I've done is to extend an invitation."

This only agitated Mario more. "I can't stand the way you're always so reasonable. Don't you ever show any passion? I spent hours feeling angry about your letter and days thinking about what I was going to say when you came back. And you just smiled when I told you, and said, 'I thought that might be the case.' Well, fuck you."

"Look, Mario," I said, still intellectual. "I don't care if you're in the book or not. I don't need you. I'm not even sure I want you. But I do think you're passing up an opportunity to be part of something really important. And besides"—I laughed—"if you're not in the book, you can't do the screenplay for the movie. Ben's doing the music!"

I looked over at Ben, who looked away. Mario glared at me. Rusty just stared.

Then Mario stood up and said they had to go. Ben picked up his jacket, mumbled good-bye to me, hugged Rusty, and made for the door.

"Good night, Mario." I stuck out my hand.

"Good luck, Toby." He reached out and shook it.

Ben's last few months in the Bay Area were all the more poignant because of the breach. He stayed away until Mario returned to L.A. and then, as if to reassure me that our bond was still there, asked if he could store some of his things in the garage and used this as an occasion to drive up to Berkeley two or three times a week.

Each of us worked to be cheerful. I told Ben I was disappointed in the way Mario had reacted to my invitation but that I knew different people had different priorities. Ben confessed he had no idea why Mario had gotten so wrought up, saying simply, "I guess that's just Mario." There was no sign that he was in any way perturbed himself.

But on the morning of his departure, when he drove up with one last load of stuff to store before leaving, Ben looked worried. I grinned as I joined him out at the garage. "What's the matter? Has Mario had a change of heart?"

He stared at me for a moment, then murmured, "It's hard to believe, but last night on the telephone he said he was beginning to have real reservations about my coming. He's afraid I'll interrupt his work. He wants to keep his apartment until I'm settled in the house. But I'm still going to go. I just have to take the plunge if I'm ever going to make it in music."

"Mario's probably just experiencing commitment anxiety," I counseled, trying to be supportive without sounding self-righteous. "You just tell him that if he doesn't want you, we'll take you back."

Ben smiled weakly and said he had to be off. We unloaded his stuff without saying anything more, and then I went inside and got Rusty. Each of us scooped a handful of rice out of a canister in the kitchen as we made our way out to the driveway. Ben was standing next to his Dodge.

"Bon voyage, Ben." Rusty sprinkled him with rice.

"Where's the *Just Married* sign?" I smiled as I brushed the grains out of his hair, then showered him with rice myself. "And remember. I'll be down in a month or two to check things out."

When I got there, Ben seemed slightly unsure but not at all unhappy about just where his relationship with Mario stood. They hadn't had sex in a long time, but they didn't exclude that possibility for the future. Meanwhile, Ben was exploring gay low life in Los Angeles. But he and Mario still saw a lot of each other, still did the things they enjoyed socially, still were working on the musical. As Ben told me soon after we began our interview, "There will always be a place in my life for Mario."

I was eager to have him tell me more about his approach to sex and love because I knew that his ideas and his ways were typical of many homosexuals involved in the gay male subculture. If nothing else, just the variety of unusual relationships I had encountered once I had begun to explore gay life opened my eyes to this: men who called themselves "lovers" but had lots of "recreational sex" in addition to the "communicative sex" they had in the context of their "primary relationships"; men who continued to live with so-called lovers long after they had stopped having sex with each other and begun to enjoy transient sexual partners and even boyfriends; men who had relationships with old lovers alongside relationships with new lovers and lots of recreational sex in addition; couples who enjoyed "three ways"—sex shared with third parties—or who lived with friends, male and female, in what were clearly "alternative family" arrangements.

In earlier years, it had been hard for me to believe that such unconventional relationships could be healthy. And I was not alone among the gay men I knew in finding it hard to relinquish my long-held view that sustained sexually monogamous relationships were both the epitome of romance (because long years and limited sexual sharing were somehow more special) and the key to personal fulfillment. Then, before I got out into the gay world and saw what was actually happening, I tended to doubt that these unusual sexual and social arrangements could actually work. This was a view I shared with many who had been burned during the course of countercultural and political experimentation, veterans of the optimistic sixties who now believed that it would be wonderful if relationships could be open and sexuality shared, but that this was rarely possible in practice because of human nature, social conditioning, social pressure, jealousy, time, the practicalities, and so on.

It was no surprise to me that many of those in whom I found this latter view were women, most of them aware of feminism if not politically active as feminists. In *The Politics of Homosexuality* I had shown that the foreignness of traditional gay male sexual and social styles was one of the things that had led lesbian political leaders over the decades to believe that they had more in common with heterosexual women and the women's movement than with homosexual men and the gay movement. Most of the heterosexual feminists these lesbians allied with equated traditional gay male patterns with the unliberated sexuality they found so objectionable in straight men. Following the lead of lesbian

feminists and feminists in general, many of the first male gay liberationists had also been critical of the sexual pastimes enjoyed by
so many of the gay men they vowed to liberate. As more and
more aficionados of the gay male subculture and sexually liberated lesbians became involved in gay political activity, there was
less misplaced moralism and more understanding of how sexually
promiscuous men cóuld be perfectly liberated. But the meaning and morality of gay male sexual styles was still a hot topic
in gay, lesbian, and feminist political circles, and as more and
more thinking heterosexuals became aware of the ways in which
many gay men lived and loved, I expected the controversy to
spread to society at large. In the testimony of classmates like Ben,
I saw material that might enlighten—and enliven—popular
debate.

How many sexual partners do you think you've had?

I don't know. That's like asking how many lunches have
you eaten. You lose count.

Can you make a guess as to an average?

Oh, well, some days none, some three or four. It sort of
depends on what you mean by sexual partner, on how
much contact it takes to make somebody a sexual partner. I
mean, there's a whole range of behavior that's really sexual
—from just touching a cock, to going down on it, to fucking
or getting fucked, to coming or not coming. Sexual activity
should be viewed as a continuum rather than as some sort of
discrete act. One night at the baths I might touch ten or
twenty people. But that doesn't mean that each of them was
a sexual partner.
   Anyway, for an average, let me guess one person a day
since I started being sexually active.

Have you ever had an extended relationship with another
man?

Sure. I have lots of relationships with lots of people.

But have you had a lover for a long period of time?

Well, in a sense. But that's an area that's very ill-defined. What does having a lover mean? I don't draw any distinction between someone I call a lover and someone I call a friend.

Isn't there a distinction between those you have sex with and those you don't?

Yes. But having a sexual relationship doesn't necessarily mean you're lovers or friends: You can have sex with somebody and not know them or even like them. Somebody's a friend when there's something special about him to you, when both people are sensitive to each other. That's what lovers are too.

What I want to say is that both love and friendship are more important than the sex. I can have sex with most anybody, but I can't be friends with just anybody. And loving someone is very special.

How about the intensity of closeness? Doesn't "lover" conjure up something stronger than "friend," a sense of closeness, or coupling?

Well, coupling's a good word to use, but it says something about how two people behave together without necessarily saying anything about how they feel about each other.

What do you mean by that?

Oh, that there are a lot of couples who don't have sex and don't love each other and aren't even friends. Coupling is one thing. Sex is another thing. And friendship and love are still other things. Sometimes they overlap, and sometimes they don't.

Do you desire to be in a couple?

I think it's just as desirable as it is undesirable. It sort of depends on how it turns out. I've never been dependent on having a partner to couple with, but when I've felt like it, I've done it. I'm kind of in a couple now, but the important thing is our friendship. Then there's sex, and that's something else again. I can go to the baths and have as much sex as I want. What's that got to do, in itself, with my sharing this house with Mario and looking forward to seeing him?

To get Ben's perspective on how his relationship with Mario had evolved, I asked him how he felt about commitment, whether he saw that in his own relationships.

I've remained pretty committed to you and your book, haven't I? I have commitments to several people in my life, people like Tom and Alex. Those commitments aren't formalized, but they're very real.

And with Mario there's a commitment. I don't really know when it came into being. I guess it's still kind of congealing. From my point of view, he exercises a lot of power and decision-making about what's going to happen. And that's okay with me. That's the kind of relationship I have with him.

But doesn't Mario's behavior have any effect on your feelings for him? Will they change if he doesn't want to live with you or he doesn't want to have sex with you or he doesn't particularly want to see you very often?

He would never decide that he doesn't want to see me. I don't care what kind of conflicts we have, we think a great deal of each other. We respect one another. We're fond of one another. We'll always care in some way about each other. And if the way we express that or experience that changes, well, then it changes.

You've described yourself as being very promiscuous. And you've described yourself as being pretty capable of commitment at the same time. Do you think there's any conflict?

No, I think it's possible to have your cake and eat it too, as long as you only take what you need and aren't greedy and don't have too many expectations. Life gives you what you need. I believe that.

And are you completely happy? I mean, do you go through life feeling fulfilled emotionally and satisfied sexually?

Yeah, I do.

At the end of our interview I asked Ben if his agreement to be in my book was a sign that he had become more political about his homosexuality. It was then that I learned why, that very first time he came for curry, he had been so careful to say that he wasn't "all" gay.

Do you remember my portraying your participation in *Sons of Harvard* as liberationist political activity, and my argument that having liberated people speak out was important because it enhanced society's understanding of sexuality and sex roles and thereby contributed to sexual liberation and to humanism?

Well, I can see that the book will help people understand a lot more about sexuality. But I don't think that books or political crusades are what will bring about sexual liberation.

Then how, in your view, is sexual liberation going to come about?

Well, it's already on its way, and I don't think it can be stopped now. That's part of what's been happening since the sixties. *Playboy* has done as much to further sexual liberation as anything else.

But don't you think that gay liberationists have played a role in making it easier for people to express their homosexual feelings naturally?

I don't know. I guess I think that they are responding to the reality of what is happening, which is something very much broader than a change in attitudes about homosexual behavior. I think that most people have become very much more open-minded about sexual expression. Gay people are focusing on their homosexuality now, but I think they'll soon get tired of being just gay or just politically gay or just anything. Ideally, everybody would be trying to explore all the sexual aspects of themselves, homosexual and heterosexual.

So you see everybody slowly but surely becoming bisexual?

It will probably never get to the point of perfect equilibrium. That would be kind of dull. But I think that unless there is some absolute disaster, things are going that way, towards a greater variety of sexual expression for everyone.

Are you moving that way?

I haven't yet, but I feel that welling up in myself. I find that the more comfortable and interested and successful I am in my homosexuality, the more able I am to continue exploring to see if there's anything in heterosexuality for me. What I'm looking for is an environment, inside my own mind and outside in the world, that is not rigidly conservative or screamingly unconventional, where all kinds of people are sharing and getting along and making space for one another. Then I can be homosexual when I want to and explore the rest of myself as I want to.

But isn't it because liberationist-minded gay people have provided visible role models, information, and attractive and legitimate gay institutions that homosexuals today are able to develop happy and integrated lives much earlier and more easily than we were able to?

That's the one obligation I think I feel towards gay liberation—to reach out to people who are tortured and unhappy and alone because they don't have any corroboration for their natural feelings. I think we owe it to them to let them know that the rest of us are here.

Ben was the gay classmate I'd known the longest, and in many ways my visit with him was only a preliminary to the real exploration that lay ahead. From Los Angeles I was flying to Chicago to visit an old freshman dorm-mate I had been particularly uncomfortable with in college. Then I was off to interview classmates in Washington, D.C., Ann Arbor, East Lansing, New York City, and Cambridge, which, because we had all spent four years there, was where I liked to think my journey had really begun.

3

WILLKIE SCHOPENHAUER

I was feeling slightly uneasy as I made my way down the dark alleyway. Though back in college I'd known Willkie better than most of the classmates I was going to visit, I'd never really liked him. For a variety of reasons—the way he looked, the way he talked, the way he moved—he had always given me the creeps.

Almost as soon as I knocked on the side door he'd told me to find, it opened a crack. Then the door swung open and a voice boomed forth: "I wore my Harvard football jersey in *your* honor." It was a gravelly voice I knew was Willkie's. "I'm very different now, wouldn't you say?"

"You sure are." He did seem thinner than he was in college, and rather macho in that jersey. But there was still that fawning smile and that hovering closeness that had always made me feel as if Willkie was just waiting to get into my pants.

With pushiness that was also familiar, he said he was late and led me down the dim corridor and into a small room. It was musty with the smell of burnt candles and sweet herbs. One wall was banked with cabinets full of wide, shallow drawers. Another was studded with hooks hung with chains and cords of different thicknesses and lengths. A third was lined with shelves crowded with metal implements.

"I've got to rush," Willkie said as he pulled the jersey up over his chest. Thick hair curled across it. His body was beefy but muscular. All the flab was gone.

As he threw a black robe over his head, I told him I was delighted he'd invited me to come see him perform. When I'd called to set up our interview, he'd told me that the whole performance would take less than an hour and that we could tape at his apartment afterward. He'd assured me that I wouldn't have to participate if I didn't want to, promising there'd be plenty of others who just sat and watched.

As he wrestled to untangle a thick white cord, I found myself thinking back to freshman year. Willkie had lived just a few doors down the corridor from me in Matthews Hall, one of the big red-brick dorms in the large expanse of elm-shaded lawn known as Harvard Yard. Its five floors of oak-paneled rooms were linked by a wide circular stairway of black granite. At the head of each landing was a common bathroom. The john on the third floor was ours.

It was there that I was especially careful to avoid Willkie. He always used to smile a little bit too leeringly for my comfort when he walked into that bathroom, and he was much too self-conscious about the little squeezes he would give those he was talking to. I couldn't have found Willkie more unattractive. He was girdled with rolls of fat. He had a thick upper lip and was so heavily bearded that he always looked unshaven. His eyes were either intensely direct or darting nervously from one place to another. Back then, Willkie looked and acted the way I imagined all "queers" did.

"I'm ready," he announced, placing his arm firmly around my shoulder to indicate it was time for me to go. "Just walk through that door and take a seat up front."

Willkie really had changed, I thought to myself. With the weight in his face gone, his features looked strongly hewn. His heavy beard now appeared as a very masculine shadow. And he stood, shoulders back, almost six feet tall.

But Willkie's now-solid torso was hidden beneath the thick layers of cloth he had donned as I reminisced. The first layer was the long black robe he'd pulled on first. Over that was a smock of starched linen which he'd belted with the thick white cord. Over all this he wore a chasuble of ivory brocade lined with red satin. Around his neck was a wide white ribbon embroidered with crosses and flowers.

Smiling broadly, Willkie made a mock bow. Then he led me to the door opposite the one we had come in. Painted across it, in ornate gold script, was the word *Sacristy*. Beyond was the nave of Saint Thomas' Episcopal Church.

Saint Thomas' was a small Episcopal parish in one of the working-class German neighborhoods of Chicago. Its walls and arched ceilings were painted white. Its stained-glass windows, scenes from the New Testament wrought in basic hues, were ringed with glass an almost fluorescent yellow-green. Vividly colored plaster of Paris statues looked out over the pews.

I was going to church for the first time in years. I hadn't gone regularly, in fact, since my freshman year at Harvard. Back then, almost paralyzed by the anguish I felt at having lost my high-school lover, I went each morning to chapel at the University's Memorial Church. From the guys in Matthews, I hid my pain by being affable in the superficial way that had made me very popular at Medford High. I was honest with no one. And neither was Willkie.

All the way through high school, all the way through college, and then in the seminary and in the parish, I never had any doubts about being homosexual. On an intellectual basis I was never bothered by it. I accepted it. But for all my intellectual acceptance, I was very hung up about it psychologically and emotionally, and very guilt-ridden. That was why I'd gotten fat—it was a way of not having to deal with sex. And that's why, once I came out, it was easy for me to lose the weight and the other mannerisms or whatever I'd used to distance people.

From high school on I was absolutely terrified that someone would discover I was homosexual. I was convinced that if anyone I knew and cared about found out, they would totally and completely reject me. I was sure they would think me a piece of filth. Well, of course, that was what I had come to feel about myself: that I was worthless, that I was a piece of shit, that I was perverted. Intellectually, it didn't bother me; emotionally, it was a disaster.

So my greatest concern was to hide that one fact from everyone else. With all of my friends, my goal was to become as close as possible, to learn as much about them as possible, but to hold this one thing back.

The organ that had been accompanying my reverie with simple harmony suddenly blared forth loudly. Others sitting in the pews eased themselves up and began to sing. I stood up and watched.

In the doorway to the sacristy appeared a white-smocked acolyte holding a long gold chain with a censer at its end. Suddenly, the golden orb swung up into the air, leaving an evanescent fist of smoke at the acme of its rise. Then the acolyte stepped forward, and a procession of altar boys emerged. Then Willkie, in all his magnificent adornments, singing distinctly louder than everyone else.

The procession led Willkie to the center of the sanctuary. Against its back wall was an altar bearing six gold candlesticks with tall white candles. In the middle, flanked by the candles, was an even taller gold crucifix. Several feet in front of this stood a bare table made of blond wood. Willkie faced the congregation, the table in front of him, the crucifix rising dramatically behind his head. Without a trace of his once-thick accent he intoned, "Blessed be God—Father, Son, and Holy Spirit."

The congregation replied with a muffled, "And blessed be His kingdom, now and forever."

From the rack on the back of the pew in front of me I withdrew a piece of paper headed *Order of Worship* and tried to follow along. I had a hard time paying attention. My mind raced back to the last time I had seen Willkie preaching to an attentive audience—a group of tourists he was guiding around the Harvard campus for the Crimson Key. The Key was a small fraternity of undergraduates who conducted tours for visitors, stopping to give little spiels in front of each historic building and important monument. Willkie had competed and, much to my surprise, had been chosen for membership early in our freshman year. After that he was much less often around Matthews. I had always assumed that this was because he had gotten caught up in the Key.

But what really happened that year was Jack Smith. I met him the first week we were at Harvard and flipped out over him. I thought he was the most attractive person I'd ever met. Very quickly we became close friends. We ended up spending virtually all our time together. I was always over at his dorm. We always ate our meals in the Union together. I was practically never in Matthews Hall, except to sleep.

Well, of course, it wasn't long before I was madly out of my mind in love with him. Not that much actually happened, of course. Jack was almost asexual at that point. I don't think he really had any definite sexual feelings of any sort. He was so utterly innocent. You probably remember how utterly innocent he was. I think that's one of the things that attracted me to him. Because, in a sense, I couldn't have been less innocent.

Well, what happened is a real dramatic story. Jack and I and his two roommates went down to Cape Cod over spring break. Someone in Jack's roommate's family had a house there. Well, spring break, as you remember, is at the beginning of April, and in New England it's still cold at that time of year. It turned out to be *very* cold on Cape Cod that week.

The house was a summer house, so it was unheated. And it was so cold the first night we nearly froze our butts off. We were all sleeping in separate rooms. And—mind you, this was Jack's idea—there was one room that had a double bed in it, and he suggested that the two of us sleep together in the double bed to keep warm.

It was so cold we literally took the curtains off the windows and the rugs off the floors and put them over our beds to keep warm. If we doubled up in the one bed, Jack said, we could double up with the blankets, curtains, and rugs, and use our body heat to help keep each other warm.

Well, we did more than that. It was one of those classic cases—I'm sure you've heard stories like this from other classmates. He pretended to be asleep. I pretended to believe that he was asleep—which, actually, I did believe. I know now that he was probably wide awake the whole time. But at that time, I guess, I believed it was possible—because I wanted to believe it—to sleep through what went on. So I took an awful lot of liberties, shall I say, with his body. And he allowed it on the grounds that he was asleep and, therefore, not responsible for what was happening.

At the time—I could tell from his erection—he seemed to be enjoying it. However, the next day he was awfully quiet and rather pensive about something. This puzzled me. I kept thinking: He couldn't have known what was going on last night because he was asleep, after all.

We slept together again that night, and the same thing happened. I fooled around a lot, and the next day he was even more pensive and quiet.

About the middle of the afternoon, he decided that he didn't want to stay on Cape Cod anymore. He wanted to go back to Cambridge: He had so much studying to do; he had a lot of work to do; he had papers, et cetera, et cetera, et cetera. He was talking very fast.

Well, I'd driven all of us down there. So I said, "Well, all right, I'll drive you back up to Cambridge." In fact, I was so madly in love with him that I said, "Why don't I stay with you in Cambridge?"

He said, "No, no, no, I don't want you to. You come back down to the Cape." So I drove him back up to Cambridge, dropped him off, and went back down to the Cape. I was utterly miserable for the rest of the break.

From that time on Jack was very, very cool towards me, very distant. The whole relationship was totally changed. In my desire not to know the truth, I refused to believe that it was because of what happened. I still believed he was asleep and didn't know. But the fact remained that, in effect, he had rejected me.

I would call him up and say, "Do you want to go to a movie? Do you want to do this? Do you want to do that?"

He'd say, "No, I don't. I can't do that. I'm busy. I can't."

Suddenly he was no longer available. When we were together, he wouldn't look at me. He wouldn't speak unless spoken to. He'd never call me.

The next thing I knew I started seeing him with you all the time. He was walking around with *you* just the way he used to walk around with me, looking at *you* the way he used to look at me, smiling at *you* the way he used to smile at me. Do you know how jealous I became of you? I wanted to kill you, I hated you so much.

U

"Love thy neighbor as thyself," Willkie urged the congregation, reading from Saint Matthew as he proceeded through the Liturgy of the Word. In the letter he had written me after seeing the class report, he'd confessed that he had loathed me back in college, saying that his feelings about me and a lot of other people had begun to change only after he had started feeling better about himself—which was after he'd become deeply involved in religion.

As a junior Willkie had attended services at Boston's famous Trinity Church because the rector there was a particularly scholarly interpreter of Christian philosophy. After graduating, he'd enrolled in the nearby Episcopal Theological School, been ordained, and taken a job as an assistant priest in a small parish on Cape Cod. From there he'd gone to Notre Dame to begin his own studies of Christian philosophy, by that time comfortable enough with his homosexuality to organize a gay student group on campus. After completing all but the dissertation requirements for his Ph.D., Willkie had realized that there were going to be no positions available for religious scholars by the time he completed his thesis. Turning to an earlier love—science—he'd taken a job editing a national science magazine, with plans to complete his thesis in his spare time. To keep in touch with the church, he conducted services as a stand-in, and he was also active in Integrity, a national association of gay Episcopalians. Though he enjoyed being a pastor, he wrote me in that first letter, he thought of himself first and foremost as a religious scholar.

I'd not been surprised to learn that Willkie thought of himself as an academic, for he had always struck me as being rather bookish. At Harvard he was one of those characters who seemed to live in Lamont Library, the modern undergraduate facility located next to the president's mansion in a corner of the Yard. After freshman year, even though he and I both moved to Lowell House, I seemed to see him only when I was in Lamont. I was sure that Willkie was even more uptight about getting good grades than I was. Why else would he spend so much time in Lamont?

Once, when I was a freshman, I was over at the basement john in Lamont Library on perfectly legitimate business. And the guy in the stall next to me sort of reached his hand under the partition. It frightened me so much that for the next several days I had nightmares about disembodied hands reaching for me. After I got over the initial fear, of course, it was perfectly obvious what was going on—the guy had been after me sexually.

It preyed on my mind, but I didn't go anywhere near that john again for another year and a half. It wasn't until I was a junior that I went back. I hadn't masturbated for about a day and was very horny. I remembered the john.

At that time the University was trying to suppress activity in the johns. Obviously a lot of straight guys had complained about hands reaching for them under stalls. They extended the partitions down to the floor so that people couldn't do that anymore, which was a very stupid thing to do. It made sexual activity even more common, because it made each one of the stalls a private room.

There were a couple of stalls that had peepholes between them. All you had to do was go into one of these, look through the peephole, and see what the other guy was doing in there. If he was playing with himself, you knew he was there for sex. Then you would pass a couple of quick notes back and forth, and one of you would go into the other's stall. I remember at times, when I was a senior, I'd stop in the basement john and find crowds of people. All four stalls would have at least two and sometimes three people in them. That was too many people for me.

That's when I discovered the basement john in Burr Lecture Hall. It wasn't as active as Lamont, which, as I say, got so busy it scared me. But it was busy enough so that you knew you could go there anytime you wanted and have sex in fifteen to thirty minutes. When I was a senior, and also when I was in the seminary, maybe once every two months the pressure would build up to the point where I couldn't stand it anymore. So I'd tromp over to Burr. Then there'd be another two months or so, and I'd do it again.

The sexual activity that went on there was almost exclusively sucking. It was very anonymous—that was important for me. They hadn't put extenders on the stalls in Burr, so you could just get down on your knees and get to everything you needed to get to underneath the partition. Of course, only that much of the person was visible, and so you never saw any faces.

I think the major reason I liked the Burr johns was that it was possible for me to have sex there without ever being seen. Of course, I had to put up with the fact that I couldn't see the other person either. But I was willing to pay that price in order to be safe. I think most of the guys who used the johns were there for the same reason: They couldn't afford to let anyone know they were homosexual.

I remember one time I went over to Burr and found two of the stalls right next to each other occupied. I knew that something was going on, so I went back upstairs and waited. A few minutes later this tall, very attractive, very masculine young guy, probably a freshman, about eighteen years old, came up with a look of fear on his face that you just can't imagine. He rushed up the stairs, obviously afraid that the guy who had been in the other stall was going to follow him, and he ran out the door and up Quincy Street towards the Yard.

It was perfectly obvious what was going on, so I went downstairs. The other guy was still there. Wanting anonymity himself, he hadn't followed. We exchanged notes under the wall. I asked about the guy who was in there previously, and he told me they'd had sex. That's exactly what that freshman had been doing: He was gay, he was horny, he went in there to get a blow-job, and as soon as he got it, he couldn't get out of there fast enough. Like I used to do—although by that time I wasn't so frightened that I had literally to run away.

Anyway, then the guy in the john blew me too. Neither of us ever saw each other either.

Now, standing in the pulpit, Willkie was ready to give his sermon. "I want to talk to you this morning about wine," he began, turning his head slowly from left to right so that every eye would fix upon him. "Did you know that even the best French wines have American roots?"

Willkie paused, cleared his throat, looked for the eyes, went on. He explained that early in this century, vintners in France had discovered that the roots of their grape vines were being killed by worms. They had escaped disaster by grafting their plants onto the worm-resistant roots of vines imported from America. Willkie's analogy: "As French and American grapevines now draw their sustenance from common roots, so we, all different, draw our sustenance from the same source . . . Jesus Christ."

"The beauty of the Church," Willkie continued, "is that thanks to its common root, it has the strength to encompass people who are very diverse—people who differ in economic status, nationality, race, sex, and . . . (I was wondering if—and how—he was going to bring up the gay angle) . . . life-style. This is why the Church became my home."

I think I've been making it clear that from the time I was in high school right up to February 14, 1973, when I was working in a church on Cape Cod, I really had no emotional growth or change whatsoever. During that entire period, my way of dealing with my sexuality and my feelings about my sexuality remained exactly the same. Then a person named Dean appeared in the parish. He was immensely attractive to me, physically and personally. We became friends, and I began to follow the same script I had followed in all of the other relationships I'd had: to come as close as possible, to be very intimate, to share all kinds of things, but never to say anything about my homosexuality.

Well, Dean destroyed my script by telling me he was gay. This he did on February thirteenth. I didn't sleep a wink that night. Suddenly I had no idea what to do; this was not the way the script was supposed to work. Anyway, the next night, with fear and trembling, I told him that I was gay too. I also told him that I was sexually attracted to him.

I was afraid, of course, that he was going to reject me. He didn't. Since he wasn't attracted to me sexually, there wasn't any sex between us. But over the next few months, he put me through the psychological process of coming out in an incredibly skillful way.

The guy is a natural counselor, a natural psychologist. There would be times when I'd be feeling really put down and depressed and he'd listen. There'd be other times when I was not simply down and depressed, but wallowing in it, using my depression as a manipulative technique to try to get something out of him. He'd see right through that and cut me off. He just wouldn't let me do it. He was there to listen when I needed listening to, but when I was there to play games, he'd shut me up. He was incredibly preceptive.

Slowly but surely I told him everything. This was the first time in my life I told someone I liked and respected that I was gay. And a great deal more. Bit by bit, to see what his reaction would be, I told him about my masturbating five times a day, my sexual fantasies, my sex in the public johns, everything. And he was perfect.

What he did, of course, was to help me accept myself. For the first time in my life someone knew all about me and still accepted me, still said that I was all right, that I was lovable, that I was a good person. And gradually, I began to feel that way about myself. I began to love myself.

The change was enormous. It took place over about four months. I lost sixty pounds, and I suddenly became a very happy person, which I hadn't been before.

This puzzled a great many people in the parish. They'd say, "What happened? You used to walk around all the time with your head hanging down. You pretended not to see people. You wouldn't speak to people unless they spoke to you first. You hardly ever smiled. But now, all of a sudden, you go around with your head up and you meet people eye to eye and you smile and say hello. You seem much happier. What happened?"

Talk about liberation. I was liberated during those four months in an incredible way. It was then that I discovered what Christianity is really supposed to be about. And it was all because of my relationship with Dean—who, by the way, is now in the seminary himself. But he's being openly gay, and I don't know whether they'll ordain him or not.

As Willkie concluded his sermon with some kind of prayer, in which everyone else joined, I continued taking notes on the back of my Order of Worship. Then, feeling a hand on my shoulder, I wondered if I was doing something wrong. When I turned to see whose hand it was, a woman bent forward and pecked me on the cheek. "Peace be with you," she whispered. I smiled and she was gone, stooping to plant a kiss on the cheek of the elderly black woman sitting next to her. "Peace be with you," she said again.

Now the whole congregation was astir. People were wishing each other peace, kissing one another, shaking hands. Willkie was making his way up the aisle, brushing his lips against the cheeks of the women, looking straight into the eyes of the men, shaking their hands. I walked over to the aisle and held out my own hand. "Peace be with you," Willkie said, winking as he took it into his own.

As he stooped to kiss the women in the pew behind me, I felt a rush of affection for this man I had done so much to avoid back in college. Once Willkie had begun to show up less and less in Lamont, I had been perfectly happy limiting my contact to the reports I would get periodically from Ted Somes, who had roomed with me freshman year and shared an apartment with Willkie the summer after we were sophomores. They seemed to go separate ways after that, and whenever I would ask Ted what was going on with Willkie, he would only shake his head and chuckle, "Oh, you know about Willkie." Once he said this in front of his friend Ned Fromm, and in the slightly teasing tone he always took with me, Ned said, "Yeah, Toby, *you* know about Willkie."

In those days, I did all I could to make Ted and Ned think I had no idea what they were getting at. And I wasn't the only one playing games that left us all losers.

I wanted to be close to Ted, and so I told him all kinds of intimate and personal things about myself. But when it came to sex, I would concoct lies about heterosexual episodes and fantasies because I felt I just couldn't tell him the truth. Which was pretty ironic because Ted had already guessed the truth.

One summer, when he was working at Mass General Hospital, we roomed together on Beacon Hill. We had been out together one night and were very drunk. Ted, I thought, was even drunker than I was. When we got back to our apartment, he went into his room, stripped completely naked, and collapsed on his bed. I mean, he passed out completely—or so I thought. I staggered in and saw him lying there and was so turned on; his naked body was so beautiful that I just stood there and looked, enraptured. I didn't do anything. I didn't touch him. I just stood in a drunken haze and stared at him.

If there was one person in the world Ted believed straight, it was Ned Fromm. And the incredible irony of this whole story is that just before we graduated, Ned came over to my room and told me that he was gay. He said he was confiding in me because Ted had told him what had happened that summer. He said that Ted was sure I was gay from that point on.

At the time, I was still so hung up that I lied and told Ned I wasn't gay. I said that I had just been worried about Ted because he was so drunk and I was just watching him to see if he was going to be okay. And Ned believed me. I remember his saying, "You know, it's really funny. Ted thinks that you're gay and that I'm straight, and the reality is that you're straight and I'm gay." The truth, of course, was that both of us were gay. And so were you, Toby. Poor Ted. Poor us.

When the Greeting of Peace was over, Willkie returned to the sanctuary, fetched a golden bowl and chalice, placed them on the table, and then blessed the bread and the wine. Solemnly, members of the congregation shuffled forward, one by one, to be fed the ritual meal and dispatched with a blessing to their places. When the communion was over, Willkie took a seat on a side bench and bowed his head in meditation. The white-smocked acolyte removed the sacred vessels, then positioned himself, censer in hand, at the head of the troupe of altar boys who had gathered at the front of the church.

Now Willkie stood, stepped forward, blessed his flock "in the name of the Father, the Son, and the Holy Spirit." The censer shot out from the acolyte, and Willkie walked over and stood behind the altar boys. There was a burst of organ music to announce the closing hymn.

For one full stanza the churchmen remained frozen, with Willkie once again singing distinctly louder than everyone else.

Then, following the shooting censer, they marched down the aisle, out the front door, and into the Sunday morning sun. I waited until almost everyone had left before joining the exodus. From the back of the church I watched Willkie greet members of his flock.

When the last one was gone, he came over, took me by the arm, and guided me to the parish house, a large, multipurpose recreation room built onto the back of the church. Near the door was a table covered with plates of doughnuts, columns of styrofoam cups, containers of sugar and powdered creamer, and an urn of coffee. Behind it was the woman who had kissed me. Willkie introduced me as an old friend from Harvard. The woman smiled, and when he moved on, she bent over and said that she had just loved "Father's" sermon. We conversed for a few minutes, and then she asked me if I wanted to meet her daughter, who was "still single."

I shook hands with the daughter, who appeared from behind the mother, and said I'd love another cup of coffee. I was thinking about what I was going to say if she asked me why I had been taking notes. It was obvious that most of the parishioners didn't know that Willkie was gay. How, I wondered, did he square this with his claim to being an ardent gay liberationist?

Avoiding the eyes of mother and daughter, I watched Willkie make his way around the room, acknowledging compliments, answering questions, shaking hands. It was clear that he would never have reached these people as he obviously had if he weren't "in the closet" when it came to his pastoring. It was also plain that he tried to convey important messages in his sermons. Still, I wasn't at all sure that people understood messages delivered so abstractly and indirectly. This was another topic I wanted to take up with Willkie.

People tend to read their own biases into the Scriptures. Anyone who really knows anything about the Bible knows that there is no biblical condemnation of homosexuality that holds any water whatsoever. Of course, I'm not talking about people like Anita Bryant who use Scripture to argue whatever they want. I'm talking about serious scholars. All the research shows that Old Testament condemnations of homosexuality were based on questions of ritual purity and not on some kind of divine commandment about sexuality. I mean, homosexual practices were part of non-Hebrew rituals and were condemned the same way that worshipping other gods was condemned. The sermonizers in the New Testament misinterpreted their forebears.

Besides, theology should be about how to live well, how to live like Christ, not about what to avoid. Biblical teachings have to be interpreted in the light of contemporary realities. How can someone say that it is sinful for a guy to go to the baths to meet someone who is there to meet someone; for them to smile at and to touch and to have sex with each other; for them to make one another feel good? How can someone say that that's sinful but that it's perfectly moral for a husband to fuck his wife every night with a total lack of concern for her as a person—especially if he's the type who slaps her around during the day, boozes it up at night, never shows her any genuine interest and respect, and is only concerned with getting his rocks off?

Sex should be about communication and caring. I think legitimate theological questions can be raised about promiscuity without caring—although even then it probably doesn't hurt anybody. But I think that's what people should be thinking about. If being promiscuous limits your ability to respond warmly and humanly and honestly, then I think you shouldn't be promiscuous. But if it can help you learn to be more intimate with people, feel better about yourself, and be more open and warm with others, then how can we condemn it? The point is not just what you do, but what happens when you do it, why you do it, what effect it has on your life and the other person's.

I haven't been very promiscuous lately because I value the relationship I have with my lover. I want that to be kind of special for me now. I've only had tricks and affairs until now. But there have been times in the past when I've been very promiscuous. Right after I came out, I went to the bars all the time and had lots of one-night stands. They taught me a good deal about myself. They left most of my sexual partners feeling good. I think that that's what theology has to be about.

When most of the parishioners had disappeared, Willkie excused himself and went off to change his clothes. I helped the hostess and her daughter clean up. Willkie reappeared in his football jersey, and we set out for our afternoon of taping, leaving the women smiling.

Back at his apartment, which was far more ornate than Saint Thomas', Willkie stretched out on his sofa and I made myself comfortable on the rug. Now that we were home from church, "Father" was willing to talk openly about his painful years at Harvard, his dramatic coming-out in the priesthood, his development of positive feelings about homosexuality and gay life, and his ideas about promiscuity, sexual liberation, and theology. At the end of our long afternoon, I returned to the matter of his ministry and asked him how his gayness affected his pastoring.

I've already given you some idea of how my theology has been affected by my involvement in the gay subculture. And then there's my emphasis on the Church as a community of different people with different life-styles who can accept each other and all their differences. I push that idea as much as possible. It's the best hope for liberation.

And the way I relate to men and women within the Church is certainly colored by my sexuality. I can deal with women in ways that are nonsexual and nonthreatening to them. And I can offer men a special sort of warmth and affection. I don't mean sexual come-ons, mind you!

I believe that my liberated sexuality enhances my qualities as a person in every way. And I think that, in general, the more people are aware of and comfortable expressing their sexual feelings, the more fulfilled they are as persons and the better able they are to relate to others. For me, that means being happily and freely gay. If I weren't a liberated gay man, I wouldn't be as sensitive, I wouldn't be as warm, I wouldn't be as good a priest.

"Look at yourself," Willkie continued. "Don't you like yourself a whole lot better the way you are now? I sure do!" And before the afternoon was over, I learned that Willkie had seen as much good growth in me as I had seen in him.

When we were freshmen in Matthews Hall, I thought you were very attractive physically, and in other ways. I liked your smile, your personality. Like Jack, you had a certain cute shyness and a disarming air of innocence. But I didn't get much back from you, so we never really became friends.

That was the period when I was so in love with Jack, and since I was getting warm feelings from him, I spent almost all my time with him. Then, of course, that awful thing on Cape Cod happened. After that, Jack wouldn't talk to me, and he started spending a lot of time with you. I thought that maybe you were having sex with Jack, and I just hated you.

By the time we got to sophomore year, I began to think of you as very ambitious, politically and socially. You seemed to be very interested in spending all your time with guys from famous families, guys who had lots of money or were in the Social Register or were for some reason or other big men on campus. I thought you were out for yourself, out to pick friends on the basis of how they might help you politically and socially, you and a lot of others. I didn't respect that. I didn't like people who cared only about using one another.

4

MARTY BRENNER

After traveling to Los Angeles and Chicago, being in Washington, D.C., was like being back home. I had spent a great deal of time in the capital as a Harvard student. More than any place else, my ambitions had led me there. I returned with a touch of sadness. Ten years earlier I would have been met at Washington National Airport and driven home to Georgetown by Larry O'Brien, one of my college roommates. This time I took the Metro to Arlington, Virginia, and checked into a Holiday Inn.

The first thing I did was to call Marty Brenner. He had been the first to respond to my letter to the class asking for help with *Sons of Harvard*.

FROM: Brenner   To: Toby Marotta
          222 Melba Drive   934 Carleton Street
          Atlanta, Ga.   Berkeley, Calif. 94710

                        DATE: *April 16, 1979*

Dear Toby,

Your recent letter, which illustrates your great commitment to gay liberation, was greatly appreciated by both myself and my lover, Ted. I am pleased that you are serious enough to compile a Class of '67 Chronicle. I suspect, however, that you may finally include a wider sampling than only a single class.

My hope is that you will awaken a need within gay classmates to "support" each other in every endeavor, including standard professional services. It goes without saying that such a minority is generally capable of communicating with each other more efficiently than others. Therefore, I urge you to put more Harvard gays in touch with each other for purely business reasons. It certainly seems to me to be more comfortable working and consulting with others who share a similar sexual orientation.

I am enclosing a summary professional bio which recently appeared within an article I wrote for a trade journal. This, of course, includes no statement of sexual philosophy, but I would be happy to discuss a more personal history with you or your representative, should you desire some. As a Vietnam Vet, I am well-versed in the politics and priorities of the sixties, and I have few reasons to be inhibited about my homosexuality, thanks to what I have learned from my 6-year relationship with Ted.

My schedule is a bit erratic, however; and I presently commute to Washington, D.C., weekly to work on a temporary assignment. Therefore, you may reach me most easily at the above address/ phone on most weekends.

In any case, I am interested in subscribing to the fruits of your labors, so please put my name on your mailing list.

Very Truly Yours,

Martin Brenner, A.I.A.
B.A. '67
M. Arch. '72

When I had called to set up an interview, Marty had asked me to come to his office for a get-acquainted meeting. His headquarters was a basement office in the big federal building adjacent to the Old Post Office in the Federal Triangle. Marty was one of the architects supervising the renovation of this original home of the Post Office Department. It was being remodeled into a complex of shops and public offices surrounding a huge glass-covered atrium.

As soon as I arrived, Marty offered to give me a tour of the big neo-Romanesque structure. First we walked up to the top tier of offices and looked down into the indoor court. Then we climbed a rung ladder into the clock tower. Its spacious, open windows looked out on the city. "People say this is the best view of the capital there is," Marty told me. "Both ABC and CBS take their panorama shots of Washington from up here."

I turned my eyes from the spectacle before me to the building adjacent, the new Post Office Building, and felt a flood of nostalgia. I had once been atop that building too. Larry O'Brien's father had been Lyndon Johnson's Postmaster General. My first hosts in Washington had been the O'Brien family.

Partly to break the ice with Marty, who was clearly feeling me out before opening up, I began to reminisce about my friendship with Larry Jr. I recalled how excited I had been freshman year when I heard that there was a member of our class whose father was intimately associated with John F. Kennedy. That was the third year of Kennedy's presidency, and I was enchanted with him. Kennedy had gone to Harvard; I wanted to go to Harvard. Kennedy lauded politics and public service; I wanted to go into politics and public service. Kennedy was elegant, competent, and tough; I wanted to be elegant, competent, and tough.

If anything, Kennedy's hold on me was only strengthened by the assassination, which took place in the fall of 1963. By Harvard's calendar, that was the first day of Harvard-Yale weekend, which that year led a dozen teams of Harvard sportsmen to New Haven to compete with their Yale counterparts. I was with the freshman soccer team. We were playing the Yale frosh on the Friday afternoon before The Game when word that Kennedy had been shot was passed along the sidelines near the end of the third quarter. The coach ordered the news kept from players on the field so that they wouldn't lose "vigah" before the game was over. We won the match, but not the opportunity to savor the victory for Mother Harvard. Back in the locker room, we were told that The Weekend was canceled and instructed to take the train back to Cambridge.

For me the days that followed were a time of rededication. Upon being inaugurated, Kennedy proclaimed that the torch had been passed to a new generation. I considered myself part of that new generation, and I saw no better way to pick up the torch than to learn all I could about government and politics from Larry O'Brien.

For hours on end I would listen to Larry Jr.'s stories—about how his father had helped Jack Kennedy get elected congressman, then senator, then President; about how his father had then turned his political talents to getting New Frontier legislation through Congress; about how, after the assassination, Lyndon

Johnson had begged O'Brien Sr. to stay on as a link between the New Frontier and the Great Society, appointing him Postmaster General to make the offer irresistible.

I listened to Larry Jr.'s stories so raptly and joined in the adulation of his father so enthusiastically that I was soon invited home to Georgetown to meet "The General" himself. This was what brought me to Washington the first time, and many times thereafter. Now from the clock tower of the Old Post Office Building, I looked out on a panorama of powerful memories. There was the White House, of which "little Larry" and I had been given a tour by Lynda Bird Johnson; the Capitol building, about which we had heard delicious tales when Vice President Hubert Humphrey came for drinks to the O'Brien household; and the Watergate complex, where O'Brien moved his office after he resigned as Postmaster General to run Bobby Kennedy's campaign for the presidency until that assassination, and where he managed Hubert Humphrey's unsuccessful 1968 campaign and was elected national chairman of the Democratic party. All this history I had shared in a very personal way, thanks to my friendship with Larry Jr. and his family.

Though I now believe that every relationship is more or less an exchange between self-interested parties, I never thought I was using Larry. I felt that I was taking advantage of a unique, Harvard-provided opportunity to learn about politics, and I saw Larry and myself as fellow student concentrators in government who were supplementing our studies with "real world" exposure. This remained the case until our politics began to diverge. Always a devout Catholic and a devoted traditionalist, Larry went to Vietnam, returned, got married, and became ever more socially conservative. When, during what turned out to be the last weekend I stayed with him, I took a baby step toward coming out to him by telling him about my new thesis topic, he made sure I would go no further by saying simply, "I think they deserve their rights, but I don't want them teaching my children."

The evolution of my own thinking made this type of refinement unacceptable. For as I came to understand the arguments made by the first gay, lesbian, and women's liberationists, I became convinced that politics consisted of something very much broader than government. I saw that it was rooted in the power dynamics in personal relationships, which were very much affected by whether

individuals were comfortable with themselves and at ease and respectful in their dealings with others. I came to believe that it
required individuals to go about their daily lives in ways that made
those they interacted with feel equitably treated and good about
themselves, thus improving the quality of life in society in ways
that would inevitably affect the political system. In short, I was
persuaded that politics involved not simply elections, law, policies,
and programs, but the individual and social behavior that affected
public opinion and thereby determined how social issues were
dealt with politically and hence how equitable and humane government and society really were. As my belief that things individual and cultural were political led me ever more deeply and
personally into explorations of sexuality, sexism, self-actualization,
and relationships, it led me farther and farther away from Larry
O'Brien.

Yet of all the old friends I parted company with in order to live
in line with my new understanding of politics, and perhaps
because I saw losing him as a symbol of my departure from the
ranks of those working for a restoration of Camelot, Larry
O'Brien, Jr., was the classmate whose memory haunted me most.
He was the person I imagined among the watchers as I marched
up Fifth Avenue for the first time on Gay Pride Day in June of
1975. His was the reaction of disapproval I envisioned when I
sent my letter to the class announcing that I was going to write
Sons of Harvard and seeking gay classmates willing to be interviewed. Though a number of old friends identifying themselves
as straight got in touch or sent supportive letters, there was no
response from Larry. But who else could I think of when the
first gay to reply was a Vietnam vet working to restore the Old
Post Office Building in Washington, D.C.?

From the stiff, professional tone of his letter, I had feared that
Marty Brenner might be slick, ambitious, and mistrusting. The
man I actually met was very genuine and only briefly on guard.
As we made our way down from his rooftop he asked, with rap-
idly apparent approval, why I was interviewing gay classmates
and how I intended to use the material. Soon his approval became
warmth—and an eagerness to share with me as I had shared
with him.

When we got together that evening, Marty told me that he

belonged to a large Jewish clan based in Atlanta. Both his paternal and maternal grandparents had emigrated from Russia to the United States. His father's parents had settled in a small town in South Dakota, then put each of their four children through college, sending his father to Harvard the same year Joe Kennedy had enrolled his son Jack. His mother's parents were Feldmans, who had arrived in Philadelphia, adopted the twelve orphaned children of a couple they had known back in the old country, relocated to Atlanta, and watched their children spread out along the coast. When Marty's father married into the Feldman family, he joined his father-in-law's business. As he and his wife became established, they started a reform Jewish temple. Once the four Brenner children were through college, Marty's mother enrolled in graduate school, got her Ph.D., and then published her dissertation. The next year she organized a family reunion, where Marty met some 250 of his Feldman kin. He was proud of his clan, and he made it clear that he felt he was putting together his own life with skill and success that were very much in the family tradition.

These characteristics certainly seemed evident in the way he had handled his homosexuality. While I and the other classmates I had interviewed up to this point had been ignorant, deluded, pained, and repressed as homosexuals in our undergraduate and early post-graduate years, Marty had enjoyed a spate of homosexual "intimacies" as well as a couple of substantial relationships with women. After graduating from the Harvard School of Design, upon moving back to Atlanta, he had turned to the bar scene for a while. Soon, however, he had found a lover, set up house, advanced his career, and developed a satisfying social life.

Marty and Ted were each committed to a "permanent partnership." They had both straight and gay friends with whom they were quite intimate, but they tended not to be open about their sexual preferences with strangers. They had bought and restored one old Victorian house after another, filling each with ever more exquisite antiques and art glass, and they moved easily among the lovers of art and opera in Atlanta, where many knew that they were a homosexual couple but few acknowledged that explicitly—at least not in front of them. Marty's parents lived close by, and though the four of them socialized regularly, no mention of homosexuality was ever made by family members either.

About each of these dimensions of his life Marty talked freely and sincerely.

About being a Jew in Harvard College he explained:

I don't think the Jewish students at Harvard were much different from the average, well-educated students. If they were brought up in this country, they were homogenized into the American way of life. They may have come from more conservative or more liberal families, but so may have the non-Jews. I did not see them as a separate group of students at all.

There was an incredibly high percentage of Jews at Harvard, up to twenty or thirty percent, far above the national average. Where I'd grown up, there were whatever the normal, small, percentage of Jews is, so in going to Harvard I went from a low-density population to a high-density one. I was pleased by that. I knew that Harvard had a cross-sectional admissions policy, and I didn't see why they'd want any more of one religion—whether it was Zoroastrian or Jewish—than of another.

So I felt a certain pride because of the numbers, but I wasn't attached to them in any way. I don't think it's right to feel pride about something like that. It gets into "hubris."

About how he was able to have "sexual intimacies" with classmates in Kirkland House:

It was easy. In those days we played a game called Diplomacy a lot. Typically a group of friends would get together for a game. The game would last from four to seven hours, say, till two, three, or four in the morning. People would be very worn out from the experience, and at that hour, especially in the depths of winter, they didn't necessarily want to return to their rooms. It was just more or less "lie where you will." And that made it very easy for certain individuals to stay together after the game had broken up and other interested individuals had gone to their own rooms. Things seemed to happen rather smoothly and weren't as complicated as you might think they could have been.

About the Vietnamese War interrupting his studies at GSD:

Soon after I started my second year of Design School, I got called for an induction physical. I was astounded and sorely depressed that a country that values education as much as this one has could decide to draft its own students. I just could not believe that after two hundred years of development, the country had gotten an insane leader. I thought it was like a bear eating its own claws. But Lyndon Johnson completely abolished graduate-student deferments, and for a short time Congress supported that decision. They eventually withdrew that support, but not before a group of students, of which I was one, had been sucked into "the green machine."

After this happened I started reading the astrology columns. I discovered that if I'd been born during a different six-month period under a different sign, I'd have been deferred instead of drafted. I had always considered astrology a lot of bullshit, but with the irrationality of everything else that was going on, it began to seem as sensible as anything else.

Well, I thought it was worth going to some lengths to avoid going into the military service, but not so great a length as leaving the country or going to jail. I found too much future, too much potential good in the country to forsake it for what might be forever. I decided I would try to get myself disqualified from the service by telling them I was homosexual.

Instead of taking my physical at the Boston Induction Center, I got them to shift the site of my examination to Atlanta. I thought that in the South I would be disqualified instantly if I was open about homosexuality. Unfortunately, it turned out that the psychiatrist at the draft induction center in Atlanta was a young, avant-garde medical student from the University of Michigan, who said he wasn't surprised that I was homosexual because I was in architecture, but that it was probably just a passing phase I needn't worry about. Well, of course, that wasn't what I was worrying about.

A month after that slap in the face I marched off to war. I was in a catatonic state, never expecting to return home again. I think only those who have gone unwillingly into the service can know what that feeling is like. It was different from simply being depressed or unhappy; it was as if one was imprisoned without hope of release. I was taken to Fort Benning, Georgia, in what seemed like a cattle car, for six weeks of basic training. I didn't speak to one other person the whole time I was there. I was then assigned to a language school and from there sent to Vietnam.

The war was unlike anything I'd ever experienced before or even knew how to experience. In school I had always had a goal. Whatever I did was going to be received and graded, and I was going to accumulate status and rewards for the future depending on the results. In Vietnam I didn't know if I was going to make it to the next day. It wasn't so much that I was in a dangerous situation, but that I was in a situation in which I couldn't control anything. It was like being a marble thrown into a pinball machine, unable to control which flipper was going to hit you and being aware that if the wrong one did, it was going to be all over. To live like that for a whole year *definitely* makes you come down from the goal-oriented approach. It makes you live much more for the day, for the hour, for the moment.

As a result, I think I was much more relaxed about my sexuality when I came back. I was much more relaxed about everything. Nothing mattered anymore. Having made it back alive, I had no need to hurry to do anything else. In some ways I'm glad I got it in such a stiff dose, because it probably would have taken me a lot longer, in the Western world, to learn that philosophy. When I came back I reenrolled in the Graduate School of Design. Somehow, academia seemed much easier because I had a different perspective on it.

About the serious affair with a woman he had during his final year at GSD:

That final year I came as close as I'll probably ever come to marriage. Until that time I'd thought my homosexuality was something I had *in addition to* a regular sexual and social life, not *instead of*. But the relationship with Dianne just wasn't what I wanted. There was a problem with communication. She had rather conventional aspirations—she wanted to be a wife, mother, and colleague—but those seemed to leave me no flexibility or independence. When I projected that type of relationship into the future, and imagined what it was going to be like in another time, another place, another age bracket, I found it depressing.

We were both finishing school, and she was awarded a Fulbright to India and Nepal. She wanted *me* to go with *her*. That seemed like a very heavy request. I had no intention of going to the other side of the world with that woman—at her request.

About that time a gay German guy I'd met traveling in Europe several summers before wrote that he was coming to America. He asked if he could stay with me in Cambridge. It seemed that telling this woman that my gay friend was going to come stay would be a convenient way to tell her about things and to bring our own relationship to an end. So I told her that she couldn't stay with me for a while, and of course, I had to explain why. That cut the relationship rather neatly.

Since then I've been in contact with her. She's now in Washington. She knows about my relationship with Ted and has found someone else that she wants to marry. Now we're friends again.

About resettling in Atlanta:

I had gone home to Atlanta the summer before I graduated and decided it was as progressive as I needed it to be. There was a job market in the area that would not be uncomfortable to compete in. And I was content to return to the home base. Needless to say, my parents were pleased to have their oldest child living close by.

There was a small but nice gay community in Atlanta, and that was all I really required. I was looking for someone who'd be intellectually and personally stimulating. I didn't need hundreds of thousands of contacts. At the time, I wasn't interested in having a host of different sexual and emotional relationships, although I could see that changing later in life.

At first I went to the bars a lot and had some one-night stands. I was lonely, and those seemed to satisfy something. I also met people at private parties. I prefer to meet anybody —gay, straight, male, female—in a private setting, because then there's already been one step in selection, i.e., you know that they are a friend of someone you know.

During this period, before meeting Ted, I was not relating well to my family. It was difficult for them. I was opting for independence. I assumed I could handle anything that came along, and I wanted to be on my own. I was very open for any and all experience. That was my Faustian period, and I wanted all knowledge and all experience. And I didn't want to share much of my life with my family. I wanted to spend more time by myself and less time with them.

It was painful to live that close to my parents then. It was painful because I had not discussed my sexuality with them, and they were always unintentionally trying to involve me with women. That's what parents normally do. But it was uncomfortable, and I didn't know how to confront them, and I was worried about that. This was still the early seventies, in the South.

About the beginning of his relationship with Ted:

I had told no one in my family about my sexuality, and I didn't want to share it with them. Not then. But all this changed when I fell in love with Ted. As I grew closer to him, I felt less defensive with my family.

We met through a mutual friend who invited both of us to go with him to see Menotti's *The Telephone*, a very contemporary comic chamber opera. It was a hot late September afternoon, and Ted, who's bearded, blue-eyed, Polish, and the same age as I, was wearing a gaily colored madras jacket and bright yellow pants. I was attracted to him, but it wasn't anything earthshaking. There were no bells, no "This Is the One" feeling. But I liked his *joie de vivre*, his ability to ad lib, and his sincerity. He made me laugh.

After that first meeting, I said I'd call him. I was tied up the next day, and we had just left it open, so I didn't call for two weeks. Later he told me that he'd been very attracted to me, and he'd waited and waited anxiously and then finally written me off. Two weeks later, when I called, he fell over.

We started seeing each other. I guess that's when the bells started. We spent more and more time with each other, then decided to live together, then got the first house, then the second. . . .

About why he had volunteered to let me interview him—and why he suspected that the other gay members of our class he knew, back in college and right now, had not:

Can you tell me more about why you volunteered to be interviewed?

Since I've done no real gay activist work, I feel this is a way I can participate with the least risk to body or future. If I went to march somewhere, I might get trampled or stoned. Why should I get stoned?

But I'm willing to support and contribute to what I trust will be a sincere effort to let the public know what the lives of people like myself have been like. I think I lead an attractive life. I guess I expect that you'll present me in a way that's likable, so that people who read the book will have a better understanding and, if they know me, will like me better. I'm not ashamed of my life in any way, and if letting people know about it will help educate them, I'm willing to do that. I certainly understand how what you're doing is political.

Are you more political than the other gay classmates you know about?

I guess so. I think that's because I'm more relaxed about my sexual status than they are, about myself in general. I feel there's no reason to hide any information. I feel secure that I have examined that which I need to examine about myself, in terms of what I am, what my goals are, what I expect out of life. If I have delusions, I'll live with them. I think that perhaps the other gay classmates I know may still not be sure what they want out of life, personally or professionally. And being unsure, they probably don't want to commit themselves to anything that might affect their futures.

Only when we got to the matter of how Marty and Ted related to the Brenner family did I indicate that the degree of openness they were comfortable with was much less than what I myself enjoyed—indeed, than what I myself often assumed to be both healthy and political. The more I prodded, the more Marty tried to explain why he chose to relate to his family as he did. The differences in our viewpoints became clearer as our dialogue proceeded.

Do you remember the first time you introduced Ted to your immediate family?

It was the summer after we'd met. I invited him to a meal at my parents' house. There were always friends of the family invited to dinner, so that was natural. It was apparent that it would be nice if we all could know each other and accept each other as friends. But there was no great announcement of our relationship.

In fact, it has never been announced. There has never been any need to specify that we're lovers. My parents have always respected my choice in friends or lovers, male or female. They would, I think, have considered it a violation of my privacy to have asked questions about the relationship, and I saw no need to be more explicit. The relationship between Ted and me simply developed. And as we became closer, he was accepted into the family like any other partner of one of the children.

Do your parents know you're gay?

It's never been said in so many words, but they recognize it.

When did they first recognize it?

Probably that summer of '74. Though they'd seen me with other gay guests at the house, I don't think it was obvious that I too was gay until they started seeing me with one particular person all the time. By then I'd stopped going out with women altogether. It took a few months. It was something that slowly dawned on them. It didn't come as a shock. After a while I could tell they'd realized and accepted it because there were no more offers to introduce me to women.

One time we were on the beach, Ted and I and my parents. We were watching the people walking up and down the beach. There were lots of good-looking men and women. My mother said, "Why don't you two pick up a couple of nice-looking girls?" There was dead silence, and then the subject changed. I suspect that that was the beginning of the crystallization in their minds. I think that Ted and I were a little better prepared for it than they were. We let them see as they were ready to see.

After that day on the beach, the situation changed. Things got progressively more intimate. Soon Ted was introduced to the siblings, all of whom he's very close to now. Whenever we go to New York, we stay with my sister in her apartment, and we sleep in the same bed, even when she's in the apartment with her paramours.

Have you been explicit with either of your sisters or with your brother?

I see no reason to be. If they asked any explicit questions, I'd answer them to the best of my ability. But I don't think it's necessary. They're all intelligent people. They don't need to be lectured or spoken down to. I think if they're curious, they'll ask. Until then I don't feel I have the need or even the right to try to make them understand something they may not be interested in or want to know.

Do you feel close to your parents?

Yes.

Would you feel closer if you had explicit discussions?

No, or I would have had them. I believe that they're willing to accept the gay part of me like they accept the rest of me. Though, of course, I'll never know till I say something point-blank. But I prefer relating to people in the easiest and subtlest fashion until it's necessary to go to a further stage. If there were some financial, emotional, or social need to go further, I would.

If there were a need to do so, you would? Let's say that you and Ted and your parents were all going to India together. Would there be a need then?

As a matter of fact, we will be taking a trip like that within the next year.

Are you going to sleep with Ted?

I would assume that we will have one room and that my parents will have another. What we do in our room is our business. It will be as if two heterosexual couples are taking a vacation together. I just can't imagine that anyone would come up with any other arrangement. Do you think somebody would suggest that we always have three rooms? At this point in our relationship that would be out of the question.

I do anticipate it being a new experience for my parents. We've never spent every meal and every day together, so it will be a closer relationship than we've ever had. I think it will be a growing experience for my parents on account of the age difference as well as the sexual difference.

How do they relate to Ted now?

They're very close to him. They like him and care for him, and they treat us like a couple. Ted will call my mother and chat about what he's preparing for dinner one night so it won't conflict with what she's preparing for the four of us the next night. The same thing you'd do with another gay couple you were dining with two nights in a row.

Do you think that they would be happier if Ted were Jewish?

Well, I have no idea. I doubt if it's come up for them like that. I don't think they've gotten to the point in their feelings about intermarriage to consider homosexual intermarriage.

Do you think that they're more concerned that Ted is a man or that he is a Catholic?

Even though he's a Catholic, Ted's the most Jewish Catholic you'll ever meet. He knows more Yiddish than most non-Jews, and he knows more traditional Jewish cooking than most Jews. Ted runs a Jewish deli. It's a very nice kosher-style restaurant. My parents have eaten there a lot. They've stopped lately because Ted always insists on picking up the tab, and they don't like to feel that they're freeloading. At least on the surface, he fits into my Jewish family perfectly, even though he is a Catholic and even though he's a man.

Are you physically affectionate with Ted when you're together?

When we're alone, and sometimes with other gay people, more than when we're with my parents or in an integrated crowd. Ted takes a few more liberties in public than I do, and sometimes that's embarrassing for me, but I can go along with it. It's the normal difference in emotional reactions between any two people. I'm conscious of the crowd. I just don't express affection randomly or without regard for who's around. If most of those around dislike or disapprove of ways I might like, I'm not sure I think it fair to impose on them.

Well, with your parents, you have a selected public with whom you're extremely intimate. And anyway, I'm not talking about passionate sexuality, but about hugging and touching and kissing, about expressing affection.

My parents aren't very affectionate with one another, and I think I inherited that. It's definitely not a part of my family background to be touching and hugging and kissing.

Do you think that you would feel closer to your parents if you were able to be more openly and naturally affectionate with Ted in their presence?

Certainly at this point in time I don't think it would make our relationship any more fruitful. Five years from now, things might be different. But I don't see that as any kind of goal. If they gradually become more affectionate themselves in public or with us, then it might happen. But the understanding now is that we all know the nature of the relationship between Ted and me. It is accepted, and any further expression or explanation of it would only be a violation of privacy, theirs and ours.

I think that I can be very close to my family and they can be close to me without a lot of "encounter" or confrontation. They like Ted, and that's enough.

Do you think that gay people have a right as human beings to express themselves affectionately?

I would say it's not exactly a right. I think that it has to do with social mores. As time goes on and the public becomes better educated, I'm sure more affection will be tolerated. But I don't see the need to be a part of that education. I don't want to be a martyr. I just don't see myself as part of that process—except as a participant in this book, which is kind of a back-door way of doing it. But I wouldn't be comfortable waving flags. I understand why the gay liberation movement is necessary, but I don't feel the need to be in the forefront of it.

Marty was an interesting case. In history, thinking, and lifestyle he was in some ways like the rest of us and yet in other ways different. In the lives of Ken, Ben, and Willkie, I was able to see the basic patterns I had found in the liberationist-minded gay activists I believed responsible for the contemporary explosion of gay life—namely, a countercultural resolve to express feelings that seemed natural despite conventional taboos, and a consequent coming to terms with homosexuality and involvement in the gay male subculture. However conventional Marty's life appeared, the shift to countercultural views responsible for my assessment that he was sexually liberated was dramatically apparent in his life story: his coming down from the goal-oriented approach . . .

[to] live much more for the day, for the hour, for the moment," a transformation in existential perspective brought about by all the senselessness he saw in the Vietnamese War and the lack of control over his fate that had meant for him. Marty's coming out had followed a rejection of external expectations and a resolution to be true to self. It was only in the way he chose to express himself as a gay, which was mainly a reflection of the way in which he had explored his homosexual interests, that he differed, in varying degrees, from the rest of us.

All five of us believed in and cherished a greater spirit, our country, basic American values, our families, and education, but in his preference for approaching these in rather traditional ways, Marty was most like Ken. For example, all of us placed great stock in being responsible for ourselves financially, but Marty and Ken cared most about succeeding in conventional professional career lines. This was less in order to wield power and status or to acquire money (though each enjoyed spending on things he enjoyed, especially when he got a good buy on an object he was sure would appreciate in value) than to be more in charge of their working lives, and hence freer personally. These professional goals they believed Harvard had done much to help them achieve.

Indeed, both Marty and Ken felt that the liberal education they had received at the University was delightful and competent—as far as it went. They believed that Harvard was always ready to make improvements, and they were confident that University officials were intelligent, sophisticated, and reasonable enough to recognize that they could only improve the quality of education by making more information about homosexuality available and by taking other steps to assure that homosexual Harvard students of today had an easier time coming out than they had had.

This belief, rather than convictions about the need for cultural evolution and the importance of liberationist political activity, was what led Ken and Marty to talk to me, for publication, about their homosexual lives. Willkie's thinking and motives were closest to my own in these matters, and he was the only other self-styled gay liberationist in our group. Ben agreed it would be good if it were easier for young people to learn about homosexuality and to find other gay people, but he thought that the political contributions of individuals were negligible in the sweep of social change and that everyone was becoming more knowledgeable about sex as the result of obvious, inevitable cultural evolution.

Ben and Willkie cared less about Harvard and had less faith in the capacity of its leaders to do the types of things that would help homosexuals, but they shared Ken and Marty's faith in reason and also tried to make decisions "rationally"—i.e., by considering all the evidence and doing that which was in their best interests. All five of us had more or less rationally come to the conclusion that we were better off accepting our homosexual feelings and getting involved in the gay male subculture. For Ken the big decision came after years of listening to his priests, parents, and psychiatrists talk about how he could eliminate his homosexual yearnings if he would only control them—specifically, when he rejected the counseling of his born-again Christian therapist and decided to "listen to his own feelings" instead. For Willkie the remembered moment was the experience of being accepted as a homosexual—more, as a very active homosexual—by a fellow religious he respected. Ben and Marty pointed to no dramatic turning point, but to insight and resolve that were the products of understanding gained through experience. Marty explored his homosexuality alongside his heterosexuality, then decided to make a life with a man because he found the idea of a conventional relationship with a woman depressing (more than anything else, because it seemed destined to curtail his freedom to live as he wished in the future). Ben had also opted for autonomy, though for him this meant preserving his freedom to enjoy his sensitivity and to express his creativity through song-writing—and sex.

Indeed, it was in the realm of sexuality that Marty most dramatically parted company from Ben and Willkie; Ken fell somewhere in the middle. Like the others, Marty had made the gay male subculture a focus of his personal life for a time (what he called his "Faustian period"); he had taken full advantage of the opportunities for recreational sex presented by cruisy gay bars and enjoyed a fleet of one-night stands before settling into his relationship with Ted. Unlike the others, perhaps because he had always been able to find and to keep lovers, Marty had never turned to the baths. He and Ted had a "partnership" that was open in principle but in practice relatively chaste, if only, he confided, because the two cared so much more about the other things they enjoyed—good food, fine china and glass, opera and the arts, stimulating company, family, security, professional success, and travel.

Partly because he had been unable to sustain a gay relationship

while living with his father and seeing his therapist, Ken had
learned how to enjoy sex with men at the baths, and he continued to go to the baths when he wanted sex, while barhopping,
partying, and dating in the hopes of finding Mr. Right. Ben and
Willkie had also come out with the help of the baths, and they too
thought them fine arenas for sexual recreation. But Ben also
enjoyed gay low life, sex scenes the mere mention of which made
Ken blanch, and while Willkie had abandoned sex in public rest
rooms and begun to go to gay bars and bathhouses after accepting
his homosexuality, he now complemented his bath- and bar-going
with participation in a number of private sex clubs whose members liked to explore the fantasy dimensions of gay male sexuality. Ben and Willkie considered sex their favorite sport; Ken and
Marty preferred tennis.

In his relative lack of experience with traditional gay male
pastimes and institutions, Marty was most like me. Before graduating from college each of us had enjoyed, if left unlabeled,
homosexual intimacies, and simultaneously had explored love relationships with women. Both of us had discreetly enjoyed male
lovers as Harvard graduate students. And both of us had formed
partnerships we found pleasing and respectable and had used
those relationships to allow members of our families and close
friends slowly but surely to perceive that we were gay. The difference was that Marty remained comfortable with this living situation—with leaving everything about his homosexuality unspoken
and unexplained and with going about life as any conventional
upper-middle-class heterosexual couple might, except in certain
social situations and in bed. Rusty and I, ceasing to find this life-
style satisfying, had become more openly and actively gay.

Ken was the only one who talked about wanting to settle down
when I interviewed him. Ben and Willkie were for the first time
involved in love affairs, yet neither of them was considering a
relationship that wasn't going to be, if not at the beginning, at
least in the long run, "open." It might have been necessity that
first impelled Ken, Ben, and Willkie to get so involved in the gay
male subculture, and it might have been their lack of interest
(in the case of Ben) and success (in the case of Ken and Willkie)
in finding and persisting with lovers that led them to devote so
much of their time and attention to transient sexual partners and
recreational sex. Whatever the origins of their involvement, how-

ever, with time and experience they had grown to love homoerotic adventure and to be enthusiastic about gay male life. They had discovered that the subculture they had been forced into could be healthy, moral, and stimulating, they had learned to approach it in this spirit, and they had no desire to give up gay male customs.

My own exploration of gay life was very much more calculated. At first my way of reconciling my homosexuality with traditional values and conventional ways was to find myself a lover of substance and standing and to devote my academic life to study of the politics of homosexuality. With Rusty I developed a critical perspective on conventional outlooks and established ways. Then I came to understand the logic of liberationist politics and set out to help spread countercultural and liberationist perspectives by making myself a liberated gay. My embrace of the gay male subculture stemmed not simply from personal and professional interest, but from political commitment.

In any event, in each of the first four gay classmates I interviewed I found—though less labeled, analyzed, and proclaimed than my own—both a countercultural opting for self-realization and supportive community resulting in a rejection of conventional taboos about sexuality and a liberationist interest in making it easier for homosexuals to come out and to join together by letting everyone know the truth about gay life. Each of them also confirmed my view that countercultural values and liberationist political ambitions didn't necessarily require individuals to abandon all traditional views or to forsake every conventional pursuit. And Marty's life taught me that one didn't have to be actively promiscuous in order to be a liberated gay man. All one had to do was believe that homosexuals could indulge in recreational sex healthily and morally and be open to the possibility of enjoying sexual variety, as those involved in the gay male subculture did. Marty felt that he had benefited from the involvement in gay male life he had experienced before beginning his partnership with Ted. His relationship had always been "open" in principle. And he said that he could envision enjoying "a host of different sexual and emotional relationships" at some point in the future.

Of course, it was the value that I and the others placed on homoerotic sexual and emotional fulfillment that made us think the enjoyment of traditional gay male pastimes so central to gay liberation. Marty seemed to value this less, and, as I had taken great pains to point out in *The Politics of Homosexuality*, by any true interpretation of countercultural and liberationist ideals, his choices could be called liberated as long as they were self-determined rather than dictated by convention.

So I had learned a lot from my visits with Ken, Ben, Willkie, and Marty, about how the trends I trace in my first book had manifested themselves in the lives of individuals. And I was sure that I would learn even more as my travels continued.

5

SANDY
ANDERSON

From Washington I flew to Ann Arbor to see Sandy Anderson. Like Willkie, he had lived in my dormitory freshman year. Unlike Willkie, he had struck me as being genuineness personified. He had come to Harvard from a small town in Michigan, bringing all the freshness and vitality his rural upbringing had endowed him with. I used to kid him about being a country boy, and, in fact, he came closer to being one than anyone else I had ever met. But he rarely let me tease him without letting me know that in his eyes, *I* was the naïf. Late in the fall of 1978, when I received a letter with his return address on the envelope, I guessed that he had seen my piece in the class report and wondered if he still thought me naïve. Then I read his note.

Ann Arbor

29 October 1978

Dear Toby—

I returned to Ann Arbor this summer, after almost a year on the West Coast including a month in Berkeley, to find an unforwarded copy of the 10th reunion book and your fine statement, which I've wanted to applaud and hug you for ever since. Consider yourself hugged and kissed many times. After slogging through half the alphabet it was quite a surprise to find your name, a beautiful heartfelt message, courage, and a coming out all in one paragraph. Such a world—in which coming out is necessary—in which it requires courage!

Well, you're wondering, who is this guy writing this? Sandy—from Michigan—freshman dorm—Gov. major—who prided himself on being less innocent than you—long-ago-lost to the world outside Cambridge and unheard of. Now a carpenter/cabinetmaker in search of another calling, married and happily separated (probably temporarily) from a deeply loved wife now living in Berkeley (Christina Olson), also a lover of India (Peace Corps agricultural work in a Kerala village), and of men (including one Rod McGregor of Berkeley and John Norris of San Francisco, whom you might somehow know) . . . a bit confused about sexuality sometimes but mostly feeling fine about bridging the worlds.

And I'd like to see you sometime here or there—wherever "there" now is—and enjoy some of your radiant good energy and share some of mine with you. Toby, hello again! Thank you for writing that. Love,

Sandy

I found it a beautiful, heartfelt message, and I wanted to let Sandy know that. I also wanted to inform him that I was doing a book on gay Harvard graduates. From the tone of his letter, the openness with which he expressed support for my coming out, and the chiding of society for making this so difficult, I knew that he was countercultural. Also from what he told me of his own interest in personal exploration rather than professional advancement, his unconventional relationships, and his desire to share "radiant good energy." That was the way countercultural people of the late sixties and early seventies "shared" with each other—even if they were Harvard classmates who hadn't heard from each other in eleven years. And since countercultural people tended also to be very political about changing culture, I expected that I could count on Sandy to be in my book—as long as the "vibes" in my letter of invitation were right.

934 Carleton St.
Berkeley, CA 94710
January 2, 1979

Dear Sandy,

I've just returned from two months in India and found your letter. As soon as I saw the return address, I recognized your writing. I used to marvel at its precision back in '63 when you lived down the hall in Matthews. I thought you very neat, very intelligent, and very wholesome.

We lost touch after that freshman year, and all I remember from the rest is a long conversation about Spinoza. You were probably the world's expert on Spinoza, you told me once as we walked along the Charles. Was that senior year? Then college was over, and you were off on your own odyssey, as we all were. I remember stopping at your name in the 5th year class report, and then again in the 10th. What has happened to my gentle friend, I wondered with a rush of warm feeling as I turned the page. I never thought I'd hear from you again.

How lovely that I have—that after all these years you've reached out with your same careful touch. And to think that you were staying just up the street all the time I was slaving away on my thesis. I could have used your encouragement then, your applause.

My coming out in the class report was easy after having chosen to do my thesis on gay politics, which made all my life from that point on a coming out. Yet the piece in the class report has produced more immediately fulfilling rewards—people. Almost as soon as the redbook was circulated, I began to hear from classmates who wanted to congratulate me for being so honest, to tell me about their own homosexuality, to socialize. Suddenly people from Harvard meant something again—for some reason, the common college history plus our gayness permitted easy intimacy and gave it special richness. Two of the classmates who got in touch with me, Ben Miller and Mario Montano, met at my house six months ago and are now lovers. Another, Ken Ryan, has moved out here from Boston.

This rediscovery of old classmates has been such a powerful experience—and the stories these classmates tell have such potential for affecting the lives of others—that I'm planning to do a book of interviews. I want to have a dozen or so gay members of the Class of 1967 talk about Harvard, their homosexuality, their lives. To help change "a world—in which coming out is necessary—in which it requires courage," as you wrote me. Will you join us?

Sandy's reply confirmed my initial hunches.

Ann Arbor

17 January 1979

Dear Toby,

I arrived back here from Mexico Friday night in the beginning of a three day long blizzard and an even longer stretch of subzero weather. Your letter was something to huddle over and soak in warmth from. And it was almost the proverbial straw that broke the camel's back. As I traveled north from Mexico City and then up through Chicago to Ann Arbor, I was becoming more and more aware of how I am no longer a Northerner, how this will certainly be my last winter here, how lasting through even one more feels crazy, especially for me—with more good friends in the Bay Area than here. You get the drift? Well, it got warm today (19°) and I went skating under the stars tonight and I'll stay this winter and I'll almost certainly enroll Friday in some more dance and art courses. But I *am* coming back out there. Maybe sooner than I think right now.

Meanwhile, the book. Exciting. Yes, please let me put my bisexual shoulder to the wheel. It's late and I'm tired so I won't/ can't say much right now except that books that are nothing but interviews don't appeal to me as much as more *written* things. So I hope you'll consider having the narrative history of each of us be something more polished and that you'll try to go a bit deeper than *Word is Out* or at least to create something that will reach a different (less converted) audience.

Tell me more.

I'm moving, soon, into a communal house. If things are moving as fast as I think, we'll probably have a place by the time you get this. Just call my old number, and there'll be a referral. If I haven't heard from you soon, I'll call you.

Sleepy-eyed love and kisses,

Sandy

When Sandy met me at the airport, I saw that the country boy of yesteryear had become a man. He was a big, strapping fellow, leaner than he had been in college, nicer-looking now that he was not so chubby. He was wearing yellow drawstring pants, a faded green T-shirt, and sandals. From the depth of his tan I could tell that he spent a lot of time outdoors. There was even a fresh, woodsy smell about him.

As we chugged off toward his "communal house" in an old Volvo, I described my morning in church with Willkie and told him how much our old dorm-mate had changed. Perhaps because they had so little in common back then, perhaps because they had gone on to different upperclass houses, Willkie hadn't remembered Sandy and Sandy barely recalled him. When I asked if he had any interest in meeting Willkie, Sandy said that he didn't keep in touch with any Harvard people, though he had seen two of his old roommates when he was out in Berkeley. In fact, he said that he wanted to leave Harvard where it belonged—"far in the past."

Sure that we were on our way to the country, I was surprised when we turned off the highway into a heavily residential neighborhood and pulled up in front of a large, wood-shingled house.

"Isn't this a rather suburban neighborhood?" I asked.

"Uh huh," he replied.

It was clear that times—and communes—had changed.

Not only was I expecting to find Sandy's commune occupying some kind of ramshackle farmhouse, I was sure that the place would be bustling. It was six in the evening—surely time, I thought, for some cooperative effort at food preparation. But there was no one around. "The whole house is away this evening," Sandy explained as he ushered me into the hallway. "We're supposed to be having dinner with a house on the next block. If you're really hungry, we can join the party."

I said that I'd had a lot to eat on the plane and that I was much more eager to catch up with him.

Sandy asked if I wanted to drop my things in his room and then led me up the stairs. At the top, by telling me who lived behind each of the four closed doors that surrounded the large landing, he introduced me to his four housemates. There was Lois, recently divorced, a feminist therapist; her eleven-year-old daughter, Peggy; Molly, a radical therapist; and Ken, one of Molly's former lovers.

"Aren't any of the people you live with gay?" I asked with some dismay.

"Right now," he replied, "I'm the only one who's involved in a same-sex relationship. I wasn't when we moved in, but I am now. It's cool with everybody."

"Even Peggy?" The rise in my voice revealed more dismay.

Sandy squinted his eyes to ask if I was being serious, then responded, "Yeah, even Peggy. Her mother *is* a feminist therapist." He was reminding me that people "into" radical therapy and feminism tend to be pretty "hip" about "relationships."

Following Sandy back down the stairs and into the kitchen, I asked how he had found his living situation. "I'll tell you all about it," he assured me, patting me gently on the arm as I gave him a patient smile. "First, I want to have something to eat."

The kitchen walls were striped with crowded shelves. There were jars of preserves of every size, covered plastic containers by the dozens, and rows of big glass bottles filled with noodles, lentils, beans, grains, rice, and dried greens. The refrigerator was full of more plastic containers, bottles of juice and milk, wedges of Saran-wrapped cheese, bowls of fruit, and bags of vegetables. Sandy pulled out a big plastic tub labeled *Yogurt*, asking, "How about some granola?"

I nodded, and he took two bowls from the cabinet next to the sink and filled them with a raisin-nut-grain mixture from one of the glass bottles. "This is my very own blend," he remarked while taking a big spoonful of yogurt and kneading it into his granola. "Want yours with yogurt?"

There was silence while we each ground away. Not until he had emptied his bowl did Sandy speak again. "I want to hear about your writing. I've been doing a lot of writing myself, lately, mostly in my journal. Have you brought along your journal?"

I told him I didn't keep a journal but that I made copies of all my long letters and had been writing some nostalgic autobiographical sketches during my trip. "But I'm here to interview you, remember. And I'd really like to catch up with my tape recorder on."

Acknowledging my hint with a smile, Sandy led me back upstairs to his room. A thin foam-rubber mattress covered with a faded Indian-print spread occupied at least a quarter of it. Wooden fruit crates stuffed with books and lined with potted plants stretched along the two free walls. In between the plants were chunks of pretty rock, colored glass bottles, and a few small statues. Tacked onto the walls above the crates were some sketches and watercolors I guessed were Sandy's. The room was crowded but clean and organized; Sandy hadn't lost any of his old neatness. And there was that woodsy smell—the smell I had noticed when he met me.

Sandy stepped out of his sandals, plopped himself down on the far side of the mattress, and pulled his big legs beneath him. I put my recorder in front of him, stretched out on my side of the mattress, and looked across at him. His thighs looked as if they were going to burst through the uncombed cotton of his pants. He watched me stare at his legs, then laughed. "Well?"

"Well, I can hardly wait to hear what you've been up to. And I'd like to begin taping right away, if that's all right."

Sandy nodded and I switched the recorder on. I fumbled for a question, but before I had a chance to open my mouth, he said he wanted to let me know "where he was at." His "rap" was a report on how he was feeling about his life right then, the type I often got—and gave—when I was in my own early countercultural period.

I'm viewing these last couple of years as a kind of vacation from the world. I'm joining the "Me Generation" for a little while. That feels very much the right thing for me to do, though I get guilt feelings about political responsibilities. I often trash myself for not being active and political right now and wonder when I'm going to get active again. But I don't want to become active out of a sense of guilt or anger. The anger's perfectly wonderful and legitimate, but I want my politics to come from a different source, to spring from joyousness and not from anger. I want to approach politics as a free spirit who is not completely bound up in the political process and who has foothold outside of it. So this is my time to involve myself with therapy, with dance, with getting really comfortable with myself as that free spirit.

When we were in college, I remember there were all these people taking advantage of the psychiatric coverage in the student health insurance. It seemed like every other person I knew was seeing a shrink. I thought that silly self-indulgence. Through my freshman and sophomore years I had a deep distrust of psychology. Even though I was aware of all sorts of conflicts in myself, I never thought of taking that route, except for a couple of brief periods when I was feeling suicidal and considered going for help. I never did.

By junior year, psychology had become my major subject, but even then I didn't want to go into therapy. My primary interest was intellectual. Over the years that's changed, and I've gotten out of my head and more into my body and my feelings.

These days I'm surrounded by therapy. Christina's in Berkeley training to be a radical therapist. Frank, the man I'm seeing, is a radical therapist. Oliver, my dance teacher, is doing therapy, even though he doesn't call it that. In the house, Lois does it for a living and Molly's doing group organizing based on a lot of the radical therapy theories. One of the things about this house coming together is that we are interested in a lot of openness with each other and in supporting each other in changing and growing. It hasn't been everything that I wanted, but it's been really good, much better than living in a situation that isn't structured for that.

"How about you?" Sandy asked suddenly. I knew he was asking for the same kind of report. In early countercultural and radical feminist circles, personal interaction is expected to be an exchange in which each individual gets as much as he gives and thereby feels equally acknowledged and involved. No provision is made for the wallflower, something I had come to see as a bit of a philosophical contradiction. Sandy had been talking for a while. He'd opened up to me. Now it was time for me to open up to him—whether or not I wanted to.

I smiled uncomfortably. I was afraid that if I began talking about myself, we'd never get back to him. "Can't I tell you about myself later, after I've gotten some of your story down on tape?"

"Okay," he said softly. "Maybe you should tell me what you want to know."

Sandy sounded wounded and looked rebuffed, and I felt a pang of regret. If anything, I wanted to welcome him closer. He seemed much more attractive than he had fifteen years ago, our freshman year, when his wholesomeness had been too much a reminder of my own townie background and feigned innocence to make me comfortable. Now his freshness was seductive. Warring with my resolve to get the facts was a yen to be more intimate. For the moment, I resisted.

"Okay," I said brightly. "How about telling me when you discovered your sexual feelings?" Sandy looked across the room. My eyes followed his. They seemed to have focused on the little statue of Hans Christian Andersen that stood between two geraniums on the crate-shelf across from us. Sandy must have gotten it when he was an exchange student in Denmark. That was where Andersen, a homosexual, wrote most of his fairy tales.

Well, I didn't have my first experience of intercourse until junior year of college, but of course I'd been thinking about sex for a long time. I masturbated all the time. I suppose everybody does. The fact that I had both male and female fantasy images was pretty confusing, though.

When I was a kid I remember being fascinated by my father's body. At our summer house there was a partition between my room and my parents' room. It didn't go all the way to the ceiling and I slept on the top bunk, so when I had the opportunity, I'd look over the partition to see what I could see.

The people I recall finding sexually attractive were guys in high school I thought really beautiful. I felt an attraction to them that I thought in some way was probably perverse, but I couldn't stop looking at their faces and chests, admiring their manliness. And I remember swim classes at the Y and feeling fascination for the powerful swimming teacher who had hair all over his chest. After going to the Y, I'd be downtown, and there was a shoeshine stand on the edge of the downtown district where I'd buy muscle magazines. Not body-building magazines—the ones I bought had pictures not of pumped-up musclemen, but of graceful bodies in provocative poses. But I don't think the word homosexual had started to reverberate for me.

Junior year in high school I had the closest thing to an experience that was homosexual. There was a guy whom I knew through drama; he was one of the two or three whiz kids in the senior class and a "big man on campus." I didn't like him much, but I had a lot of respect for him. One day near the end of the year, I was walking into the auditorium as he was walking out. Nobody was around, and he grabbed me in the crotch and said, "I'm hot for your bod." Then he went running off down the hall. I was terrified. I wasn't sure what that was all about.

I do remember covering a paperback called *Sexual Histo-*

ries of American College Men with the cover of *The Russian Revolution,* so that it would look like I was reading a real boring book when I was really reading about the sex lives of college men. I remember seeing stuff about homosexuality in that. But it never occurred to me to approach men for physical contact. I was just in awe of the perfect bodies around. I had a couple of good friends, one of whom I was sort of attracted to, but in terms of emotional things I was much closer to my women friends. They seemed more interested in people, in books, in ideas.

My first experience of genital involvement with another person was with Ingrid, a couple of years after I met her in Denmark. You remember, don't you, that I was an exchange student my last year of high school? Denmark opened me up to a lot of things. There was a lot of drinking in my Danish high school and that stimulated me to experience a lot of emotional stuff.

Before leaving for Denmark I'd had a girl friend, and I remember getting incredibly aroused with her. We'd kiss each other so wildly that both of us would have bloody lips the next day. But there was no question of taking off clothes or going anywhere in that direction. When I came back to the States, we'd have sex all over the place, but she still wouldn't allow penetration: She was going to stay a virgin for her husband. But we had a lot of fun together. And I had a lot of orgasms. I don't know about her; I didn't know about women's orgasms then.

Then I went to Harvard. I still considered myself a virgin because I hadn't entered a woman sexually. I'd fallen in love with Ingrid, and I believed that sex was something that belonged only together with love. There was a woman I went out with freshman year whom I slept with several times. I remember lying awake all night once with an erection, but I wouldn't make love to her because I wasn't really in love with her. I had a couple of other women friends with whom the situation was very similar.

Then, junior year, Ingrid came to the States, and I had my first real intercourse. That was incredibly wonderful and exciting, and we were doing it like crazy for a couple of weeks. Then one day we were sitting out at Walden Pond looking out at the water, and she turned to me all of a sudden and said, "You know, I could have a child." That scared the shit out of me, and after that, when we slept together, we didn't really have sex because I was so aware she might get pregnant. Of course, part of what she was laying on me was her strong desire to get married. And although she didn't want children, she was reminding me that I'd be responsible if one came along. But I didn't want to have a kid. I didn't want to be tied down.

Sandy turned his eyes back to me and grinned self-consciously. "What else?"

"That's beautiful," I said, taking his hand into my own. I massaged his bony knuckles with my thumb, then squeezed his calloused palms with my fingers. "Tell me about your roommates. You roomed with Rip Stone in Adams House as well as Matthews, didn't you? How did you two get along?" I remembered Rip as an earthy preppy from New York City, and I'd never been able to figure out why he and Sandy roomed together.

I got along with Stone very well. I remember feeling real close to him at times. I also remember times when he treated me with that very bored New York kind of condescension.

At the end of freshman year it was vital for each of us to get into Adams House. It was amazing that year: Adams had two thirds of the applications. That said a lot about which direction people were moving. Adams House had a kind of turtleneck, beatnik image. All the other houses seemed boring and lackluster. Adams seemed like where I belonged.

So Stone and I got together this irresistible roommate group with Morgan Blaine and Ashok Aman Adani. Adams House was artsy and radical. Stone was an artsy New York preppy. Blaine was an economist and a New Englander. Adani was an Indian from Tanganyika who'd been through the British private school system. I was a midwesterner from a public school. We had geographical balance, different majors, different backgrounds—we were a dream ticket for a house priding itself on diversity.

After we moved in, I didn't need much interaction outside the house. I felt incredibly well-nourished. I liked the self-selected group of people who were attracted to Adams.

There were lots of opportunities to get to know a lot of different people. I remember that as one of the things I really liked about the dining hall. It was this grand wood-paneled room with high windows and a lot of space. As you'd get your food, you could look around and decide whom you were going to sit with, what kind of conversation you might have, who looked like they were in a good mood, whether you were going to sit alone or join someone who was sitting alone or sit with a group. Three times a day there was this wonderful opportunity.

That was my real education from that point on. The peer-group interaction was the high point of the educational experience. Lots of talk at night in the rooms and out on the stairs that led to the library. That's where it really happened.

One of the things about Adams House is that it had just about the highest percentage of public school graduates of any of the houses, something like seventy or eighty percent. And it was nearly balanced Midwest and East, with a fair number of westerners and southerners. Good, interesting people.

My intuition is that Rip and Morgan became sexual buddies. I'm not sure, but that was my intuition. I wouldn't call them lovers. I don't use that word lightly. But there was a kind of homosexual ambience which I always felt when the two were together in the room.

I interrupted: "Did you see any other signs of homosexuality on campus?"

By the time I was in Adams House, I was aware of homosexuality, aware that certain poets and writers pushed buttons in me that others didn't. I knew about Keynes, Forster, and Auden. I was aware of the Bloomsbury group. I was aware of the possibility of sexual freedom, and I think I had a picture of a real liberated future for myself.

I remember eyeing a lot of people, but I wasn't really aware of any overt homosexual response. I remember being real uncomfortable with effeminacy, and I'm sure I sometimes correlated that with homosexuality. I was bothered by Cartwright Shane, my freshman adviser, and by the kind of attention he paid to me. I always felt like that was supposed to lead to something, and that made me feel uneasy.

I knew from the graffiti in the johns in Lamont that things were going on. A lot of the stuff referred to was taboo and mysterious and thereby interesting, but I don't remember really wanting to suck cock or to get fucked in the ass or any of the specific activities that were mentioned.

Remember, I'd had a dynamite relationship with my girl friend in high school. Hers seemed like the most wonderful body I'd ever touched. The naked male body had appeal for me, but I didn't allow myself to go in the direction of actual touching. Homosexuality seemed forbidden, and while having contact with another man's cock seemed exciting, it did not have the total magic or rightness about it that heterosexual experience did.

How about the Adams House crowd? Two other classmates who got in touch with me lived in Adams, and one told me that he chose Adams because of its reputation for being gay. Didn't you see any gay people in the house?

Well, there was an English tutor, Clark Copley. He was this fat, very effeminate, very dirty-witty guy who was friends with Rick Bly, the history tutor. I thought they were both disgustingly fat. They had a circle of admirers who were clearly into everything decadent. I made a lot of assumptions about that.

Copley was always eyeing me. I lived right above him. He'd make little remarks about what a chicken I was, what a naïve farmboy. I was really intimidated by him. He was especially intimidating because in some ways he was what I aspired to be—a very bright man of letters.

He was a teaching assistant in a course on Proust. You had to read French to be in it, which I didn't. But I went to the first meeting because I wanted to get the reading list. The next day I was going up the stairs, and Copley saw me and said something in French. He damn well knew I didn't know French.

So I think I associated gayness at Harvard with certain cliques, certain types. I think I assumed that a lot of the preppies were homosexual or had had gay experiences. I rowed freshman year and was surrounded by preppies. I thought that there was something gay about their style or manner. And I overheard a lot of sexually explicit locker-room conversation.

But it wasn't until senior year that any of this became real for me. That year there was a suite of juniors down the hall. Two of them were really fine people, each bright as a pin, really intelligent. One was very artistic, always doing collages and things. He was fairly effeminate, but that didn't bother me much in him, and we became good friends. The other had a beautiful body. We used to swim together a lot, and I remember wanting to touch him.

At some point, Simeon, the artistic one, propositioned me. He really laid it on heavy and managed to half-seduce me, but I really wasn't into it with him. But during that I learned that he'd been sleeping with Wyatt, the other guy. So shortly thereafter I asked Wyatt to sleep with me.

We did sleep together, but we never took off our underpants. We'd already developed a platonic relationship, and crossing the sexual line was real difficult. I remember that I woke up in the morning ready to cross the line, but he wasn't. He was real insecure about his sexuality. He was threatened by what was going on between him and Simeon. He sort of put me on a pedestal as a person, and he didn't want me tarred with the same brush Simeon was.

One night Simeon tried to carry off a three-way. The idea was to have a Roman orgy in my room. But it absolutely fizzled. Wyatt was caught in the middle 'cause both of us wanted him, and he felt attacked.

That was as close as I came to any real homosexual experience at Harvard. It was enough to let me know that there was a world out there that might be explored at some point. My image of myself was that I was a straight man who was also interested in men. I'm not sure when the word bisexual began to have any meaning for me.

Those times were so fucking repressive. I'm not one to wallow in regrets, but when I think about what I missed out on in terms of all kinds of wonderful contacts with people, I'm pissed. There were so many nights I slept alone. The one thing that would have put blood into my studies would have been sex. Paradoxically, everyone seemed to believe that repression would keep everybody working. The truth is exactly the opposite.

"Well, what did you do after graduation?" When Sandy paused, looking as if he was expecting some kind of response, I tried to keep him talking by asking another question.

"Oh," he said, "that's when I joined the Peace Corps and went to India." His eyes brightened. I knew he was thinking he'd found a way to involve me in conversation. "You've been to India too, haven't you?"

"Yeah," I replied. "Rusty and I first went to India together in 1971. The trip was probably what cemented us together as a couple." I wanted to acknowledge Sandy's interest but to keep him talking about himself. "Did you go into the Peace Corps to get out of the draft?"

Senior year, the draft was my big dilemma. My sense of self-preservation said that there was no way I was going to go into the Army. Politically, I wasn't going to support the war or have anything to do with it. But I didn't know just how I was going to keep from getting involved.

That year I took Henry Kissinger's course in International Relations. He was flying back and forth to Washington to consult with the government, and everything he said indicated the war wouldn't last long. The *Boston Globe* and *The New York Times* were editorializing against the war. I was so convinced of the power of the Eastern Establishment that I thought that if *The New York Times* said the war was bad, then it would just have to end. I didn't want to be sitting in jail for three years for refusing to fight in a war that was going to end in six months. I had a real fear of withering away inside prison walls.

At that time, the option of declaring myself homosexual wasn't real. It seemed like a cop-out, and a cheap way out besides, since all I'd really done was to think about having homosexual experiences. But I felt okay about the Peace

Corps. I'd wanted to join it since it was started, and I specifically wanted to go to India.

I was in India for two years. The last eight months I had a very happy sexual relationship with my cook. Before that, I'd stay over at farmers' houses if I was a ways away from my house in the evenings. But once I started sleeping with Vijay, I'd be on my bicycle riding home by the light of the moon every night to get more of that nice touching. It was playful and happy sex. That was my first homosexual relationship.

"By now Vijay is probably a proud husband and father," I said with a laugh, rubbing Sandy's shoulder. "From all I've been able to gather, many males in India feel perfectly comfortable about having sex with other males, but few can conceive of identifying themselves as gay or leading gay life-styles. I think there's no concept of gay because there's so little awareness of the psychological insights that have done so much to shape Western culture and because the pressures to marry and produce heirs are so deeply rooted. Children are the best hope adults have for improving their material status and getting cared for in their old age. Weren't you devastated by the poverty?"

India wasn't nearly as bad off as I expected. That might have been because I was in one of the fertile agricultural areas in the South. Most of the people I encountered, maybe eighty percent, were quite secure in knowing that they were going to be eating in three months, knowing that if something happened to them, they could get the necessary health care, knowing that they had a roof over their heads and certain luxuries that gave their lives a little extra spice. They certainly had access to what we call culture. Every village had activities in which music and dance were available to the people. Of course, the other twenty percent were hopelessly oppressed, but that's not so different from here.

The most striking thing was the amount of freedom that people had in scheduling their lives, the amount of leisure, and the amount of good conversation that afforded. My contact was mainly with farmers and farm workers, but also with a fair number of merchants. They worked when the season demanded it, when the land had to be tilled, when something had to be planted, when the weather suddenly changed, when the harvest was ready. At those times they might put in eighteen hours a day. The rest of the time, when it wasn't necessary to work, they didn't work. They visited their relatives twenty miles away, or took a bus and went to temples that were important to their particular religion, or sat around and talked.

Paradoxically, my time in India seemed like a continuation of my time in college. The Harvard house system seemed to reflect an awareness of the importance that conversation and casual encounters play in our development. In India, at least in the village I lived and worked in, I found much of the same appreciation.

I think another thing that was paradisiacal for me was the absence of television and automobiles. Those two things have always been repulsive to me. I came to hate TV during high school. It seemed to take my parents away from me; it reduced the amount of conversation in our house; it was mechanical noise blaring absolutely banal and often ugly, inhumane, antilife messages. Our whole lives seemed dependent on automobiles that cost great sums of money and that polluted the environment with exhaust fumes, noise, and ugly commercial strips. To live in a society where these two machines were not present was wonderful.

When I came back from India, I found that I had a different outlook on the world. My attitudes and values had changed. Of course, while I was away, the thinking of a whole lot of people in the United States had evolved in much the same way mine did. I'm thinking about the growth of hippiedom and the whole new generation who were looking for ways to avoid high-consumption life-styles and who were seeing that their relationships with other people and their own happiness were far more important than the media version of happiness. It's totally obscene that people should devote so much of their time to doing stupid and unfulfilling work just so they can buy things they don't need. They're just perpetuating an incredibly wasteful mechanism that they've been programmed to support.

Sandy gazed at me intently. "Didn't you like the simplicity of life in India?" I could tell from the tone of his voice it was going to be harder to escape this time. Sandy was just too uncomfortable being alone on stage, too addicted to the joys of conversational exchange, too firm in his belief that it was important to share.

I bit my lip, then began, "Well, my experiences in India were very different from yours because Rusty's a Parsi. You know, a Zoroastrian." I was afraid I was going to have to begin a long digression right there.

"A Parsi? I didn't know that. So it was all very upper-class and Western for you."

"Well, yes," I said, surprised. I rarely encountered someone who knew what a Parsi was.

One of the smallest of India's many minorities, the Parsis are descended from Zoroastrians who in the seventh century fled from Persia, now Iran, to escape invading Muslims. According to Rusty's father, who warned me that he was simply passing on oral history, only three boatloads of Parsis managed to set sail from ancient Persia, and only two made it across the Arabian Sea to Surat, just north of Bombay. Left alone by the local Hindu ruler on the condition that they make no efforts to convert his subjects, these Parsi pilgrims prospered greatly. When the British colonized India, the Parsis became court favorites and were drawn in disproportionate numbers into the military and civil services. Fairer than most Indians, and distinctive because of their Persian names and facial features, they were generally educated in British-run schools and exposed to all the amenities of the Western world. In India, most of the Parsis lived in Bombay, the country's commercial capital. The next largest concentration could be found in London. Rusty, whose real name was Rustam, that of a mythic Persian hero, lived more like an Englishman than an Indian.

"Well, tell me about Rusty," pressed Sandy. "He was a big shot at Harvard, wasn't he? How did you two become lovers?"

"If I get into that long story, we'll never get back to you."

"But I feel uncomfortable doing all the talking."

Suddenly I knew what to do. "Look. I've got an idea. You said you were interested in my writing. And I don't want to get off the track by going into the whole story of my relationship with Rusty now. So what if I just give you a sense of how Rusty and I got together by reading one of my pieces. It's real romantic—that was the most romantic time in our lives, remember—but it summarizes a lot of what happened."

"That's a great idea," said Sandy. "We can alternate. You read me some about your life. I'll tell you some more about mine."

I reached over to my shoulder bag and pulled out a folder containing my story. "Okay. I'll read you a piece about the beginning of our relationship. But remember, it's very self-consciously loving and a little cute."

"Good." Sandy giggled. "So are you."

I smiled, cleared my throat, began to read:

The story of my relationship with Rusty is more than anything else the story of my growing up. This is partly because Rusty, ten years older and a born teacher, has worked so hard to help me grow. And it's partly because living with Rusty has meant adapting to and learning from the ways that he himself has grown. I didn't follow along without kicking and screaming all the way, he'll tell you, and he's right. That should give you some idea of how strong his personality is.

It was the force of that personality that drew me to him when we met. With his unfailing memory, he remembers the very first time we laid eyes on each other—at an evening meeting of the Lowell House student governing committee, when I breezed in late, smiling my apologies, and tried to include him in my charm. Later, and many times thereafter, he told me he had found my rudeness outrageous and my brassiness irresistible.

I don't remember that first meeting, which took place early in my junior year. But my memories of Harvard are more than anything else a haze of powerful experiences through which Rusty became the central presence in my life. Music brings specific scenes to mind more vividly than anything else. Whenever I want to see us back then, I listen to the score from the movie *Mondo Cane*, music we enjoyed countless times while lounging on the gold rug we'd picked out together for the main room of his Lowell House apartment. Rusty was then the newly appointed senior tutor of Lowell House, one of the nine housing units to which Harvard freshmen were assigned after living together for a year in the Yard.

I got to know him during the course of student business. That session of the Lowell House Committee, which I went to because I was Lowell's representative on the Undergraduate Council, was only the first of many committee meetings we both attended. During the spring, after moving from the student council to the Educational Policy Committee, I persuaded the EPC to ask

Rusty to be one of its three faculty advisers. (Another who accepted our invitation was David Riesman.) This gave me an excuse to spend long hours with him discussing educational policy, mostly the issues of pass-fail grading and dorm visiting hours for women that were in vogue. The College didn't admit women then; the Yard and the houses were all male, and women were allowed in student rooms for three hours a day on weekdays and from noon to midnight on Saturdays and Sundays. We were fighting for more weekday hours, not yet even dreaming of overnighters.

Having been active in student government in high school, I was fascinated with how influence was exercised and policy made at Harvard and thrilled that I had made friends with one of the University's rising stars. At the age of twenty-one, Rusty had traveled alone to the United States and earned a master's degree in geology at the University of Arizona. After getting his Ph.D. at Harvard, he'd been invited to join the faculty of the Geology department. Soon afterward, he was appointed senior tutor. He taught a popular undergraduate course in the natural sciences, ran a series of imaginative freshman seminars, played ace billiards, and was well loved by the circle of sensitive and competent administrators who gave heart to Harvard College.

I was impressed with these men. And because I wanted more than anything else at that point to become part of that circle myself, I took every opportunity I could to become part of Rusty's life. With his perfect manners, he welcomed me into his home. With his open heart, he accepted me into the ranks of his student friends. These were legion. Rusty knew hundreds of students. I had to work to have him for myself.

It was my brassiness that permitted me to make progress. Assuring my roommates that we had to tend to important student business, I would leave word with his secretary that he should call me, and tape notes with this message to his door. Telling my dates I had to consult with the dean, I would take them home early and then sit in his stairway waiting for his return. Usually when he found me camped in front of his door he'd ask me in for a nightcap. Because I didn't drink, he made me "pink elephants"—soda water with maraschino-cherry juice and a dash of bitters. Often we'd talk over scotch and pink elephants till two or three in the morning, when, yawning with fatigue, he'd shoo me out the door. Gradually he let me get close.

By the end of the term I felt close enough to announce that I was moving in for the summer. That did not seem as suspicious then as it might now. Rusty was only one of many resident administrators who let student friends, particularly those who could not afford to stay in Cambridge otherwise, "crash" in their rooms on campus during vacations and between terms. Rusty's guest room was frequently filled, and people also slept on the low divan in the TV room, on the couch in the main room, and on the floor.

It was to make the floor in the main room more comfortable that we went rug-shopping in the middle of that first summer we lived together. In the rug department at Sears, when he wondered aloud whether he should purchase a long rectangle of velvety gold weave, I registered my approval by plunking myself down on it and announcing that it felt like lion's fur. We carried it back and laid it the length of his large living room, which looked out over Lowell's carefully landscaped courtyard, across to the Master's Residence.

That stretch of "lion's fur" became our favorite place to while away long summer evenings. Two or three times a week I'd come home from my job in the Admissions Office and find Rusty ready to cook dinner. While I leaned against the refrigerator in his narrow kitchen and told him what the director of Financial Aid had said about this or that, he'd dice and fry onions, add a blend of cumin, coriander, turmeric, and ginger, incorporate a cut-up chicken, and then simmer the whole thing into a fragrant, spicy stew. This was curried chicken, and we ate it with large quantities of rice, yogurt, and chutney. Then, holding our stuffed bellies, we'd lie on the lion and listen to records, usually beginning with Rusty's favorite, the score from *Mondo Cane*.

For him that music conjured up the natural wonders and the cultural oddities that were featured in the filmed travelogue. For me they evoked the varied facets of the man who lay facing me. I would look into his almond-shaped eyes and bring my face so close to his that I could smell the sweet residue of curry seeping through the pores of his olive skin. Then I'd smile my broadest smile, inviting his. Then we'd touch. He'd place his hand on my shoulder and I'd put my hand on his waist and we'd lie there, gazing into each other's eyes, smiling. But we never let our bodies touch. I made sure of that.

By the fall of my senior year I had become more relaxed about touching, and we often hugged when we were lying together on the rug. The bulge in my crotch showed that I was aroused, but our intimacy went no further. Rusty was completely comfortable with his homosexuality, but he knew that I was not.

There were a number of homosexuals in his wide and varied circle of friends. On the assumption that most people at Harvard—at least those he wanted to keep as friends—were sophisticated enough to deal with people without regard for their sexual persuasions, he would mix gays and straights at his parties. I didn't meet those standards of sophistication. Often, when the parties were over and we were cleaning up, I would express loud dislike for those of his guests who struck me as being too "weird" or too "effeminate" or too interested in students to be "okay." Most of the time Rusty just ignored me. But if I got too insistent or abrasive or personal, he would icily ask me to leave. Then I'd stay away and pout until I couldn't resist coming back, respecting him in spite of myself for his integrity.

Rusty's way of being open about his homosexuality was to keep a copy of Donald Webster Cory's *Homosexual in America* prominently displayed in the bookcase that was built into the wall next to the fireplace in the lion room. I noticed it the very first time he invited me in but resisted asking him about it until well into my senior year. Then, late one evening when we were entwined on the rug, I asked him why he displayed that book.

"To inform people who care to know that I'm homosexual," he replied.

I froze, pulling myself away and averting my eyes to show him I was mortified. "I don't believe you."

He stared at me, silent, then said simply, "No matter."

I refused to believe that homosexuality had anything to do with Rusty, just as I refused to believe it had anything to do with me. Although I had had sexual contact with so many of my male friends growing up in Medford that I assumed that every boy had sexual intimacies with others in his gang and on his team and in his classes, I didn't call those contacts homosexual. What that word conjured up were the disgusting things that dirty old men did to boys who pulled their pants down in the park after dark. What I did with my special friends was to "make love."

When I was sure I was in love with Rusty, I was ready to make our relationship sexual (though still not "homo"-sexual). That's when I discovered that Rusty wasn't ready for me. He had a rule about not having sexual relationships with undergraduates, and he told me we could do nothing more intimate than what we were doing until after I graduated—if then. When I pressed him, struggling for the first time to talk explicitly about my sexual feelings, he told me he found me so uptight about sex that he wasn't at all sure he ever wanted our relationship to be physical. What he enjoyed about me—most of the time—was my companionship.

Late in the spring of my senior year, Rusty asked me whether I wanted to spend that summer in India with him. Soon afterward, one of my roommates told me that a friend of his had seen him in a gay bar. I rushed over to his apartment, told him I had heard an ugly rumor, and was informed that it was true. To register my disapproval, I stalked out. For the next few days I avoided his room and sulked whenever I ran into him. When he finally pulled me aside and asked why I was punishing him so severely, I only shook my head and looked sad.

Then one evening, deciding finally to forgive him, I knocked on his door, sauntered into his living room, and announced that I had decided to go to India after all.

"Not with me," he said without hesitating.

When I began to protest, he started to lambaste me. When I

retreated into a pout, he taunted me in rage. "I dare you to say fuck," he finally shouted. At the time I didn't "swear," and I had never said the word *fuck* out loud. But the more I resisted, rooted there by the power of the confrontation, pleading to be excused because of my upbringing, the louder he charged that I was prudish, provincial, and self-righteous. Finally, tears streaming down my cheeks, I said it: "Fuck." The next thing I knew his arms were around me.

The night we graduated from college, I went to my roommate George's bachelor party determined to celebrate by taking my first alcoholic drink. Like everyone else at the party I drank scorpions, chalices of sweet pink froth with fragrant white camellia blossoms floating in them. I downed six, partly because I wanted a garland of camellia blossoms to take to Rusty, who was leaving without me for India the next morning.

When I arrived at his apartment, we sat down on our rug and Rusty opened a bottle of champagne. As soon as I caught a whiff of the sweet-sour grapes, my stomach began to churn. Rusty saw what was coming and thrust a large ceramic ashtray beneath my mouth in time to catch it. Then he pulled me up and led me to the guest room, where I groggily peeled off my clothes and flopped onto the bed. Silently he took off his own clothes, lay down next to me, and pulled me close. In the warmth of his embrace I ejaculated. Then I rolled over, my head swirling, and fell asleep. When I awoke the next morning he was gone.

"Sweet," Sandy said as I looked up at him. "I wouldn't have dreamed you were pursuing an older man. You know what summed up my impression of you back then? The phallic symbol incident. Do you remember the time we were walking by Memorial Church and I referred to its steeple as a phallic symbol? You asked, 'What's a phallic symbol?' I was amazed that you could be a student at Harvard and not know what a phallic symbol was. And when I told you, you looked like I had just said the worst kind of obscenity and went into your naïve Toby routine: 'Come on, that's not true. People who think that way just have dirty minds.' You were very upset."

I laughed. "That's amazing. I don't remember that, but it doesn't surprise me. Some of my ingenuousness was feigned, but a lot of it was real."

"That episode really symbolized you in my eyes," Sandy continued. "I found you very sincere and open and fresh, unlike a whole lot of our classmates who never seemed quite fully aware or alive. And you had that easy smile and that boyish athletic look. There was probably a buried desire to touch you or to make something of it. But all I remember is the visual delight of looking at you and watching you move. You seemed so innocent. I felt awfully worldly and wise compared to you."

I reached over and rubbed his thigh. "Did you really find me attractive?"

He blushed. I could see that I had embarrassed him. To let him off the hook, I asked another question. "How about you? When did you first have a significant relationship with a man? I mean, with someone other than your cook."

He wrinkled his forehead and looked thoughtful. "I guess it was after my trip to Mexico, when I was involved with Lucy."

After getting out of the Peace Corps, Sandy had moved to Ann Arbor, gotten involved in leftist politics, and done a lot of antiwar organizing, supporting himself by delivering newspapers. Like most leftists, he thought it important to explore avant-garde personal arrangements and cooperative living. After enjoying two relationships with women, each lasting about a year, he had plunged into an affair with a man who was a carpenter, the man who taught him carpentry. Yet his first lover turned out to be pretty ambivalent about his homosexuality, and when the relationship became unpleasant, Sandy went off to Mexico. It was when he returned to Ann Arbor that he got involved with Lucy . . . and then Rob.

That trip was very rejuvenating. I did a lot of drawing, explored beautiful places, had a couple of strange gay experiences, soaked in the quiet of the villages again, and I came back feeling on top of the world.

A few days after I got back, I went to visit Lucy and found that she was breaking up with her husband. She asked me if I'd build a back porch on her house, and she offered to let me live in the garage in back of the house, which was a really neat space. So I said yes.

I'd always liked her energy, but I don't think I'd ever had sexual feelings toward her. So I was pretty surprised when the third day I was there she pretty much point-blank asked me how I was feeling about her sexually, confessing that she was interested in me. I remember that I was surprised. After all, she was the wife of a friend of mine, and they were just splitting up. But we started sleeping together that night and did so for the next three months.

It was delightful. It was the first time since my relationship with Vijay that I was having a fun sexual relationship that was just that. Although she pushed all kinds of romantic buttons in me, that wasn't where either of us was really at, and we didn't pretend to be. Her sex life with her husband had been pretty unsatisfactory. She had a once-a-week relationship with another man, but it wasn't really serious.

By then Lucy had thrown away the bourgeois marriage standard. She was subscribing to *Ms* magazine, which was new then, and was reading Masters and Johnson for her work. She was a sex therapist, and we talked a lot at night about the people she was seeing. I just couldn't believe some of the stories she told me. There were husbands and wives who'd never seen each other naked—they'd always have the lights off. There were lots of women who'd neither masturbated nor had orgasms—even at the age of thirty-five or forty. Then there were the men who'd always come within a minute and then pull out and turn over. I realized just how lucky I was.

Lucy had a daughter, Sally, who was one of the most wonderful and precocious children I've ever known. And she had lots of friends who were always dropping by. The energy in the house was so high that people from all over the block came and hung out there.

Pretty soon the house started growing. A friend of mine named Joanne needed a place to stay, so we put her up in the basement. And then Bob, Joanne's boyfriend, needed a place, so we took him in. Meanwhile two young friends of Lucy's who were like her adopted brother and sister came from New York for the summer. And the household next door was breaking up and their two kids were going through hell, so Lucy volunteered to let them camp at our house too. In this tiny little house at one point there were five kids and three adults, with me out in the garage.

It was a delicious period. I was spending lots of time with the neighborhood kids. Everybody's fathers were gone during the day, and I became the neighborhood dad. And at home, I was wife for the summer. I took care of the dishes and the house while Lucy went off to work. Then I'd put in a few hours on the porch, play with the kids, and go bicycling or read. I was reading a lot of women's poetry that summer, and I was very occupied with the question of sex roles.

Near the end of that summer Rob McGregor came to visit me. He was a Peace Corps volunteer who'd arrived in India just before I left. I got Vijay a job with him. Later, when I learned from one of the other volunteers that he was very active homosexually, even experimenting with S & M sex, I started worrying about my poor Vijay. I corresponded with Rob for the next couple of years, hoping he might say something, but he never mentioned sex in his letters. I just assumed they were having sex.

Rob was from Berkeley, and on his way back from India he came through Michigan to see me. We talked for a whole afternoon and really enjoyed each other. I wasn't aware of any sexual attraction. I was having this wonderful relationship with Lucy at the time. But I was really delighted with his company.

During the course of our first conversation, I finally asked him if he'd ever slept with Vijay. He looked at me quizzically and said no. I said that that surprised me because I'd been sleeping with Vijay almost every night. It turned out that Rob had been going out and getting sex and that he had never even thought of broaching that subject with Vijay. And Vijay had never come on to him.

The house was so crowded that Rob had to sleep out in the garage with me. The first night we both fell right to sleep. The second night I felt an incredible amount of sexual tension and began to realize that I was going to make love with him. It scared me because it had all the earmarks of a real equal relationship, not just kidding around. It seemed more like what I'd experienced with women; most of my relationships with women had been fairly long-term, monogamous, and romantic. Rob suddenly became my first romantic gay lover. The whole house soon picked up on what was happening and showed its approval.

There was just so much love in that house that summer! We'd sit down to dinner at night, and the place was just hopping with improvisational dance and theater and laughter and rolling on the floor. Joanne and Bob and Lucy all loved Rob, and I loved them, and we all loved Sally and the other kids, and they all loved us. For the two weeks that Rob was there, I experienced how I would like to live. Not all the time maybe; I'd like a quieter place sometimes. But it was just wonderful for Rob and me to be lying out in the garage and have Joanne and Bob come out and sit down and talk while we were in bed. And it was wonderful to be lying in bed with Lucy naked in the morning after making love and have Sally crawl in beside us and ask us incredibly fresh questions.

It all had to end, of course. The garage wasn't heated. Rob had to go on to Berkeley. Neither Lucy nor I wanted to live with each other. And so, as the summer ended, we each found a place. Only Lucy and Sally stayed behind in the house.

Sandy looked at me and sighed, "Wow. Those were really heady times, weren't they? All that stuff we did in the name of building humane society. Did you and Rusty get into all that?"

From the tone of his voice I knew he was expecting me to continue our exchange. Again I picked up my manuscript and began to read:

Exactly five years after I graduated from college, Rusty resigned his positions at Harvard, and though I remained enrolled in the University's Graduate School of Arts and Sciences, I moved off campus with him. We left our respective apartments in Lowell House, where I too had become a resident tutor, and went to live in an abandoned pool hall in one of the working-class neighborhoods just outside Harvard Square. In the spirit of the counterculture, we had struck out on our own so that we would be freer to be ourselves and more able to relate to others in ways we felt more natural, honest, and intimate than those encouraged in "the system."

To support ourselves, we had decided to start a mineral business. Our plan was to import clusters of the natural rock crystals that were found in the quarries honeycombing the hills around Bombay, to sell to mineral collectors and museums of natural history. We wanted work that would permit us both to live as we wished and to spend long periods of time in India with Rusty's family.

Rusty was at the height of his career at Harvard when he re-signed. The late sixties were years of tumult that made as many University administrators as they broke. During 1966–67, my senior year, there was only a hint of the political ferment that was soon to turn Harvard topsy-turvy. By the end of the 1967–68 school year, antiwar fever was high, SDS had grown prominent, and national rather than student politics had begun to dominate campus life. In April of 1969, this politicization reached a peak when University Hall was occupied and the police called in to bust the sit-in. There followed strife among the faculty and a month-long student strike.

More than others who were "over thirty," Rusty kept pace with the student tide, trying to explore it, to channel it in healthy directions, to explain it to his more removed colleagues. And just when he was sure that his sympathy for the students would mean the end of his Harvard career once his term as senior tutor was up, he was thrust to the top of the institutional ladder: The day before the occupation of University Hall, the dean of the faculty asked him to become director of the multimillion-dollar Science Center that the University was planning to build between the Law School, the existing science buildings, and the Yard.

Rusty accepted the position with every intention of using it to promote the humanistic education he had begun to advocate. In an article for a new student newspaper called *The Independent,* he defined this as "the task of exploring new life-styles, anticipating tomorrow's society, discovering new personal challenges for the individual, and searching for the wisdom that is to be." Unfortunately, he found that the demands of his new post kept him not only from contributing to the type of education he espoused for students, but also from continuing his own education. During 1971 and 1972, it was discussing the existential and moral dilemmas posed by his success in the system that drew us together on the gold rug of his Lowell House apartment. The more we talked, the worse his feelings about being involved in the Science Center grew. Toward the end, he came to view the very building as an incarnation of the growth-oriented, resource-devouring society he believed it so necessary to reorient.

As Rusty had become prominent in and then disenchanted with life and education at Harvard, I too had become more involved in the University and then less happy with the life I found there. During my first year of graduate school, I was asked to be a freshman proctor and adviser. When my draft board refused to grant me a deferment to complete my master's in public administration at the Kennedy School, I transferred to a teaching program in the School of Education, knowing that I would be able to get a deferment if I taught in an inner-city school. The next year I took a job in an all-black junior high school in the North Philadelphia ghetto known as "The Jungle." The following year I taught in an all-white high school in a poor section of Boston, completing my degree at the Ed School and again proctoring in the Yard. But as I became more comfortable with my homosexuality, I became less satisfied with the prevailing ethos that it was okay to be homosexual but not good to be open about it. Shared disenchantment with the cultural status quo drew Rusty and me even closer.

Late in the spring of 1971, he invited me to take the trip to India I had missed in the summer of 1967. This turned out to be a most romantic adventure. From the airport in Delhi we were chauffeured to a large military farm where Rusty's elder brother was the Commandant. There we were installed in the main guest cottage, vacated a few days earlier by General William Westmoreland, and made to feel that the estate was ours. There were genteel carriage rides to different stables and pastures; long jeep tours to see the wild game in the foothills of the Himalayas; banquets to meet the Commandant's official retinue and greet the neighbors. In between family activities, back in our honeymoon cottage, we read *The Greening of America, The Pursuit of Loneliness,* and *Future Shock*; smoked marijuana plucked from the tops of the plants that crowded the sides of the roads; and made hot love in the humid afternoons. I loved India, and I loved Rusty's large Parsi clan, and I loved him. And he, feeling for the first time I might be big enough to share all his worlds, loved me.

It was just a few months before our trip to India that Rusty had resigned as head of the Science Center and given up his tenure. The dean had asked him to spend the next school year teaching his old course and seeing if there were any jobs in the University that appealed to him. We spent most of that year planning how to make a life for ourselves once we cut the institutional cord. I was by that time enrolled in a Ph.D. program, and while I worked to make as much money as I could by teaching in both the Government department and the Ed School, Rusty set out to turn his little capital and our love of India into a mineral business.

I organized a small picnic on the banks of the Charles River to celebrate his last lecture in Nat. Sci. 10, the course on energy, evolution, and the environment he had presided over through the sixties. The lecture was in many ways a political valedictory. To illustrate his major themes, he alternated slides of beautiful natural settings with photos of pollution, crowding, and rot. It was time for a dramatic reordering of American priorities, he told the crowded lecture hall; it was a time to replace the production and consumption that had made America great with the conservation and cooperation that had to evolve if the country was going to adapt to future conditions.

At the end of his lecture, envisioning a more humanistic future, he read a poem by Roger McGough from a volume he had given me shortly after my own graduation. It was called "At Lunchtime: A Story of Love":

When the busstopped suddenly to avoid
damaging a mother and child in the road, the
younglady in the greenhat sitting opposite
was thrown across me, and not being one to
miss an opportunity i started to makelove
with all my body.

At first she resisted saying that it
was tooearly in the morning and toosoon
after breakfast and that anyway she found
me repulsive. But when i explained that
this being a nuclearage, the world was going
to end at lunchtime, she tookoff her
greenhat, put her busticket in her pocket
and joined in the exercise.

The buspeople, and therewere many of
them, were shockedandsurprised and amused-
andannoyed, but when the word got around
that the world was coming to an end at lunchtime, they put their pride in their pockets
with their bustickets and madelove one with
the other. And even the busconductor, being
over, climbed into the cab and struck up
some sort of relationship with the driver.

Thatnight, on the bus coming home,
wewere all alittle embarrassed, especially me
and the younglady in the greenhat, and we
all started to say in different ways howhasty
and foolish we had been. Butthen, always
having been a bitofalad, i stood up and
said it was a pity that the world didn't nearly
end every lunchtime and that we could always
pretend. And then it happened . . .

Quick asa crash we all changed partners
and soon the bus was aquiver with white
mothballbodies doing naughty things.

> And the next day
> And everyday
> In everybus
> In everystreet
> In everytown
> In everycountry

people pretended that the world was coming
to an end at lunchtime. It still hasn't.
Although in a way it has.

"Great poem. Great poem." Sandy grinned appreciatively. "That's exactly how I had come to look at life and love by that time too."

When I asked him if Rob had shared his views, he explained that in the summer of 1974 he had gone to Berkeley to see if they could establish some kind of long-term relationship, but that Rob had become very excited about exploring the gay scene in San Francisco. The "glitteriness" and materialism of this turned Sandy off, and he was also uneasy with all the constant cruising and anonymous sex. So he returned to Ann Arbor, lived for several months in a shack in the country, and then took a job leading a group of American students to Denmark. While on tour he met Christina. It was with her, rather than Rob, that he worked to develop a committed but open relationship.

At that time I was carrying around this real strong notion I'd gotten from reading a book called *Das Energi* by Paul Williams that whenever somebody is in loving interaction with somebody else, everybody who's aware of it should be happy. The only really positive, humane response to people loving one another is happiness. So I was just not going to be jealous. I was not going to be exclusive in any way.

I was kind of shocked that Lars, Ingrid's lover at the time, wanted to be exclusive and to exclude me. But I was willing to accept that as part of the way things were. I was happy that Ingrid and Lars loved each other. But I didn't want that kind of love.

After about five or six weeks in Denmark I met Christina at a party. I had been seeing her around for a couple of weeks and delighting in her physical presence. I liked her style, her color sense, her clothes, her eyes, her body.

When I saw her at this party, I went over and sat down and started talking to her. At first I feared she was bored with me, but soon I saw that she was really liking me. By that time everybody had had a lot to drink, and soon we all started dancing. In the course of the dancing, Christina and I started getting real passionate, groaning and hugging and kissing our way around the dance floor.

We slept together that night. It was probably the most powerful sex I'd had up to that point in my life. I remember feeling like we were two skeletons in space moving in rhythm with a whole spectrum of other creatures that were radiating around us. As if we were part of a vast web of connections with all of life. It felt like we were Adam and Eve beginning the world.

A real part of the connection between us was that we were in harmony about where we wanted our personal lives to go. We agreed right from the beginning that if we continued as a couple we didn't want to live together all the time. We wanted to live down the street from one another or maybe to live together for six months and apart for six months. We wanted to completely squash dependence and possessiveness, to retain our independence and creativity. There was a famous Swedish journalist, Jan Myrdal, who spent half each year apart from his wife. And there were Sartre and De Beauvoir. They were our models.

I was sure that feminism was the most powerful political force of the decade, maybe the century. I was reading Doris Lessing and feminist poets, especially Marge Piercy and Adrienne Rich, and I was something of a propagandist for feminism myself. My ideas and Christina's seemed to click perfectly.

"Were you able to pull it off in practice?" I interrupted. "Rusty and I began opening up our relationship at about that time, and it was really tough going. Ideals are one thing, feelings another. . . ."

"We really had to work at it too."

Christina had come to Ann Arbor in the fall of 1975, and they had gotten married so that she could get a work permit. For the next six months they were sexually monogamous. Then, in the summer of 1976, Sandy began to sleep with John Norris, an old friend who was planning to move to San Francisco. Though Christina had given her okay, she soon started to express reservations. And that fall, when Christina started sleeping with a guy from their food collective, Sandy himself was upset. That made Christina resentful. They fought more and more. They decided to travel separately that summer.

When they were reunited in Ann Arbor that fall, Sandy fell madly in love with her all over again. To make some money, they decided to go to Washington and pick apples. After the harvest, they got a place together in Portland, Oregon. Then once again they began to feel that they were stifling each other. This was in the spring of 1978.

That summer, Christina decided to move to Berkeley to study radical therapy. Sandy went along to help her get settled and to visit Rob and John before returning to Ann Arbor. Just before he left, he had a birthday party that drew together almost everyone he'd been seriously involved with during the previous five years. Also present were two of the guys he'd lived with in Adams House his senior year. It turned out that their lives had been just as political, if not so countercultural, as his had.

What was most fun about seeing them again was that, in a certain way, they were just the same. Both of them had been through a whole lot of stuff. Max was divorced and living with a new woman. Ed had been all over the country doing different things, and at the time he was a cobbler. But basically their styles of relating to me and to other people were just the same as they'd been at Harvard.

Max was pretty involved politically. He'd had a lot of practical experience lobbying the legislature and working with state government. The woman he was living with worked for an environmental group. They were heavy-duty politicos in a very old fashioned New Left sense. They were very suspicious and critical of Christina and me because of our interest in therapy and the consciousness movement. They more or less maintained that such things were objectively reactionary. After a while, we began to avoid those topics. Ed was also very political, but he seemed in a place a little closer to where we were.

It had not come out in previous conversations that I was bisexual, though they knew that I was staying with Rob and that Christina was staying someplace else. But at the birthday party things were pretty explicit. There were three of my old male lovers—Rob, John, and Bob, Joanne's lover—and

there was a lot of openly displayed affection, especially because I was saying good-bye. I think Max was particularly
bothered by John, who is a delicate flower of a person, manly
but wonderfully delicate in his manners and taste. And there
was a lot of conversation about gay topics. A story had just
appeared in the papers that high-school students had voted
Anita Bryant the most hated woman in America—everybody
was real amazed and pleased by that.

These were the first old classmates I'd encountered since
leaving Harvard, and it was very clear to me that I'd changed
a lot. Having Christina there along with my male lovers
made me especially aware of how much my notions about
relationships had changed.

"But how about you?" Sandy said with a yawn. "How did you
and Rusty go about opening up your relationship?"

I caught his yawn, stretched, sighed. I couldn't bear to read
again. "Well, though we talked a lot about having an open relationship, we didn't really have sex with others for a long time,
mostly because I was very uptight about Rusty's having sex with
someone else and he didn't want to hurt me. Like you, I was comfortable with sex in the context of relationships but freaked out by
the idea of having sex with strangers. I was completely inexperi-
enced with recreational sex as it is known in the gay male subculture.

"Anyway, once Rusty started going to the baths, I had a few
sexual encounters with people I met through friends in Cambridge,
and a relationship or two in New York City when I went there to
do research. But I didn't feel comfortable going to gay bars alone
until after we moved to Berkeley. My first one-night stand was
with someone I met at the White Horse. I still haven't gotten into
the baths. It's been mostly research that's given me a sense of
what the gay male subculture is all about."

"You're going to sleep with me, aren't you?" Sandy said without
batting an eyelash.

I knew exactly what he meant. If it had been earlier and we
had been fresher, he might well have been initiating a conversation about our having sex. We had grown progressively more intimate during the exchange that my interview of him had become,
especially after he had remarked on how much I had changed

since the time I insisted that people who saw phallic symbols in steeples had dirty minds. After that, I had flirted with him, and he had flirted back. We had both known that flirting was all we were going to do because I cared more about getting his story on tape and he was more interested in learning something about me and my writing.

But that didn't mean we couldn't enjoy the physical dimensions of our attraction. During the course of the evening, Sandy had gone from his disciplined cross-legged crouch to various sitting and lying positions on the mattress. Now his long body was stretched out next to where I knelt gathering up the pages of my manuscript. I stuffed them into their folder, switched off the tape recorder, sat back, and gazed down at him.

"Well?" He grinned up at me lazily.

"Well." I smiled back.

Slowly I reached over and wrapped my hand around his ankle. He had big feet, workingman's feet, and there were callouses where his boots rubbed too tightly against his toes.

I let my fingers slide over to his instep, felt its soft flesh, then slid my hand up beneath his pants, grabbing hold of his calf. "These are carpenter's muscles, aren't they? Where did all the baby fat go?"

He laughed and closed his eyes.

I pulled my hand out from under his pant leg and placed the tips of my fingers on his stomach. There was a tightening of muscle. He wrinkled his nose. "That tickles."

I put my hand on the side of his head, rustled my fingers through his curls, began to massage his scalp with my fingers. His face was plain but pleasing—squarely set eyes, something of a bobsled nose, dimpled chin. With his eyes closed, his long lashes curled upward. His eyebrows were so brown that his freckles looked almost golden in contrast. His hair was the same brown of his eyebrows bleached many shades lighter by the sun. He smiled without opening his eyes.

I bent over, compared the white of his teeth with the red of his lips, brought my mouth right up next to his. "You smell like the forest," I whispered.

He sniffed once or twice, giggled, whispered back: "It's rosemary. Oil. I use it in my hair."

A minute later he was snoring.

❋ ❋ ❋

When I had called to set up our interview, Sandy had invited me to spend a day camping with him before going on to East Lansing. The next morning at daybreak, he woke me with a warm squeeze and urged me to get ready. With the early morning work crowd, we wound our way back into Ann Arbor and then out the other side. By midmorning we had driven halfway across the state of Michigan, making our way west to Sandy's favorite stretch along the shores of the Wisconsin River.

We arrived there in time to feast on fresh cheese, bread, and juice in the late afternoon sunshine. Then we hiked a ways upstream along the shore, picked our way through the woods, and climbed a steep incline to the top of Ferry Bluffs, a precipice some 150 feet above the river. At the edge of the cliff, huddled together, we sat and watched the sunset dapple and shade vast tracts of unpopulated Wisconsin forest. Each of us honored the spectacle by keeping silent.

We had spent almost all the drive talking about politics. Sandy was interested in the conceptualization of political outlooks I had presented in *The Politics of Homosexuality*, but he was sure that his own ideas fit neatly into neither the radical nor revolutionary categories of New Left thinking I had outlined. He believed it important to experiment with more humanistic ways of living, but he didn't think this a realistic way of precipitating cultural revolution, if only because the culture was so shaped by the media, the Establishment had so much influence over the media, and the Establishment was itself under the control of corporations that acted mainly in the interest of maximizing profits. In fact, Sandy wondered if it weren't downright dangerous to see living a good life as in and of itself political. As far as he could see, this idea had only encouraged the narcissism and the high-consumption life-styles he saw and objected to in so many of those belonging to what he called "the consciousness movement." This, he feared, was composed of children of the sixties who remained less true to the ethos of the counterculture and the ideas of the Movement than "more political people" had.

In my judgment, as I told him, his views were very much those popular in the New Left in its early years, and of the counterculture as it took shape beside that, before it evolved as time and logic required it to. For Sandy remained convinced that the most important political work was to check the power of huge, growth-oriented corporations, in all the traditional ways used by community organizers and by developing cooperative economic arrangements that could replace capitalistic ones. Compared with the task of making the economic system more socialist, he viewed the pursuit of self-knowledge, and the experimentation with unconventional sexual, emotional, and social relationships called for by that pursuit, as a sideline, almost a self-indulgent one. He had little sense that life-style politics had produced a healthy evolution in contemporary culture. In the gay male subculture in which I was discovering such liberation, he saw mainly sexual objectification, fear of intimacy, and hedonism. In the affluent and industrious gay ghettos I viewed as such triumphant manifestations of countercultural and liberationist movement success—dramatic evidence that those movements had succeeded in making society more pluralistic by getting people with unconventional life-styles to carve out a place in the system that reflected their own special wants and needs—he saw only capitalism, consumerism, and gentrification.

The issues Sandy thought most important were "economic" rather than "cultural." He was interested more in fundamental economic arrangements and their consequences than either in how contemporary American mores made people feel about themselves and relate to one another or in how these cultural and psychological factors affected the distribution of wealth and status. He was anarchist where I was libertarian, and socialist (in analysis and strategic perspective if not utopia) where I was liberationist. Listening to Sandy made me aware of how poorly the first radicals had explained the theory of political and social change responsible for their embrace of liberationist politics; of how myopic, confused, and divided everyone was when it came to understanding what had come about as a result of the counterculture, the Movement, and the early gay, women's, and lesbian liberation movements.

I tried to help Sandy understand why I thought liberationist politics had been such a grand success. I reminded him that the theory of the cultural radicals who believed in revolution through consciousness change (the people Charles Reich had *really* described in *The Greening of America*) was that a more humane, pluralistic culture would ensue as individuals became more comfortable with themselves. In their view, social change was first and foremost a function of psychology. They wanted to make individuals more self-aware, self-confident, and secure, because they believed that this would permit them to treat others, especially those less well-endowed and fortunate, with dignity, maturity, respect for individual difference, and an appreciation of social diversity. They assumed that good character was the key to improving human relations. In addition, they assumed that those who "got themselves together" could prod, stir, help, and inspire others to follow their lead in getting comfortable with themselves and learning how to deal responsibly with others. Thus, ever-growing numbers of people would treat one another more and more respectfully. The changed way in which people would relate to one another would be the basis of a new morality that would make the culture more humane.

And the radicals didn't expect that this "revolution in consciousness"—which has in fact been more an evolution in consciousness—would be limited to interpersonal relationships alone. They believed that as individuals with countercultural consciousness and morality assumed places in the power structure, the governing class would become more sensible, equitable, realistic, and responsive; that as more and more of them went into business, there would be a proliferation of adventurous but ethical free enterprisers; and that as more and more of them assumed positions in large corporations, the "machine"—beginning with individuals and cliques and slowly moving up—would become clearer about its moral priorities with respect to the outside world and more equitable and accommodating within. In short, individuals interested in "growth" and "liberation" would produce a "counter"-culture whose members would infiltrate the system, slowly but surely permeating the Establishment and reorienting the culture. Thus would evolve a more humane and democratic capitalism.

This, I insisted to Sandy, was what had happened, what was happening. Though people bewailed their demise, the counterculture and the Movement, as they were known in the sixties, had fragmented as individuals eager to be more true to themselves and more intimate with others had clustered together in groups that made common cause of what they considered most important to their individual self-actualization. Race, religion, and national background were most important for some, especially those who felt disadvantaged because of, or conflicted about, those realms of their lives. Gender was most important for most liberationist-minded women. Their sexual orientations were what growing numbers of homosexuals had come to feel was their most vital trait, though most homosexual men and women eager to explore their sexuality and find support among like-minded peers discovered that they were drawn by their interests and their natures not to homosexuals of both sexes, but to others of the same sex, to other "lesbians" or "gay men." Since male and female homosexuals had created and enjoyed such very different subcultures before the arrival of the liberation movements, it was not surprising that they had coalesced into two very different types of gay community as they had become more liberationist-minded and liberated.

Moreover, I argued, as people of all kinds with countercultural interest in self-realization and supportive community had come to terms with and fulfilled the personal and social dimensions of their self-actualization, they had inevitably begun to focus on other aspects of their lives: on the occupational or professional facets of their self-expression; on the convenience, opportunity, and luxury added by material assets; on the rewards that came from keeping up with old friends, settling into long-term relationships, living healthily, putting down roots, parenting. Indeed, it was their very quest for liberation that had led those true to countercultural ideals back into the system—not, as before, primarily to please parents, impress teachers, win the applause of elders, make money, exercise influence, and enjoy status (though all these, with the right attitude, could be given their place) but in the countercultural and liberationist spirit of expressing themselves more fully, of relating to others more equitably and maturely, and of going about their daily lives realizing and promoting their ideas about what the good society should be like. The counterculture, and even the Movement, had been absorbed by the system, not squelched by it, or coopted by it (though countercultural individuals had been required to make accommodations with traditional attitudes and values in order to keep their cultural evolution "organic").

The result, at least to the extent that I could document it in the spread of gay life, was indeed a more humane and democratic capitalism—for all that this was evolving much more slowly and painfully than most of us from the sixties had originally hoped and expected. And despite the fact that there was a long way to go before all that had happened and was happening would be completely realized, thoroughly understood, and finally assessed. If anything, the backlash represented by the Moral Majority and the New Right was evidence of how pervasive, and hence threatening, the "new morality" had become. And this was being documented statistically, most professionally by Daniel Yankelovich for his forthcoming book *New Rules: Searching for Self-Fulfillment in a World Turned Upside Down.*

In the face of all my arguments, Sandy remained skeptical. And he was especially reluctant to grant that the personal was political, if only because he feared I was being naïve about how the world worked and perhaps even counterrevolutionary in my "apoliticalness." He just wouldn't believe that social disobedience had been to the seventies what civil disobedience had been to the sixties.

Sandy did admit that he thought it important for each individual to do as much as he or she could to make every individual feel fully acknowledged. And he agreed that one important aspect of this was working to overcome the conventional jealousies and dependencies that prevented those who wanted to from relating sexually to individuals outside their "primary relationships." He and Frank wanted their relationship to be "open." Though each of them still felt a certain degree of jealousy about the other's sexual involvements, both of them worked to abide by liberationist ideals, which they tended to call feminist, when it came to dealing with "issues of possessiveness." They spent a lot of time talking about their feelings. They worked through pangs of jealousy and dealt practically with "bad vibrations." They hadn't gotten to the point where they always told each other the details of the sexual intimacies they enjoyed with other people, but they did keep each other informed about their sexual interests, fantasies, intentions, and "secondary relationships." And each was careful never to make the other feel dismissed or replaced.

Long before I had shown up, Sandy had told Frank that he wanted to spend a few days rediscovering me and that this might include having sex with me. Frank had been told about our plans to go camping. He would also hear about all that went on.

Sandy was the personification of openness and honesty about feelings, and he brought out the same in me. As we watched the moon replace the sun over the Wisconsin, I told him all about my relationship with Rusty, about how he had guided me through the early throes of my sexual awakening, about how each of us had made painful mistakes as we went about learning to enjoy sexual intimacy with others in the context of our primary relationship, about how each of us had grown and changed as we had explored, experienced, learned, and aged.

The intimacy of all that talk about our primary relationships was what finally drew us into each other's arms. In the moonlight we continued the exploration of each other's bodies I had begun after our interview the night before.

6

DAVID FREDRICK

At the time of my journey, I remained convinced that cultural evolution was proceeding as it should and that individuals should go about their daily lives as they believed all people might, even as they operated within the system. But I had become aware that working in the system required compromises and accommodations and had begun acting on the assumption that it was necessary to be an idealist without illusions—as John F. Kennedy had defined himself. It seemed to me that the problem with the strategy of revolution through consciousness-change as originally conceived was that it demanded so much of human nature in a world that was so imperfect. If not human nature, then social conditioning, seemingly unavoidable misunderstandings and misinterpretations, and the need to survive in rough economic times kept even the most good-hearted and committed members of our generation from being saints. That this might be the fault of "the system" didn't make much difference if one chose to work within that system, which I did. Unlike many other veterans of the sixties counterculture, the Movement, and the early liberation movements (including people like Sandy, though in this he was unique among the classmates I had interviewed), I continued to believe that democracy, culture, and capitalism in America were the best hope for the values I believed in, if only because comparison showed ours superior to any existing society when it came to producing and extending affluence, equity, liberty, hope, and opportunity. I did what I did, lived as I did, in order to improve life as it was in the United States—in order to make the American experiment more successful.

So I carried the warm glow of Sandy with me as I set out to visit David Fredrick, but I was not without wariness and skepticism as well. To some extent, this was because I had found my dealings with him sobering. Though largely a product of letters, our relationship was a complicated one. I liked David. But I didn't really trust him. He intrigued me. He also frightened and fatigued me. I had seen aspects of myself in each of the classmates I had interviewed, had become clearer about who I was and what I was doing as a result of getting to know them, to the extent that I could, given my purposes, obligations, and time limits. Not all of the aspects of myself I saw reflected in David were ones I was proud of—not the myopia, insecurity, and impulsiveness, not the willfulness, opportunism, manipulativeness, and poor judgment.

It was not that these traits weren't usually mitigated or outshone by nobler ones, in David as well as myself. Awareness of our less-than-admirable traits was one mitigating quality we shared. I liked to see this saving grace in myself. I hoped I was going to find it in David. The stage had certainly been set by all that had preceded the visit I was now about to make.

It seemed that nature itself was providing a prologue when rain began to pour as my bus to East Lansing pulled out of the station. The bright blue skies I had shared with Sandy gave way to dark clouds and wailing winds. The Michigan countryside became drab and gray.

I shivered and thought of David. We had carried on such an unusual correspondence. We had had such a strange first meeting. I had brought along all the letters we'd exchanged so that I could reread them before interviewing him. I wanted to get some sense of what he had really been up to, to get some perspective on my own thinking. I reached down into my knapsack, pulled out my David Fredrick file, and turned to his first letter. It was the first one I had received when the class report came out.

East Lansing, Michigan
September 23, 1977

Dear Toby,

I've just read your statement in the 10th Anniversary Report of our Harvard class. I don't understand. What are the "politics of homosexuality"?

I have often wondered what I would say to someone from my Harvard class ten years later. I've decided to talk to you because I find your statement quite extraordinary. It certainly beats the tales of woe and success of all those lawyers, bankers, doctors, and assistant college professors. I took the coward's way out and failed to return the questionnaire. I have become a bureaucrat's bureaucrat, and it would have taken a novel at least to make that sound interesting. I have sometimes considered the irony that I, the English major, should have wound up in the middle of this thing called government, wheeling and dealing with state cops, attorneys general, labor unions, and the like. Here I am right in the middle of whatever it was people like you were studying about.

Do you understand the problem? I was not prepared for this. The only political type class I ever took was a course in Marxism from Herbert Marcuse when I was in graduate school in California. I used to try to crack jokes with Angela Davis. That was before she became famous.

I have been functioning in this government for five years. And I have zipped my way up from College Trainee to Division Director. My title, if you can believe this, is "Director, Classification and Compensation Planning Division." I have somehow seized control of the heart of the personnel system of the government of the State of Michigan. You see, I was given the unique opportunity of recreating the classification structure of the merit system.

Quite frankly, Toby, I just pretend to know what I'm doing and make up the new classification structure as I go along. I've got people convinced that I'm brilliant. Harvard—the name—sure helps. But I have this deep-seated anxiety that sooner or later someone is going to find out that everything I know about government comes from Shakespeare—with a little Marlowe thrown in.

Toby, I have written a novel about being homosexual. I have elaborate theories about the metaphysics of homosexuality. But what on earth are the "politics of homosexuality"? If I could understand that, I might be able to use it in my job.

Or maybe you could tell me how one gets out of this mess. I have been trying to convince the upper command structure of the Michigan State Police to permit a moderately paced evolution of human rights within their department. Unfortunately, the only way I could explain to the new State Police Colonel what was happening in his department was by superficially describing the Marxist theory of revolution. I'm sure they ran my name through the "red" file after that. I just might be in somebody's computer. Hell, I did know Angela. I used to be a conscientious objector. And when I was a missionary in Japan, I used to go to a "peace" coffee shop run by Japanese radical students just outside Misawa Air Base, mainly to speak English with native speakers. Let me tell you, it wasn't easy being a neurotic waning Christian in a small boring town in northern Honshu. That was back when I was sleeping with two women in Tokyo and a man in Kyoto.

Anyway, I got fired as a missionary. Actually "released" is a better word. I think they were afraid of mental and sexual aberrations. I got drunk one night and tried to explain to an old Methodist my sexual attraction to Jesus. And then I told the head honcho missionary that I wasn't committed to the Church because I didn't want to be committed to any institution, even if the Church *was* the body of Christ.

When I got back to the States I gave up Christianity and became a bureaucrat. I also became an astrologer. I once taught a class in astrology to inmates at Jackson Prison. I found that throwing in a few lines of Shakespeare while explaining what sign makes the best con added a little class to the class.

Another reason I'm writing you is that you're an Aquarian. Aquarians are tolerant people.

I think that when I left Harvard College, that bronzed John Harvard in front of University Hall should have quoted Shakespeare at me: "There are more things in heaven and earth, Horatio, than are dreamt of in your philosophy." That's what I wanted to say on my questionnaire from Harvard. But all by itself it sounds arrogant, and what I really feel is kind of awe. I'm actually very happy with the way things have turned out.

Now if I could exit from this damn bureaucracy with style, I could get on with the next outrageous act of this drama.

Occasionally now, as my lover and I are practicing giving each other more space, I go down to the local bar and ogle young men who are about the age I was when I was at Harvard. In those days I wandered through the streets of Cambridge looking at young men secretly.

You must have known Sean McBride. I'm sure I was sexually attracted to him but was too embarrassed to notice it. In the red-book—that 10th Anniversary one—Sean said "we were so split, both collectively and individually." Sean always was so elegant. That's a beautiful phrase, and it can mean absolutely anything you want it to.

I sometimes wonder if the young men at the bar are as good.

Toby, I've very much enjoyed talking at you. I hope you haven't minded listening. Please don't feel any obligation to reply. I just wanted to get this off my chest.

Thank you,
David Fredrick, '67

I looked up and out into the gray, wondering what David was now going to say.

It was almost on a whim that I wrote you that first letter. I saw your piece in the class report as a kind of advertisement, like the advertisements for sex partners in porno magazines. The report obviously wasn't a porno magazine, but how else would a Harvard man do it? And I took it as a kind of homosexual dare. I figured that if you dared put it there, I dared to get in touch with you.

I had certainly found David's letter fascinating, powerful in its honesty and personality, attractive in its humor and intensity. I remembered trying to respond in kind. A copy of my reply came next in the folder. I picked it up to see what I had written.

> 934 Carleton Street
> Berkeley, California 94710
> *November 4, 1977*

Dear David,

Your letter was deeply moving—so moving, in fact, that it has taken me until now to summon the wherewithal to answer it. I've been working for almost four years on a thesis on gay politics, and the prospect of breaking loose from my academic distance and analytical style is frightening. One is supposed to leave aside feelings when producing social science, and so I'm in the strange position of writing logical, objective, dispassionate prose about the importance of intuition, feelings, and emotion.

Anyway, the point of my writing is to tell you that your letter was deeply moving because of its honesty and its intimacy and its warmth. What a poet's gift for words you have, what lovely meter and flow. I have a harder time letting myself flow when I'm writing. I'm much better in person.

My God, it's just occurred to me that you might not have the faintest idea who this is. You may have forgotten that you wrote me a letter. We are, after all, complete strangers. Had you ever written so intimately to a complete stranger? I mean, before you wrote all that to me? This is my first try at anonymous written intimacy. I'm writing to you as I might talk to someone on a foreign train, someone I'm unlikely to talk with again.

That, by the way, is what I've come to believe about anonymous sex: it's anonymous intimacy. Isn't it ironic that people able to converse intimately with strangers are thought sensitive, sophisticated, and social, while people able to enjoy sexual intimacy with strangers are deemed amoral, animalistic, and incapable of healthy and sustained emotional relationships. That's one way society keeps people from being sexual with more than one person, I think, and that's why I've come to believe that it's liberating for individuals as well as for society when people who want to be sexual with one another go ahead and be so—even if it's only for a night or for an hour or for a blind dark minute. I see problems only when someone can be intimate with other people in those anonymous sexual ways but not in more personal and more substantial ways. Or when someone isn't sensitive enough to the customs of those around him when being sexual. But then the challenge is not to eliminate a person's capacity for short-termed sexual intimacy but to encourage in that person the capacity for other types of relationships and to assure that he has places for sexual recreation apart from people who might be offended by this. As you can see, I'm quite a believer in traditional gay male patterns.

Yipes, my fingers are typing out of control. But only because I'm a little bit stoned and shaking because of what I'm going to do. Which is not to tell you about Rusty (who loved your letter and joins me in saying that we would one day like to meet you). Instead, I'm going to tell you about another David.

Almost from the time I started doing research in the Tenderloin, I noticed this David walking to and from work. He's a therapist at the Tenderloin Clinic, which provides mental health services by gays for gays. When I dropped into the clinic, I was invited to attend its gay men's "rap," a weekly self-help group attended mostly by older gay men, some psychotic, some alcoholic. David ran the group the first time I sat in, and he tamed the tigers with such poise and charm that I was touched. He was a model man by my political standards, strong but gentle—the type of man who validates my vision of what a society free of sex role stereotyping would be.

So I was really taken with David and wanted to get to know him and was very sexually attracted to him. But being a good political man myself, when it came to getting involved, I had to wait for David to meet me halfway, for him to want me as I wanted him, so that I could reach out without making him feel that he was some kind of sex object I was pursuing without regard for his feelings. Anyway, after the next week's rap group, he asked me if I wanted to get together. I said yes, and we spent a nice lunch hour discussing politics (what political gays always do on their first "date"). I invited him to come to dinner at my Tenderloin apartment. He accepted. We spent most of that evening talking about personal things (which to cultural radicals is the

essence of politics, though not for David, because he's a Marxist).
Then we had the most loving, playful, personal sex.

The only problem was that I couldn't see David for the next
five days. When he left for the clinic the next morning, I asked
him if I'd ever see him again and he said yes, perhaps for lunch
the next week. Had he viewed our luxurious lovemaking as a one-
night stand? Did he want to keep his distance? I was disappointed
and confused, but I nobly acquiesced when he told me he wanted
to spend the next five days with his lover, the members of his
collective, the members of his study group, and his women
friends. He lives in a commune and is very big on his responsibilities to the men in his collective. I admire those who take collective living seriously, though that kind of life isn't for me. I'd rather
be freer to involve myself in situations and relationships that crop
up suddenly and unfold spontaneously—I'd rather have spent the
next five days with David.

But I'm telling you all this to answer your question about the
politics of homosexuality. You see, people really are learning how
to be sexually and emotionally intimate with one another more
easily and more frequently. I'm an example of this. David's an
example. You are too. Especially because we're men, conditioned
from adolescence if not before to focus mainly on achievement, to
avoid being vulnerable, and to hide our attraction to one another,
whenever we reach out to other males, we help create values and
assumptions that make the world more human. That's why homosexuality, in and of itself, is political. That's why, to answer your
question, being intimate with someone of the same sex is the cor-
nerstone of the politics of homosexuality.

So you see, this is a very political thing I'm doing, being so
intimate with you, a strange man, and being intimate simultaneously with Rusty, with whom I'll share this letter, and with David
the therapist, for whom I now realize I'm also writing. And I've
just thought of another David, another lover, another from our
Harvard class. Let me send this to all of you as a measure of my
trust, our intimacy, my love (see, I'm promiscuous!).

Toby

Rereading this made me laugh. I had really let him have it—
my whole philosophy of political living and loving. And I still
wasn't sure just how he'd taken it.

When you wrote back, I was worried that you'd gotten too
heavily into that relating stuff, all that pseudopsychology out
in California. I thought, "Oh, my God, not that crap." But I
just couldn't resist replying to see what would happen. I
decided that I would in no way try to respond to you as a

normal human being. You were a fantasy who answered my letters. I kept writing you the most outrageous things, and you kept answering back. I thought, "Hmm, this is interesting; he's kind of weird himself."

David's reply to my letter came next in my folder.

East Lansing, Michigan
November 10, 1977

Hi,

I'm the original David who wrote you. I didn't really expect you to write back, let alone to see you become an epistolary whore with real and fantasy Davids. But my God, Toby, three Davids with one letter!

Actually, it's not all that surprising—Davids often are beloved. Unless they fuck up, like David Eisenhower. I suppose there are those who love David Eisenhower, but I'm not one of them.

I want to say thank you for your letter. It makes peculiar sense. It's fascinating that you have no real idea of whom you're talking to—as I have no real idea. I have only a vague memory of a person at Harvard who is ten years younger than you are. As for me, just think of Michelangelo's David or the David in the Bible—king or shepherd, depending on whether your fantasies tend more to the regal or to the idyllic. I think I can say on behalf of all the Davids—excluding David Eisenhower—that we try to be a good experience.

To whom am I speaking? Or, which one of you do I relate to? I might actually have an easier time relating to gay counselor David. I get the impression he doesn't understand your brand of politics any better than I do. And I flunked being a scholar. I was bored with graduate school, and was feeling terrifically guilty about having committed sodomy with my male roommate. Then a beautiful blonde from Radcliffe moved in next door. It was my last great heterosexual experience.

So there are some things I have difficulty relating to. And then there are things that you take more seriously than I do—like mixing sex and politics. You see, I mix sex and religion. We're God fearin' folk out here in Michigan.

Maybe I want to explain why I wrote you that letter. I was reading through that Harvard thing and found what you'd written. I wanted to say, "Hey, I'm glad you said what you did. I'm gay too. I know it took a lot of courage to say it." If you can imagine Mary Tyler Moore saying that to you, that's probably how I'd have sounded. Of course, I'm not Mary Tyler Moore, so it sounded different. I cast upon the waters an anonymous self-portrait to an anonymous person. I've always wanted to find a bottle with a note in it, so I decided to send one. I wanted to believe in serendipity.

And now you've returned after so many days. Of course, you must have realized now that I've already looked up your stars. I really enjoy astrology much more than Transactional Analysis. I see you love power, you little devil. I find that intriguing.

As for sex, I like it. I used to worry about being sexually inadequate, first with women, then with men. Now I'm thoroughly pleased and delighted whenever something beautiful happens.

You've thrown in Rusty, I'll throw in Tom. What's a few more anonymous people? Tom is my—I hate the word—"lover." Tom and I have been together for a couple of years, we've meant a great deal to each other, we love each other—and now we're both nuts. I think he's crazier; he thinks I'm crazier. Actually, all that's happening is that I'm going through a major personality change in order to quit smoking.

It's strange. About a year ago—maybe six months ago—I became totally disenchanted with what I was doing. And I began having dreams again like I did when I was a kid. I wondered how good I could really be. I wanted to take all those childhood dreams, synthesize them into one, and see if I could make it come true. It was like creating a new David (how many would that make?). I was in the midst of this particular personality change when I wrote you.

Toby, your letter is not an easy one to answer. This one may be hard to understand. I'm a person, a real person sitting here, waiting for snow to strike tomorrow night. And you're a real person, now somewhere in San Francisco, three hours earlier and probably warmer. I am somewhat awed that you answered my letter. I want to thank you for restoring some of the faith I want to have in people. I thank you for what you said, what you shared. As for intimacy, I'm not promiscuous, but I'm easy.

I want to say, and I've never said this to a stranger before, I love you—at least for a blind dark minute.

Write again—please, only if you want to.

David

David had taken seriously my invitation to be intimate, if not my explanation of why that was political. During the next year, as he was making dramatic changes in his life, he shared with me in long, rambling letters his deepest hopes and fears. Late in May of 1978, he wrote that he had left his job in the Civil Service Commission and begun to write a murder mystery featuring a gay detective:

I hope you got my postcard from the Orient. I returned to Lansing, went back to my job for one day, and decided I couldn't take it anymore. So I called a friend of mine whom I've known since junior high (I beat him running for class president in ninth grade) who is now a psychiatrist. I asked him if it was reasonable that I could be cracking up. I was tired out, sick of everything, utterly bored. I thought that maybe if he wrote me a letter, I could use up my eight weeks of sick leave. I felt like I was trying to get out of the fucking draft again. He said it sounded reasonable and that he'd write me a letter if I needed it.

The next day I went to work and talked to my boss. He's an honorable man. I said, "Boss, I just can't take it anymore. Everything is falling apart. The vacation in Japan was fine, but it reminded me of the time I was a missionary and how insecure I felt.

"I need to take some time off. I've talked to my shrink friend. More than anything else in the world right now I want to write a murder mystery using a gay detective. I want to kill off a state senator and get the gay detective hired by the Michigan State Police. The shrink thinks that makes sense. Maybe that's because he's crazier than I am."

My boss, who knows I'm a fairy, is a fairly big man in the government. He understood that I was physically and mentally exhausted, and that writing a book might be good therapy.

Four weeks later David announced that he had finished his book and given it to his friend Leonard, whose brother made Hollywood movies.

I do believe that I have finally gone over the edge. I know that Leonard will read my book, because he owes me a favor. I know he will be honest with me, especially after I was honest with him about what I thought of his brother's movie. It is as if I said to him, "Leonard, I want to know if this detective story I've written is any good." It didn't seem real to me when I was doing it. But now it looms large in my consciousness that he is actually going to tell me if it's any good. Which is a naked lady in my heart called terror.

I've never done anything this bold before. I mean it's true: all English majors want to believe they're better than Shakespeare or, at least, Robert Penn Warren. Actually, I'm something of a slut compared to other Harvard English majors; my idols are Ross MacDonald and A. Conan Doyle. I might aspire to writing the sequel to *Hamlet*—call it *Horatio*—but in my heart I know that I would goddamn well prostitute my talents for money or popularity.

The problem is I don't know how much of a whore I'd have to be. It took me two years to figure that out at Harvard. But it was easy once I got the knack of it. All I had to do was figure out what would please people and then do it. I've always been like that. I simply attach myself to a situation and then figure out what works.

(Toby, I think I'm getting drunk. I don't often do that. But my detective drinks. Wild Turkey bourbon. And that's what I'm drinking now. Robert Penn Warren said it was all right to drink after writing. So I figure it's all right to drink now . . .)

I have dared to dream that Leonard might even like my book. It's a funny thing, dreaming you might be good enough. I don't know of any deeper yearning than that. But, Christ, today the world tries to make you think you don't have a right to dream such a thing.

Have you ever wondered how good you really are, Toby? Fuck, man, you went to Harvard. You're one of "the best and the brightest." How good are you? Professionally, morally, humanly? Isn't there a clarion call in the natural state of being human that causes us to dream and maybe even to attempt to find out how good we can really be?

At the beginning, I had sent David reassuring responses to his letters because I empathized so with his anxiety. I had spent four years working on my thesis because I was sure it would be published if it was definitive. I wanted to make a big contribution to liberationist politics. I wanted to impress my old professors and classmates with my scholarship. I wanted to establish myself as a professional writer about gay life. Like David (was it because we were both males in our mid-thirties or both Harvard men who felt we had yet to measure up?) I was burning with desire to see just how good I could be.

Partly because I was reluctant to interrupt my professional striving in order to work out problems, my ambitions were producing real strains in my relationship with Rusty. Despite the differences in our ages and experience, there had been a certain equality of contribution and responsibility that gave our relationship balance at the beginning, the stage for that set by the fact that we had both left Harvard without assets. While Rusty started his mineral business, I invested my energies in income-producing teaching and research. But this situation changed when we relocated to California, where Rusty moved into the major leagues of the mineral world while I spent more and more time on my thesis. To support myself I looked for work related to my interests, but that was hard to find. After my research project at San Francisco State fell through, I took a job doing ethnographic research in the

Tenderloin, San Francisco's heavily gay red-light district. This exposed me to gay low life—very soon I began to focus my research on the male prostitutes that made downtown San Francisco their turf—but it paid little and it required me to maintain a residence and spend hours on end in the Tenderloin. The more I invested in my career, the more desperate I became to make my thesis fine, to get it published, to have it pay. If nothing else, I *had* to show Rusty.

I had one contact in the publishing world, an editor at William Morrow whose ex-wife was married to the brother of one of my college roommates. I had gone to see this editor with a first draft of my thesis, and because he'd been friendly and encouraging, I'd written him a year later to report on my progress and to propose some additional books, including *Sons of Harvard.* After replying that all my ideas had potential and that the book about Harvard sounded especially promising, he passed my letter on to a literary agent, who called and said he thought my work timely and was especially interested in the Harvard book, which might make a good movie. One of the first people I told about this was David Fredrick.

934 Carleton Street
Berkeley, CA 94710
August 3, 1978

Dear David,

Are you still dreaming? I am. And I've just had a big dream confirmed in reality: I've found an agent eager to sell my manuscript on the politics of homosexuality and to hustle me advances for new books. The new book that excites him most is the one I've been thinking about almost from the time you wrote. Well, at least from the time that Ben Miller, Ken Ryan, and other gay classmates began to drop in and become friends. It's a book on the class of 1967—maybe I'll call it just that, *The Class of 1967*— but by that I mean us *special* members of the class of '67.

What I envision is a series of interviews with the gay guys who got in touch with me after seeing my statement in the class report. I'll have them talk not only about what they've *really* been doing since Harvard, but also about what they were *really* doing back then. People could use their real names or pseudonyms. I'd guess that six of those who have made contact so far would be willing to participate, and I'm thinking of writing a letter to everyone in the class to see if I can enlist six more. The book could have an extraordinary impact—on gay people, on Harvard, perhaps even on society.

Now the question is: Will you be in it? It would be a way for us to become flesh-and-blood people to one another after a year of being just correspondents. It would be a way for you to make your contribution to the class report. It would be a way for you to start yourself on the road to print. It would bring you together with the rest of our exclusive class of '67 club, because we'll all have to get together for publishing parties, news releases, film script consultations . . . no, wait, let's not blow this thing out of proportion. All I really want to do is to ask you if you'll help me with a project that I'd enjoy doing and that I think could have significant consequences.

So, David, if this doesn't add to the whirlpool that is your life at this point, I don't know what will. You said you were yearning to break out of old molds. You wrote in your last letter that you were working to develop a personal slant in your writing. Good old earnest David. Want to talk on tape? (Remember, all those old profs will be reading this;)

Yours a little bit crazier,

Toby

David's reply came a few days later.

East Lansing, Michigan

August 8, 1978

Dear Toby,

Quite frankly, I think your idea is fraught with difficulties, but terrific. I'd love to be in your book. My life is so fucked up now, why not fuck it up a little more? Maybe I'll use a pseudonym like David Fredrick. If I ever publish a book, that's probably the name I'll use. My own name reminds me of my life as a bureaucrat. Which, as far as the State of Michigan is concerned, is over. I could no more go back to that job than I could become a concert pianist or an opera singer. (I had thought about going back to try to change the system through subversion, but bureaucrats react fiercely and defensively to changing commas on a form. But I'm still thinking about trying to get "women's jobs" paid the same as "men's jobs" if they rank equally on my classification system.)

Let me list some of the difficulties I see with your idea. You may have already thought of some of them.

1. I would imagine that most of us are egotists. I certainly am. So there is a danger of some or all of us pontificating in magnificent clichés. Hell, we'd want to sound at least as brilliant as Bertrand Russell, if not Socrates. You would have to design your questions to bring out the human side. I suspect most of us have one.

2. It's important to maintain "the best and the brightest" myth and the Harvard mystique without making it obnoxious. There's a subtle balance. People want to believe that Harvard is surrounded by a golden aura, and yet it is very easy for them to hate Harvard. Some people do so automatically. Again I think the human aspect of our characters must come through. Maybe, to bring out the human side, you ought to sleep with everybody and then tape the conversation afterwards. (I meant that as a joke, Toby. Come back from your fantasies, I have a few more things to say.)

3. I think it's important to put being gay in its proper perspective. Being gay is important to me, but so is a good meal. I am not a career homosexual; it's merely one fascinating aspect of my character.

4. I don't care much for the title. *The Class of 1967* sounds like a TV show. It displays a lack of originality that just won't do if you're trying to maintain the mystique of Harvard. I, of course, will suggest other possibilities which you'll probably hate with equal passion:

> *From Crimson to Lavender:*
> *Fair Harvard, Thy Sons: '67*
>
> *Out from Cambridge:*
> *Twelve from '67*
>
> *Veritas: Wistful and Gay*

Hate 'em, don't you? Well, maybe one of the people you interview will make some succinct, pithy remark that will simply leap out at you and say: "Hi, I'm your title."

Those, at any rate, are my suggestions; you can ponder or ignore them as you wish.

Meanwhile, I am neurotically involved with killing the Senator all over again. The Senator is my murder victim. Leonard is now in Japan and won't be back until October. So until then I have this little fantasy that I'm doing okay rewriting my detective novel.

So, I want to encourage you. If there's anything I can do to help, just let me know. One of these days I'm going to have to figure out how I'm going to make a living. But right now I don't want to think about it. My therapist wanted me to think about that, so I fired him. The last thing I need right now is some well-meaning therapist who thinks a person ought to work for a living.

David

I was high at having gotten a contract to have both my thesis and *Sons of Harvard* published when I actually met David for the first time. This was in the fall of '78, when Rusty and I went to

Detroit for the gem and mineral show, en route to India. The night before we set out for the long drive, just after we'd finished packing boxes of specimens and display apparatus into the truck in which Crystals of India was carried, there was a call from David Fredrick. This was the first time I had heard from him on the telephone, and when I asked what had prompted him to call, he said simply that he had had a premonition that he should get in touch with me. I laughed and told him that he could see me in person if Lansing was anywhere near Detroit.

By driving and sleeping in shifts, Rusty and I made it to Detroit in three days, leaving Berkeley on Sunday morning and arriving at the Holiday Inn that was show headquarters late on Tuesday night. At eight the next morning there was a call. It was David, saying, "I forgot to ask which Holiday Inn you were staying at, but I knew I'd find you. This is the first one I tried." I invited him to drive down from Lansing that afternoon.

When he appeared at the door, he looked not like the wild-eyed author I was expecting but like a bureaucrat. His skin was pallid. His face was strapped in glasses with chrome-plated frames and lenses tinted gray. He wore a loose-fitting black leather car coat, held his lean body tense, and clutched a lighted cigarette. I gave him my biggest smile as I eased him into the room. "Did you have any trouble finding us?" He hadn't. "Was it a hard drive?" It wasn't. He found himself an ashtray. He said he'd enjoy some bourbon, Wild Turkey if we had any, "that's what my detective drinks."

Before anything else he wanted to tell me about his book. Dively, his gay detective, is hired by the Michigan State Police to investigate the murder of a prominent state senator, whose wife hates homosexuals and loves Anita Bryant. The murder is solved with the help of an astrologer. David's friend Leonard liked the book but found the writing strident. If I wanted to read it, there was a copy in the car. I said that I did, and then David seemed to relax.

Book business finished, he began to talk about his past. He had been born and raised in Grand Rapids. His mother, a lifelong Republican, hated FDR and the Kennedys and had threatened to disown her sons if they ever became Democrats. Harvard was the "den of iniquity" that Roosevelt and the Kennedys had attended, and David had been permitted to enroll only because he was awarded a sizable scholarship.

He had seen the word *homosexuality* for the first time as a high-school senior, during the trip he had made to Cambridge to check Harvard out. Feeling a little lost and out of place on the bleak spring afternoon of his arrival, he had happened into Cahaly's, a little grocery store on Mt. Auburn Street, and picked up a magazine that said something about the gay world on its cover.

It had an article about homosexuality in it, and the article said that homosexuals could tell each other by looking one another in the eye. I said, "I wonder?" And it hit me all at once that that was why I'd felt so out of sync. There'd been absolutely no information whatsoever, not even about heterosexuality, back in Grand Rapids.

David spent most of his first year at Harvard trying to figure out where he was: "I was a hayseed; I didn't know the difference between James Joyce and Joyce Kilmer." The big discovery of his sophomore year was Radcliffe.

By that time I had read F. Scott Fitzgerald. I thought of myself as another midwesterner who had gone east and picked up certain social skills. I had learned how to bullshit. I had learned how to translate my midwestern charm into a kind of eastern sophistication. All the girls I was attracted to turned out to have fathers who were ambassadors.

Senior year David and his roommates moved to an apartment off campus "to lose their virginity." David lost his with a Simmons student from Grand Rapids. For weeks afterward he was terrified she would get pregnant. And later that year, when he visited his roommate's country house in New Hampshire and was asked to share the guest room with a Yalie, he had sex for the first time with a male.

He asked me if I had ever had sex with a man. I said no, but I remembered that article. I went over and got into his bed and started shaking. Finally I calmed down and stopped shaking, but I couldn't get an erection. So we got into our beds and masturbated.

When I got back to Cambridge, I went to the Health Center and saw a psychiatrist. She said, "Well, if you've waited till you're twenty-one to do this, it will probably go away."

The only other person David told about his homosexual experience was Sean McBride, whom he had met in the Lyman Reform School tutoring program run by Harvard's Phillips Brooks House. Sean had said, "God, another friend of mine just had the same kind of experience." Now David realized he'd hoped Sean would say, "Well, am I next?"

We were having a great laugh about this when Rusty came into the room with one of his collector-customers, a strong and enchanting woman to whom I introduced David as one of the gay classmates I was going to write a book about. She was intrigued. David was charming. I was impressed.

And I liked David. As in his letters, he was curious combinations—vulnerable and aggressive, humble and ambitious, practical and otherworldly. I loved his intensity. I was tickled that he fancied himself Rasputin but looked like Clark Kent. So I promised to read his detective story and asked him if he'd like to come down again to see the mineral show, which was scheduled to run through Sunday. He came on Sunday.

When I had finished the first draft of my murder mystery, I didn't know what to do with myself. I was going through some very major changes in my life. I didn't know if I wanted to be, or could be, a writer, if I ought to go back to the government job, or what. You'd written me about your idea for this book of interviews with the Harvard fairies. I had responded positively and then didn't hear anything from you. It got to be a very big issue for me whether I should, or could, call you. I was afraid that if you became a real person, even if only a voice, I'd be terribly disappointed.

But I did call, and on the telephone you said that you were coming to Detroit in a couple of days and that you were staying at a Holiday Inn. I didn't know which Holiday Inn, but my intuition told me that it was the one near the Armory. As it turned out, I tracked you down and got through to you about six hours after you arrived. I thought that was a pretty good trick.

I was utterly fascinated. I had to know what you looked like, what you were as a person rather than as this fantasy that answered my letters. I had no idea what you meant to me or would mean to me. You were just someone I had picked out of a catalogue and whom I was finally going to meet. Then you opened the door, and you had those brown glasses on and a look like you have on your face now, that big smile. I'd been feeling extraordinarily self-conscious. I'd thought to myself, "Oh, my God, I'm going to wilt." Then we sat down, had a drink, started talking. You kept talking about gay politics and I kept asking, "What do you mean?"

What I really wanted to know was what you thought of my book. I wanted to be able to talk with someone who could at least give me a decent opinion, someone who was some kind of equal. I thought you were very intelligent. I knew you were interested in writing. I knew that you were not writing anything like I was writing and that there was no need for any competition.

And then you were . . . how can I say it? . . . you were somebody from that goddamn experience at Harvard. Harvard matters to me, but I can't tell you how except to say that it is a standard that I've always had to measure myself against to understand what I've accomplished. I mean in intelligence and style. I've always believed that one could do practically anything at Harvard and get away with it as long as one did it with style. At that point, your opinion of my book was more important than anyone else's. You could tell me if it had the Harvard style.

But for me to show a virtual stranger something I had written was terrifying. I was afraid of appearing foolish, of flunking out of the class of '67 after all these years. I was afraid I'd lost the old intelligence and style.

You called me the next night, the night you started reading it, and said you really liked it. I could hardly believe it. It was very important to me because I had no idea if I could pull the thing off. I didn't even know for sure what I was trying to pull off.

By the time I got to the mineral show, I had decided that there was one thing I wanted to do very much. That was somehow to get into bed with you—just for the experience, just to see what the hell it would be like. Would I be totally overwhelmed and terrified? I was trying to make you a real person after you'd been a fantasy for so long. And, after all, you did call me that one night when you didn't have to.

And then when I went in, I was surrounded by all those rocks. I used to collect rocks when I was a kid. I felt very comfortable around Rusty. First of all, he was an Indian, and I knew a little bit about that. And he had gotten a Ph.D. in geology and then taught the "rocks-for-jocks" course, and I knew a little bit about that. And he had been senior tutor at Lowell House, where I had spent time with Sean McBride, and I knew a little bit about that. And then somehow he had thrown over all that to become a merchant in gems and minerals from India. You had written me all these things, but I couldn't really put them together until I saw him. He invited me to come into your booth, and he told me about the different rocks. I met your friends from the museum. I got to sell some things to customers.

Still, I was waiting around for you, waiting to get my hands on your body, while this very nice Indian gentleman, who was your lover according to the description in the Harvard book, was telling me about the mineral show. And you were definitely flirting with me. It was pretty obvious that that's what you were doing. And I had gotten some psychic information—things like "Don't worry, David, you'll be satisfied."

But I didn't know if anything was really going to happen until we started talking about going out after dinner and Rusty said he didn't want to go. You said you wanted to tell me about the other gay guys in the class and to talk about gay politics. Rusty made it clear that he didn't want to hear anything more about gay politics. He went back to the Holiday Inn alone.

Then the question for us was where to go and what to do late on a rainy Sunday night in Detroit. I had the strange feeling that you wanted to go back to the motel room and have sex right there in front of Rusty, but I didn't want that. I would have been incredibly self-conscious and freaked out.

I don't remember whose idea the motel was, but I remember shaking as I went up to that glass booth and explained that only one of us was going to spend the night. You had told me that you had to get back before midnight because you were leaving for Cambridge early the next morning. I said we were going to discuss business. The guy in the glass booth didn't care. But I *am* from Grand Rapids. I felt I had to say something.

I knew we were going to go to bed. My psychic counselors told me that. But suddenly I realized that I was going to have to deal with the reality of the situation.

Once we were in the motel room you lay down on the bed and I got a fairly strong sense that you didn't really want to talk about gay politics. So I lay down on the bed beside you and unbuttoned your shirt.

I am fascinated by the physical form of men. I have often had the feeling the first time I'm with somebody that I'm unclothing the Michelangelo by David, or rather, the David by Michelangelo—notice I switched that. I could tell from hugging you earlier that you were in fairly good shape. I was fascinated by that, and terrified somehow. I was feeling very inadequate and not particularly desirable. I don't think of myself as desirable especially. I feel that people find me cadaverous and unattractive. I was flattered that you found me desirable.

You had moved all the way from being just a letter to being a person to being a warm physical body I was lusting after sexually. I was utterly fascinated by you.

Afterwards, I was exhausted. I was relieved. I felt it had been a magical experience. I had managed to get through it. I knew that I was going to fall in love with you. That was going to be the price I paid for spending a few hours with you in that sleazy motel room on a rainy night in Detroit. We were like characters in a Ross MacDonald murder mystery.

I had enjoyed David's detective story so much that I called him from Cambridge to tell him I would be happy to pass it on to my agent. He was delighted about that, exuberant about the time we had spent together, and eager to know when I was going to return from India. I didn't know. I was going to India to help Rusty, and we were planning to venture deep into the heart of the Indian subcontinent in search of new mineral localities. I told him I'd call as soon as I got back to the States, probably right after the first of the year.

About a month and a half later, when Rusty and I were deep in the Indian jungle, I sat down to write David a letter. As I was describing how the moon over an abandoned Hindu temple nearby conjured up visions of past civilizations, I realized that I was once again talking not only to David Fredrick but to that other David in our Harvard class—the one with whom I'd had a brief but intense affair the very summer Rusty and I had abandoned sexual monogamy. This David was a preppy on his way into the heart of the Establishment. He had never told anyone about his homosexual feelings. He had been introduced to me by the sister of one of our classmates, but had never been other than formal or said anything about my being gay until one time, when we found ourselves alone, he confided that he was in love with our mutual friend but wanted to make love to me. Like David Fredrick (was this the similarity that fused them in my mind?) he was complicated, theatrical, ambitious, unsettled, and otherworldly.

I didn't put all this in my aerogramme. I just mentioned in conclusion that writing him had once again made me think of another David and signed off, "I must tell you about him. When we meet."

Early in January of 1979, when Rusty and I returned to California, there were two letters from Lansing awaiting me, one with the message "please read the other letter first" scrawled on the back of the envelope. The first letter read:

East Lansing, Michigan
November 17, 1978

Dear Toby,

I want to thank you for a dream.

Your literary agent rejected my book today, and that struck me just as a lot of other things were going wrong. Including the fact that I don't have as much money as I thought I did.

I still don't have any real idea what I'm going to do. Winter is coming on, and I have to get the hell out of here before it strikes with fury. I was thinking today about going to Australia. I've always wondered what things were like down there. Two guys from New South Wales came through Michigan and were quite impressed with what I was doing with the personnel system.

Maybe I can find a place in the bureaucracy there. There's something in me that's telling me to get as far away from here as possible. Things are coming apart too fast, and I don't want to crack up in a cold climate.

I had wanted to see you again. Everything looked so good, so possible there for a while. I loved dreaming about what you and I could do, what all of us could do. It seemed like a veritable gold mine, all that talent there together. I had all kinds of schemes going on in my head, even one for rewriting the United States Constitution on a human rights basis. I had great plans for you, Toby, and for your four degrees from Harvard. It was fun thinking about it.

I went to Grand Rapids, talked with my mother, and told her I was gay. The old woman handled it very well. She was very rational and understanding. She even liked my book, and she's read all kinds of murder mysteries.

Look, I don't know what to say to you. I fell in love with you until you faded. Even back when I was in Cambridge, I knew there was something unreal about Harvard. It's an old phantom that shows up every now and then. Maybe it's all pizzazz and no substance. I swore I would never again be taken in by the Harvard mystique.

There comes a point when the Grand Rapids in my head clicks on and says it's time to get on with life and give up all that foolishness. I've got to find some work somewhere. I truly am fascinated with the idea of going down under. Maybe then my ideas would come out right side up.

I want to say good-bye, and thank you. It's been good knowing you.

That sounded almost suicidal, and I was feeling unfairly manipulated as I turned to the second letter. This one assured me that David was still around.

> East Lansing
> *Thanksgiving, 1978*

Dear Toby,

The oddest things make me happy. I got your letter yesterday. I don't understand what you're trying to say. But I was happy you remembered my name, more or less.

After I wrote you I realized that I was thoroughly pissed off at your agent. So I wrote him an angry letter. I figured he must be either chicken-shit or stupid.

Look, Toby, I want you to understand a few things. I told you in Detroit that I was all set to enter Nirvana but I had to find out about two things: you and my book. As of last Friday I had not heard from you, and your agent rejected my book.

This put me in a certain state of mind, not a happy one. I decided that I had had enough, that none of this was real, and that I could probably now enter Nirvana. That's when I wrote you.

So Saturday I realized that nothing mattered, except that I had awakened. I was in hopes that I wouldn't. So I had a whole day's time to fill up, and I thought I'd take a look to see if there was anything that mattered. I couldn't find a thing.

On Sunday I realized there was one thing I wanted to do. I wanted to let your agent know what I thought of him. The first letter I wrote started out: "Dear John. There are some men who have enough intelligence to stand in awe of a worm. I don't think you have that much." Well, it went on like that. I was hurt and angry. The letter I actually sent him was slightly milder.

After I wrote that letter, I figured I could enter Nirvana. Except that I had begun rewriting an old book. *Three Sons* is *my* book. It's the one I've loved and hated the most. I realized that once I'd told my mother I was gay, I could tell anyone. So I rewrote the book very autobiographically.

Then I got your aerogramme. It was terrific. It fit in so well with everything else that was going on. You've always gotten me confused with other Davids and now you're confusing me with myself. I tried to tell you that I'm not anybody. I'm not real; I'm a chameleon. But you insist on pondering two Davids, and I have no idea who either one of them is.

Which Toby are you? There was one of you I met in Detroit. You were different from your letters. I felt you could understand, if not me, at least some of my dreams. I also wanted to believe that, as a person, I mattered to you. I kept wondering when you'd say, "No, David, you don't really matter." But you never said that.

But there's another Toby who clicks on in my head, usually late at night. He stands in front of me and mocks me and laughs at my foolishness. Then I hear little voices saying, "David, you've been taken in by Harvard again. We've done okay without using it, except as something nice on a résumé or in an application."

Lately, I don't know which one of those Tobys you are. If you hadn't written me that goddamn aerogramme, I could have reduced you to that phantasm in the night. Now I don't know again. *You* might still matter.

Goddamn, you piss me off, Toby. What the hell is this shit? "I must tell you about him. When we meet." Well, piss on you.

Be thankful that you've only got two Davids to cope with. I was fractured when I met you, and you've hastened the process. There's one of me that would sincerely like to hold you all night long. There's another of me that would like to fuck you passionately, as if you were some stranger in a blind alley. There's still another of me that would like to play with the world with you.

And there's something about you that terrifies one or two of me. They're the ones that hear you laughing at me.

There's another one who's terrified because he knows that if we fall in love with you, we will fall in love very deeply. And he knows that that may cause more pain than we can bear in our life.

So if you would simply send me a postcard, I could let go of you. Just say good-bye.

I'd planned the Second American Revolution. You and I and the rest of the Harvard crowd were going to start it. Can you imagine the ways those guys could find to explain how human rights and ecology are incompatible with our present system? I wanted to use the Harvard connection to do some good, to change things instead of just perpetuating the same old shit. But to do that I needed money. With my book on the Best Sellers List I could finance the revolution. But it all depended on the book. And your agent "wasn't interested"—wasn't even able to figure out what that Harvard connection meant.

It was a nice idea. I can't do it by myself. In all honesty, I can't do it without you. It's too outrageous for most people. But what can I say? My gift offering to the Revolution was rejected. And I honestly don't know what you're trying to say to me. Look, just send me a postcard.

I want you to know that Revolution is a full-time job. And that my feelings have gone so far that if I can't love you and reflect love in you, I can't stand being around you.

Toby, a postcard would do . . .

David

P.S.   I'm going to pay the rent for December. So I can be reached here. There are some other people I want to go talk with. Who knows, maybe I can get the Revolution going without Harvard.

I sent David a postcard saying "Revolution *is* a full-time job." I hoped he would see that no one accomplished anything by wallowing in self-pity. I wasn't sure what he wanted from me. I didn't know how I was going to reconcile my belief in the importance of being honest with others with my professional ambitions —with my desire to keep David a character in my book.

A week later I called and said I thought he'd reacted immaturely to my agent's lack of interest in his manuscript. I told him that getting published was a matter of finding the right person for a book and that I had gotten to know an editor in California who might be interested in his.

On the phone and then in his next letter David was apologetic. But when three months passed without a word from me or my editor friend (I was totally absorbed in revising my thesis for publication), there came another unnerving letter. It began:

Not only is Neptune by transit squaring my Mercury, but Saturn by transit is squaring both my moon and ruling planet, Uranus. All of it together is like having a dream in which you know the Titanic is going to sink, and you know you're on it, and you're trying to find your glasses so you can read the directions to safety.

Without helping me understand the astrological allusions, David went on, among other things saying that he'd been offered a job reclassifying city employees in Morgantown, West Virginia, and that he had to decide whether to take the job before the week was out.

I wrote back that I'd just delivered his manuscript to my editor friend and that I'd bring my friend's assessment when I showed up to interview him—in Lansing or Morgantown—at the beginning of June. David's response was a postcard saying he'd decided not to take the job in Morgantown and so I should come to Michigan. I was relieved he was willing to have me visit. Yet even as I traveled to Lansing, I didn't know whether he was actually going to let me tape him.

As far as I was concerned, the only safe script left between us was your book. That was the plot line we'd agreed to play. I saw that as the safest possible way for us to relate. I had no idea what it was you really felt about me, especially after I'd sent you all those strange letters.

But you had to come here. That was the only way I'd play it. I deserved the same treatment you were giving the other members of the class you were interviewing. Even though I wanted very much to see you, it had to be done the way you did it with everybody else. You went to them. You had to come to me. That was the only way I could protect myself from whatever was going to happen.

But I was going to be in the book because I had told you that I would be in the book. Us midwesterners have an old-fashioned sense of morality when it comes to keeping agreements. I was always clear that I would keep my word.

Every time I thought I had him figured out, David would confound me. After meeting him for the first time in Detroit, I had been quite convinced that he didn't know or care anything about gay politics; when I returned from India, I found his letters full of talk about "the Revolution." Arriving in Lansing to interview him, I carried the news that my editor friend hadn't thought his book very professional. David had seemed extremely fragile in his letters, and I was fully prepared for my news to precipitate a collapse. Instead, during the first few hours we were together, he accepted my news gracefully, said he still didn't know what to do with his book, and explained exactly how he'd felt about me from the time he responded to my "advertisement" in the class report to the moment I'd asked him if I could turn on my machine and record his perspective on all that had happened.

The trust that David demonstrated in agreeing to let me write candidly about our relationship endeared him to me all over again, and after dinner, as we walked into the living room to tape some more, I put my arm around his shoulder and drew him close. He blushed, took off his glasses, nuzzled his head against my neck. Then I broke away to put a new cassette in the recorder, and he settled himself down on one side of the couch. When I plunked myself down on the other side, he stretched out, nestled his head in my lap, and said he was ready to go back to work.

It was then that I asked him each of the questions I was asking all the others: how he had learned he was homosexual (that article in the magazine at Cahaly's); when he had had his first homosexual experience (the Yalie in New Hampshire); whether he had talked about his homosexuality with anyone in college (Sean McBride). For the record, David repeated many of the stories he'd told me in Detroit. His responses to my questions were beautiful little anecdotes, but nothing in honesty and intensity next to his letters.

Then I asked David about his life after graduation: the year of grad school in San Diego, missionary life in Japan as a conscientious objector, his return to Grand Rapids and his stint as a teacher at a local high school, his move to Lansing and his job in the Civil Service Commission. I was especially curious about how he met gay men in small-town Michigan (he'd go to the bars—Grand Rapids and Lansing each had a pair—and offer to do the horoscopes of men he was interested in); how he felt about sexual promiscuity ("I'm not a sexual mechanic but I enjoy one-night stands"); and why his relationship with Tom had become attenuated ("He began to feel that I was more involved with the characters in my detective story").

Inevitably our conversation moved from how isolated from one another we had all been back in college to how afraid most people were of making themselves vulnerable by talking about their feelings honestly. As I had found with Sandy, verbal intimacy led slowly but surely to physical intimacy. We pulled each other's clothes off, made love with the familiarity of old school chums, and then drifted off to sleep.

Earlier that evening David had asked me if I wanted to go on a picnic with some of his astrologer friends in the morning. Most of these were associates of The Aquarian Arc, a metaphysical bookstore located near his apartment complex. When I awoke the next morning, the roar of the wind and the pelt of the rain told me that there wasn't going to be a picnic.

In retrospect, I wonder if I would have left with a different impression of David if the sun had been shining. I had already gotten most of the information I needed to write about him, and I'd been looking forward to seeing what people involved in astrology were really like. Before I had seen how intelligent David was, I had assumed they were all kooks. Now I was curious.

I lay awake for a while listening to the rain. When David stirred, I rubbed his shoulder and whispered, "No picnic." He groaned, then reached over and rubbed the top of my thigh. We dozed.

When I next came to, it seemed even darker and stormier than before. David had gotten up, and there were sounds coming from the kitchen. I was just about to pull myself out of bed when he appeared in the doorway, naked, holding a cup and saucer. Placing them carefully on the bedside table, he stretched out on the covers and asked if I wanted to talk about astrology over morning coffee. I nodded enthusiastically, said I wanted to record everything, and bounded out to the living room to get my tape recorder.

Once I too was settled back on top of the covers, David recalled how skeptical he had been when one of the students in a world religions class he taught suggested they investigate astrology. I registered my own skepticism by smirking. He responded sharply, "I know you find this all very hard to believe. I dismissed it too until I began to do horoscopes for fun and people marveled at how accurate they were."

Partly to goad him on, I replied, "You wrote me that you had looked up my stars. What does that mean? Can you tell what's going to happen to me?"

David looked annoyed. "No, no. This isn't crystal ball stuff. That's not what astrology's about."

"Come on," I insisted. "No one's ever done my horoscope before. If I tell you when I was born, can you tell me something about myself?"

David looked even more annoyed. "I already know when you were born. I got your birth date from our yearbook. I told you. I've looked up your stars. I've already done your chart."

"Well, tell me about myself. I'd really like to know what you found out."

"I bet."

"I would, David. Even if I do tend to be very skeptical about things that don't have some rational explanation . . ."

"Typically Aquarian," he said. "You see, you're a typical Aquarian. Very rational."

"What does being rational have to do with being Aquarian?" I sensed I was drawing David into this conversation in spite of himself.

"Well, Aquarius is fixed air. Air is the wind. Fixed means . . . well, fixed. Aquarians tend to have very set systems. They are the next-to-the-last sign in the zodiac, so they tend to be very broad and progressive in their thinking. But their thinking is set. They don't change their minds very quickly. They will, but only through a rational process. Anybody who tries to live this way just has to be kinky."

"Kinky. Why do you say that?"

"Nobody can really live rationally at this time in history. The world just doesn't work that way. Still, Aquarians keep applying their progressive ideas, trying to go forward. . . ."

"In the face of impossibility?"

"They go against pretty big odds. It takes a lot of self-confidence to base everything on reason, which is, I suppose, like basing everything on morality. There's only one sign in the zodiac after Aquarius, which is my sign, Pisces. That's mutable water."

"What does it mean to be a Pisces?"

"No, no," he said. "I can't do that. It just wouldn't sound real."

But now I was intrigued. "Just for fun. How about if I give you some birth dates and you tell me what the people are like. Our gay classmates. I'll go through the yearbook and give you their birth dates. You tell me what you can about them on the basis of their signs. Come on. Just for fun."

David weighed me quietly, looked away, looked back, shook his head. "Typically Aquarian," he muttered. "Always some reasonable test."

Not to be derailed (typically Aquarian?), I proceeded to give him the birth dates of each of the gay classmates I had already gotten some sense of. With each one, though he had no idea whose birthday I'd given, he described basic traits I'd come to see in those people myself. I shook my head in disbelief.

"There's something to this," he assured me, now recovered from his pique. "Want to stop?"

"No," I said. "There's one more. March 5, 1945."

"That's a day before my birthday—a Pisces. Poor baby. He must be somewhat similar to me, though he may have a different rising sign. I have Aquarius rising. That's probably why I'm attracted to you. I'd have to know what time he was born to say for sure, but at heart he would probably be like me—terribly insecure, but lovable."

"What else?"

"For a Pisces, life is one continuous crucifixion; one keeps hoping for little resurrections. Elizabeth Taylor's that way. Ted Kennedy. Those Pisces have risen to great heights, but they always seem to have to bear up under terrible personal sacrifice."

"Are you like that?"

"Oh, sure. Wait till you read the book I wrote before my murder mystery. It's very autobiographical."

I asked next if all of us in the class of '67 had anything in common astrologically.

"Well, there would be certain similarities. We were all born within a relatively short span of time, so the slow-moving planets would have been in the same signs in our charts—Neptune, Uranus, Pluto. I think that has given us a very strong sense of self-righteousness or something like that—a sense of rightness. Our whole generation uses that word 'right.' We have an odd moral sense. It's not really old-fashioned moral. In the sixties we all got to thinking, 'Hey, somebody's fucking up our world, and we've got to do something about it.' The whole antiwar thing. None of us wanted to have anything to do with what the government was doing in Vietnam. When they kept pushing it at us, we kept saying, 'It ain't right.' "

"Are you trying to tell me that the whole antiwar movement came about because of where the planets were?" My voice was thick with sarcasm. "Don't you think it had anything to do with the international situation—with history?"

"Well, sure. Everything's interconnected. Everything interpenetrates. That's the whole idea. The positions of the planets and the cycles of history are correlated. Astrology is another way of talking about history."

"How so?"

"The history is the history of consciousness." David was beginning to get excited as he talked. "Everything is consciousness. We're just a particular form of it—imitation gods. The earth is also consciousness. It has the consciousness of a planet. And it's changing its consciousness in relation to other planets, which also have planetary consciousness. That means there's a big change coming. And that has also affected our whole generation."

"What's the change?"

"We've grown up right when the Age of Pisces is changing to the Age of Aquarius."

David told me that the constellations of the zodiac moved across the sky behind the sun as the earth revolved around the sun. "Over thousands of years, that changes the angle of the constellations behind us. Two thousand years ago the constellation Pisces moved into the background. Now the constellation Aquarius is arriving at center stage."

"You mean the heavens are moving from your sign to mine?" I thought maybe he was saying something about how each of us would be affected by the changing heavens.

"Well, yes, but a historical level, that's only incidental. The shift in constellations marks a change in the nature of the age. The Age of Pisces, the last two thousand years, was primarily expressed by the building of great institutions. This was symbolized by the arrival of Jesus Christ. The sign Pisces is depicted by fishes. Jesus was symbolized by a fish. Churches were the great institutions of the age. But now human consciousness is changing to a more Aquarian, a more rational perspective on how to live. The sign Aquarius is depicted by a water-bearer pouring water on the ground. The water's supposed to represent knowledge—both spiritual, or intuitive, and rational knowledge.

"We've just come into the Age of Aquarius. Uranus rules Aquarius, so Uranus is doing a lot of ruling. Right now Uranus is going through Scorpio, which is very sexual. When it moved into that sign, three or four years ago, attitudes about sex began to change. By the time it gets through, which will be in three or four years, there will be totally different attitudes toward a lot of things that are in Scorpio—homosexuality, death, the occult. As soon as Uranus moved into Scorpio, Lenny Matlovich and Karen Ann Quinlan became public figures. Matlovich was a soldier who challenged stereotypes about homosexuals. Quinlan's case got people thinking about conventional ideas about dying. Things got brought to light. Attitudes began to change."

I was aghast at hearing David attribute cultural and political trends I had spent so much time researching to the movement of planets. At the same time, I thought it my social scientific duty to find out more about his astrological theories. To get his perspective on the consequences of the attitudinal changes he spoke of, I probed further. "Do you think that America can survive such rapid cultural evolution?"

"I think the future is very exciting, though very frightening, because it's a fantastic opportunity to build. Attitudes and institutions that have been sanctified in people's minds for centuries are going to have to be replaced with more workable ones. Even the very small changes that have already taken place, like changing the Mass from Latin to English, have wiped out a lot of people. Just imagine how people are going to resist the changes that have to come as we go about learning how to live more rationally."

"What to do?" I asked. Then, "What are *you* going to do?"

"The only thing I can say is that in a few years there's going to be one hell of a mess in this country. There are really only two things any individual can do: go down with the ship or help build something new. If there's a chance to be part of something new, I want to get in on the ground floor. That's why I'm so eager to be in your book. It's coming at just the right time. Its significance could be far greater than you've imagined."

I loved David's complexity. He could be totally rational one minute and positively wild-eyed the next. And there's always been something about craziness in a person I've found very erotic. It's almost as if it stirs in me a desire to heal by getting so close and giving such pleasure that the demons are driven away by the sheer intensity of my affection. This was what happened with David.

From where he lay beside me, I pulled him over on top of me and locked him tightly in my arms. For several minutes I clung to him, slowly moving my hands up and down his back. He was completely passive. My mind wandered.

Then suddenly, almost before I realized what was happening, the feel of his body began to change. His muscles tightened. His skin turned clammy. As if powered by some inner sexual desperation, his body began to churn back and forth against my own.

Hoping to calm him, I dropped my hands to his buttocks. He groaned, still writhing, then put his hands on my chest and reared back. His eyes were closed. He was panting heavily.

He tossed his head once, then again, and again, punctuating each of these movements with a loud gasp. Then he drew in, held, and released his breath, collapsing back into my embrace. A final spasm passed through his body, then all was still.

Slowly the softness returned to his flesh. His body became untensioned weight.

But a few minutes later, when he lifted his head again, he was not at all the David I had pulled into my arms just minutes before. His cheeks were now delicately flushed. His eyes seemed wider than before and almost cobalt blue. Moisture bunched his hair into tiny ringlets that cascaded down onto his forehead and framed his entire face in curls. The David I now found in my arms looked like a young Greek god. His gaze was dreamy. He seemed barely aware that I was there.

To bring him back I broke the silence by remarking on how dramatically his look had changed. There was a moment more of silence before he refocused his eyes. I remarked again about how his appearance had changed, and he said that that often happened—that sometimes, when he looked into the mirror, he couldn't even recognize himself. I reached up and touched his now-rosy lips with my index finger. I wanted to reassure him. To reassure myself.

Ignoring my gesture, he rolled over onto his back and gazed up at the ceiling. Then, in a whisper, he said that he was ready to tell me about the "psychic side" of his life. By this, I sensed, he meant something more than the astrological stuff.

When I got back from Japan in 1972 I taught advanced
placement English, World Literature, and World Religions
at a Grand Rapids high school. I walked into the World Religions class the first day and said, "Look, I don't know anything about World Religions, so we're all going to have to
contribute." One guy, for his contribution, went around
Grand Rapids and dug up speakers. There were a couple of
ministers, a yoga teacher, a witch, and an astrologer. The
astrologer talked about classes in astrology and psychic
awareness. Out of curiosity more than anything else—I was
really skeptical about all this back then—I took the astrology
class. For some reason it all came very easily to me. I learned
how to do horoscopes in two weeks. People always responded
as if I had hit the nail right on the head.

Then I took the psychic awareness course. I felt I had
nothing to lose because the instructor said that if they didn't
demonstrate your psychic ability to your own satisfaction,
they'd give you your money back. That sounded like a good
deal. So I took the course, which took forty-eight hours
spread over a week. I was very skeptical all the way through
that too.

At the end of the week they were ready to show me that I
had psychic powers. After being blindfolded, I was given the
name, age, and address of some man who they said had a
physical malady—they had all the information written down
on a card. They told me to try to learn more through the
psychic processes they'd taught. "Is he in a wheelchair?" I
asked. Yes, he was. "There's something about two bones
fused together at the base of his spine?" Yes, there was. "And
there's something wrong with his lungs: One is missing; the
other looks like it's bubbling; there are little energy patterns
shooting all over the place. Maybe it's cancer?" Yes, it was.
Well, I went on and on, each time hitting something that the
instructor had printed on his card. I was astounded.

For the next two years David worked to refine his psychic
powers. After having success after success in fathoming the past,
sensing more than he could see about the present, and foreseeing

the future, he had come to believe in the supernatural. Now he was constantly in contact with "spiritual guides" who told him what was happening and gave him advice. I wasn't sure whether he was describing actual voices or using some kind of metaphor for his intuition.

> What all this stuff has done is to cause me to look at the world in ways I'd have thought simply insane when we were back at Harvard. The whole idea of reincarnation now seems very plausible to me, for example. And when I think about being gay in connection with that, I say, "Well, this is my lifetime to be gay." I've probably had several lifetimes in which I've been gay and others in which I've been straight. The metaphysical perspective was what permitted me to look at being gay in a way that didn't have anything to do with right or wrong; it had to do with what was happening in my current lifetime.

By this time, the rain had begun to pound against the windows. The darkness was eerie. David was now sitting cross-legged next to where I lay.

Once again his visage had changed. His skin had gone from a rich olive to a lifeless yellow-gray. His cheeks seemed gaunt and flecked with liver spots. His hair was matted, his eyes black, his gaze distant, almost disembodied. Slowly, his voice sinking to a guttural chant, his breathing labored, he continued:

> They told me before I met you that I'd like you very much. They described it in more graphic terms than that. They said it was all part of a kind of collateral history that parallels earth reality. It began when we were together in Greece. Someday when I know you better I'll tell you about that.
>
> There's something spooky about some of the information I get from the spiritual guides about what is going to happen in the future. It doesn't seem to match with current events—though I did get something about the Three Mile Island accident. Other psychics get the same kind of information, and that's why I think there's something to it.
>
> Many prophets have talked about a big transformation between now and the end of the century. It's a spiritual transformation, a consciousness transformation, but it may

translate into history as some kind of cataclysm. There are various years suggested: 1984—because of Orwell—'92, '98, '99. But all in the next twenty years.

Poor Southern California. A couple of prophecies say there'll be land disruptions. The shelf that Los Angeles is on could fall into the sea. If there were a nuclear war in the Middle East, for example, it might not involve us directly, but the tremors might reverberate through the earth and knock Los Angeles off the continental shelf. I keep looking at that. It's very serious. Twelve million people live there. Even if it sinks slowly, there'd be a twelve-million-person refugee problem. What would that do to people psychologically? Or to the economic system?

What are we going to do when we run out of gasoline? What kind of decisions are we going to make? What about inflation? Nobody seems to know what's happening. My spiritual guides keep telling me that this is really Armageddon.

David's voice had risen from a hollow whisper to a quaking rant. His whole body was shaking. He looked like a madman.

I was frightened. I didn't know what to make of this. Was David just play-acting and I fantasizing to while away a stormy morning? Was I being manipulated by a classmate who wanted me to portray him as an unusually prescient psychic and astrologer, distinguished from other gay sons of Harvard by the uniqueness of his intelligence and style? Had David turned to metaphysical perspectives to deal with his own neuroses or to find some excuse for his homosexuality? Did he consider astrology another interesting if unsubstantiated perspective on the real world, or did he let it guide his decision-making? Had he turned to the supernatural in a desperate effort to make sense of the mindlessness and tumult he saw in the world around him? And given the state of the real world, did this make him singularly adaptive or certifiably mad? I just didn't know.

Toward the end of David's recitation about Armageddon I had become so uncomfortable that I suggested we go out. David had gotten up, gone into the bathroom, and returned looking like the rumpled bureaucrat who'd met me at the bus station the afternoon before. "What's the matter?" he chuckled. "Did I frighten you?"

After devouring the remains of the previous evening's dinner, we spent the afternoon touring Lansing in the rain. We stopped first at the Aquarian Arc, which was a homey little bookstore, and had coffee with Alba, the pleasant housewife who ran it. She told me that she and David had first met in ancient Rome. Then we stopped in at Lansing's two little gay bars and drove up Michigan Avenue to the lighted state capitol. I told David about my trip to Washington and mentioned that Marty Brenner had gone through a period of being interested in astrology. David said that more and more intelligent people were paying attention to unconventional metaphysical perspectives. ·

Later that night, just before we went to sleep, I said to David, "You know, if I'm going to write honestly about this visit, I'm going to have to say that there were times when I thought you were crazy."

He was silent for a moment and then, with all the boldness and intensity that had drawn me to him from the start, looked right into my eyes and replied, "I know."

7

NICK BOLLMAN

After going so far afield with Sandy and David, arriving in New York City was another homecoming. This was where I had first felt at home being a gay man. It was also where I had resolved to present myself to the world as a gay professional.

Keeping my homosexuality and my politics divorced from my professional life would have been a surer way of pursuing a career. The system rewards competence and expertise, and the conventional wisdom in its academic sector, among others, is that these are minimally related to an individual's personal life and politics. I had begun my research on gay political activity believing this to be true, then changed my mind as it became clear that my admitted homosexuality, my growing identification with liberationist politics, and my open-mindedness about traditional gay life were the things that permitted me access to gay leaders and any degree of honest conversation with them. As I came to believe that my personal explorations of homosexuality and the gay male subculture enhanced my professional work, and that it was important in the light of both liberationist politics and scholarly ethics to acknowledge this, I began to refer to myself not as a social scientist who happened to be gay and was interested in the study of gay life, but as a gay social scientist.

All of this happened during the course of my thesis research in New York City, but I had great doubts that I could make my professors back at Harvard understand it, especially in the state I was in intellectually and personally then. For when I was in the Graduate School of Arts and Sciences, those most responsible for the study of minority groups, social change, and social policy were a group of senior professors who have since achieved fame and notoriety for being intellectual progenitors of neoconservatism—Edward Banfield, James Q. Wilson, Daniel Patrick Moynihan, Nathan Glazer, and Daniel Bell. Then, as now, these "neoconservatives" were known for their skepticism about "alternative lifestyles," "the new morality," and "gay and women's lib."

At the time, I just couldn't conceive of getting through to them. For all that their own ideas and understandings had been shaped by their particular ethnic and working-class backgrounds and middle-class life-styles; for all that their own political and fraternal sharing with like-minded peers had done so much to advance their careers; for all that they themselves loved to debunk the myth of value-free methodology and objective social science; for all that they had made their own marks by skillfully challenging conventional wisdoms of every sort, I was sure that they would be very conventional in their response to my contention that immersion in gay life is, at least for most, a prerequisite for understanding it. Although I remained very much in agreement with my professors about the form good social scientific research should take and standards for assessing it, when it came to the study of phenomena so unexplored, misunderstood, psychologically charged, and socially controversial as homosexuality and gay life, I felt obligated by the academic values we all shared to operate on the basis of my own scholarly judgment. So I viewed my personal explorations of gay life as not only political but professional, and spent most of my time thereafter with other gay people rather than with Harvard colleagues.

It is a truism in gay political circles that coming out is a never-ending process. Both because so many at Harvard were so genteel in their dealings with us, and because Rusty and I had chosen to opt out of that genteel world when we decided to make more of our gayness, coming out professionally was a very big step for me. I didn't take that step rashly.

In my judgment, at least when it comes to revealing one's homosexuality to nongay people, coming-out decisions are made much more rationally than is generally assumed. Yet no matter how carefully one has calculated the costs and benefits and then prepared the way for any particular step, until one is very far down the line, one can't help but have fears that one is doing something that will result in irreversible damage. That's why so many homosexuals remember so many steps of their coming-out process so vividly—the time they first had sex with someone of the same sex; the period in which they first realized they were homosexual; the occasions on which they learned about and met other homosexuals who were truly impressive; the circumstances under which they came out to various friends, family members, and neighbors; the decision to let co-workers know; the resolve to build a career as a gay professional. When you present yourself as a gay in the world as it is today, you do so with the knowledge that there are many people who will never think of you in any but those terms. When you proclaim yourself a gay professional, however strongly you maintain that the experience and exposure you gain by virtue of participating in gay life significantly enhances your expertise, you know that there will be many who will never believe you competent. Very few people, particularly men, are able and willing so to risk and to sacrifice the professional dimensions of their self-actualization. Very few can bear the cost to ego and livelihood involved in being thought deficient as workers, earners, and providers. That is why there are a lot of professionals who are secretly homosexual and a lot who happen to be gay, but relatively few gay professionals.

The occasion I chose to symbolize my coming out as a gay professional was the gay pride march in New York City, held on the very day I completed my field research in June of 1975. Though I had gone a long way toward declaring myself gay professionally before that, taking the first step two years earlier when I had proposed to do my thesis on gay politics (fully aware that this would lead most of my colleagues to suspect I was homosexual), I viewed my participation in that march as a final staking-out of the turf on which I hoped to make it. By "making it," I meant succeeding not only as a gay man and as a politically enlightened and moral person, but as an authority on gay life and a cultural philosopher who would be listened to by the Establishment. However unconventional my ideas about professionalism, my commitment to being a competent professional remained as strong as my loyalty to the University, country, and system that so enshrined expertise.

So I had very mixed feelings as I marched. On the one hand, as never before, I felt that I was with "my people." I saw myself as a new recruit to liberationist politics. I felt as if I had finally joined the noble line of gay political leaders I had interviewed. I believed I was walking with people who would one day be regarded as moral and political pioneers.

Before I'd come to New York City, I'd known but a handful of homosexuals. It was true that I'd been friendly with the playground instructor who "liked little boys" back in Medford and intimate with many of the kids I'd had sex with. But until I got to Harvard, I hadn't known anyone with the self-awareness and intelligence to understand what it meant to be homosexual, with the sophistication to enjoy his homosexual side without letting that compromise or interfere with his personal and professional responsibilities. These were the types of homosexuals I met at Harvard, few in number but very significant in helping me accept my homosexuality.

But by countercultural and liberationist standards, these Harvard homosexuals were "closeted." For them, homosexual behavior and gay life were a periodic, pleasant diversion, an additional dimension of experience and existence but not something that should be central to one's personal, social, political, and professional identities. Like most with conventional cultural and political perspectives, the homosexuals I knew at Harvard had a hard time understanding why so many homosexuals of my generation made so much of their homosexuality—why we were so bent on "flaunting" our gayness. They seemed neither to understand nor to appreciate liberationist politics.

But if I felt for the first time as I marched that I was with other gay people, I also felt very alone. Oh, for a while I walked with new friends I had made through the Gay Academic Union. Jonathan Katz and John D'Emilio are the ones I remember most vividly. They were the first other people doing research on gay life and gay politics I had met, and I considered them colleagues in the sense that they too had opted for liberated life-styles and liberationist politics in the face of likely professional hardship, uncertain security, and only an outside chance of making it in the system. Yet, because they and so many of the other gay academics

I met were anarchist and socialist in their perspectives, I felt that few of them were heading in the direction I thought we needed to go (toward a more humane, democratic capitalism) in the ways I thought most effective, in the media age, to get us there (through liberationist politics). That is why running into Nick Bollman right after the march had such impact. It was as if I no sooner gave up Harvard people for gay people when Nick appeared to show me I could have both.

We met by accident when the apartment selected by my last interview subject as a postmarch meeting place turned out to be Nick's. I hadn't known Nick very well in college, but I instantly recognized him when he walked into the apartment, and he recognized me. I conducted an abbreviated interview and then stayed on to visit. I just had to find out how Nick and I had ended up marching in the same direction.

Though we spent only a few hours together, our meeting was extraordinarily affirming. Nick was a golden boy. He was making it professionally in the social service agency network, which—like every human social and organizational collectivity I've investigated, including the most radical lesbian feminist ones—had its own leaders and followers. He was socially conscious, active in "new politics," and excited about getting involved in gay politics. And his personal life was as rich and full as his professional life. Nick was handsome, well-built, and sexy. He was living with a hot lover in a nice apartment on the Upper West Side, having lots of recreational sex, and continuing to see his ex-wife and stepdaughter. Nick made me feel proud to call myself, as he did, a gay man. It reassured me to find that we thought very much alike when it came to gay men, gay politics, and sexism.

Where our thinking differed, to the extent that we explored it, was in the realm of social policy. Though we both thought of ourselves, when it came to conventional political labels, as liberals, my ideas were more neoconservative than his.

For I had been influenced enormously by my professors at Harvard. Ed Banfield had convinced me that we know so little about social reality that the best way to advance knowledge is to stir up debate and to stimulate relevant research by making good arguments. (The arguments he made were provocative enough to engender the undying wrath of revolutionaries, radicals, and liberals unaware of, or unable to stomach, his intellectual approach.) James Q. Wilson, Banfield's student, was logic personified, one of the most facile arguers I had ever encountered, and one who made me want to argue back. Nathan Glazer was a student of American society generally, and his forte was extending the ideas of others in original and practical ways. He had helped David Riesman write *The Lonely Crowd,* a pioneering study of American character and culture in the decades before I began to look at it, and he was best known for *Beyond the Melting Pot,* the study of ethnic groups in New York City he had written with Daniel Patrick Moynihan. Though I had served as a teaching assistant in Moynihan's course on social science and social policy, I knew him less well than the others, yet his whole career seemed to illustrate the liberationist view that taking controversial positions was public service of political consequence.

I had always liked Glazer the most, and not just because my intellectual style was most like his and because he had whatever it took to work collaboratively with strong men. Glazer was the nice guy in the group. He was much more sensitive when dealing with idealistic students than the others, much more paternal in his put-downs of the overzealous, uninformed, and slow to catch on. The day James Q. Wilson, who was originally my thesis adviser, passed me in orals on the condition that I drop my research on school desegregation and get into something new, Glazer, who was also one of my examiners, walked back to Gutman Library with me and said he'd be my thesis adviser if I wanted to start afresh.

That appealed to me because I liked his work. His intellectual claim to fame was that he had dumped the melting pot. *Beyond the Melting Pot* revealed that for all the popular talk about homogenization, and despite conventional belief in its desirability, American society was actually composed of innumerable ethnic subcultures characterized not only by their fealty to the nation and their adherence to most traditional values, but by special customs, distinctive ways of thinking and acting, and unusual traditions and institutions. These didn't necessarily make minority group members more violent, antisocial, wayward, or incompetent than others, Glazer illustrated. Just different. Indeed, enriching to society precisely because they were different.

I had seen enough of life in ethnic Boston to think Glazer's argument very realistic. And I thought I had hope of gaining his attention when I began my research on gay politics, because I believed I could show him that gays in New York City were

becoming a lamb chop in the urban ethnic stew he had assayed at
such length in his major work. Indeed, I believed I could convince him that the emergence of gays as an important minority
group reflected political, cultural, and social trends that were as
significant to America in the sixties and seventies as the trends
he and Riesman wrote about had been to America in the forties
and fifties. (After reading *The Cultural Contradictions of Capitalism*, I came to regard Daniel Bell, Riesman's successor as Harvard's Ford Professor of Social Sciences, as the neoconservative
most attuned to the type of cultural evolution I had focused on,
though even he seemed blind to the relationships between contemporary drives for self-actualization and supportive community
and the counterculture, the liberation movements, and changing
sexual mores.)

I was very eager for Glazer to pay attention to my work. His
group was fast becoming the major intellectual force affecting
contemporary culture and politics. At a time when even Larry
O'Brien and the liberal political establishment dismissed most
Harvard intellectuals as idealistic "pointy heads," the neoconservatives were being listened to by ascendent conservative leaders,
if only because they were thought to be so realistic. They *were*
extraordinarily realistic. They were also good-hearted, well-inten-
tioned, intelligent, and powerful. So I admired their intellectual
gifts and acknowledged their influence and did my homework in
the hope I'd be listened to. I was sure I had some very timely,
very realistic news to report: that gays were becoming a big, powerful group in the big cities; that gender and sexual orientation, as
bases of life-style, community, politics, social problems, and social
policy, had become almost as significant as ethnicity; that these
developments were the result of moral ambitions, political activities, and existential outlooks particularly characteristic of my generation; and that I could document and explain all this.

I enlisted Glazer to be my adviser when I decided to write
about gay politics, because I judged that he would be the neoconservative most inclined to let me in the door, to listen to me without feeling uncomfortable, to see the significance of what I was
saying, and to certify my effort, if not my conclusions, in terms the
Establishment would respect. He did the first and the last, and for
that I am grateful. But that was all he did.

For a time I was hurt and angry because I couldn't get Glazer
to pay more attention to my work. In some ways, these feelings

did a lot to motivate me professionally, and I'm not entirely sorry that I had to settle for *pro forma* thesis supervision. So I found it easy to forgive Glazer's busyness, but I took it as both a scholarly and a political challenge to open his eyes not only about homosexuality, gay life, and the counterculture, but about the ways of liberationist politics. I knew I could count on Nick Bollman to help me.

Nick was born in Looking Glass, Oregon, where his father ran a pig farm and was town manager. His move to Cambridge was a move to "the city." It was a very important step for him, leaving his family, leaving the country life behind to make his way independently. He'd resolved to put himself through Harvard without asking his parents for money, but when that first Thanksgiving vacation came along and he couldn't afford to go home, he had a hard time. In a way, that was what led to his first homosexual experience.

I had a scholarship and I worked, but I knew I wasn't going to have enough money to go home for Christmas if I flew back for Thanksgiving. I went to somebody's house for dinner, but it was a long vacation, and after that I was back in the Yard, essentially by myself. It seemed like everyone else in the dorm had gone somewhere for the vacation. I was really homesick. I felt terribly alone.

Barely aware of what I was doing, I went to the Huntington YMCA. Somehow, I knew that that was where to go to find men. I'd heard stories, you know, about queers and YMCAs.

But none of that was really conscious on my part. In those days, I just drifted into situations, quite literally without being conscious of what I was doing. Sometimes, I think, I remained unconscious of what was happening or had happened even after it happened. So there I was at the Y, but I wasn't really aware of why.

I was in the john. I was standing at the urinal, and there was this other man who I remember as very unattractive and, I think, quite fearful. I was just barely eighteen and looked young, but I must have also looked willing.

Anyway, I finished up at the urinal and started walking

away. And he finished up and started walking after me. I didn't really know what I wanted, but there he was, fifteen feet behind me. I walked out of the Y and across the street to the middle island on Huntington Avenue. I had to wait for the traffic. And by the time the traffic had stopped, he had come up to my side and turned to me and said, "Do you have the time?"

And I said, "No, I'm sorry, I don't."

I now know I was supposed to say "Yes." That "Do you have the time?" does not mean "What time is it?" but "Do you have time to do something sexual with me?"

Anyway, I said, "No, I don't have a watch."

And he said, "Oh," and then, "Well, you want to come back to my place for a beer?"

And I said, "Yeah, why not?" I certainly wasn't nonchalant. I probably squeaked when I said it.

Well, "his place" turned out to be not his apartment but the basement of the building he lived in. He was the super, and he'd set up a little room in the basement so he wouldn't have to bring anyone he picked up upstairs to his apartment. I had to wait outside while he went in through the upstairs and came back around and opened the basement door for me.

I followed him into the room. It was full of things packed in big boxes. There was one broken-down couch with the springs showing through. Immediately he grabbed me. At that point I just sort of fell apart. It was so wonderful.

I was not attracted to him sexually. He was ugly. But I needed to be touched, and his touch felt so wonderful. He went down on me. It was a very quick blow-job. I came in less than . . . well, forty-five seconds at the most.

As soon as I did, he got up and went into the next room, where there was a slop sink. I heard him spit, then turn on the faucet and wash his mouth out. Then he came back to me and said, in a very fatherly way, "Listen, that can happen to anybody."

I said, "Sure, I know."

And he said, "You know, sometimes what I do before I go out with a woman is jerk off. Then I can play longer before I come when I actually have sex with her."

And I said, "Sure. Me too."

Like most Harvard undergraduates, Nick dated women who went to the good women's colleges in the Boston area. As was also the custom, much to the official distress of the proctors, tutors, masters, and deans responsible for dorm life, he sometimes—without violating the rules about visiting hours—had sex in his room with the women he dated. Though he was "sexually shy," he enjoyed those heterosexual experiences and would have had more if he hadn't felt that there was some kind of impenetrable barrier between him and the women he went out with. Somehow he could never really feel comfortable with them. Somehow, when he was with them, he was never really comfortable with himself.

My self-hatred in those days didn't have to do with the homosexual feelings per se, though I guess that was part of it, but with the lying. That's the one thing I have always prided myself on not doing. I hide things. Everybody protects themselves. And I sometimes tell fibs if I think it's necessary. But I don't lie. And that was so much a part of me that having to tell a lie—even not really knowing it was a lie, if that makes any sense—was just intolerable. Not consciously recognizing my homosexuality as something I had to deal with, and yet knowing deep down inside it was there, was telling a lie. And I hated myself for that.

Nick's undergraduate years were not actively homosexual. Besides the man he met as a freshman over Thanksgiving vacation, with whom there was actual if rather brief sexual contact, there were only a couple of flirtations with teaching assistants and friends. Nick's only sexual relationships were the occasional experiences with women he'd been raised to believe sex was all about: "So there were parts of me, parts of my ability to experience, to share with another person, that were unreachable—for women, and also at that time, for men. That hurt me and made most of my life seem unreal."

Right after graduation Nick went to San Francisco. That was the summer of 1967, what he remembers as "the summer everyone grew their hair long," what I would describe as the summer the counterculture as it grew up in the Haight-Ashbury district of San Francisco was discovered by the media. Nick supported himself by painting houseboats in Sausalito, just across the Golden Gate from the city. About every third weekend he would go into San Francisco and get picked up: "I would let myself be sucked off. That's all I did until I met Jeremy. I was passive."

Like so many others in our class, Nick was determined not to let himself be drafted into a war he believed immoral. When his draft board refused to defer him for the Peace Corps, he enlisted in the Navy, enrolling in Officer's Candidate School and finishing at the top of his class. After being commissioned, he threatened to resign if he were assigned to a position that had anything to do with Vietnam.

At that time no officer had resigned his commission to publicize opposition to the war. When Nick made it clear he was ready to, his commanding officers decided to post him at a weather station in Norfolk, Virginia. That was close enough to Washington, D.C., for Nick. He used his weekend passes to work in the antiwar movement, helping to plan the May 1970 Mobilization Against the War and to organize a group called Commissioned Officers Against the War. To his political friends, it looked as if Nick were too busy to have a social life. As it was, he did his socializing back in Norfolk.

It was a male-dominated atmosphere in the Navy, and I learned to be comfortable with men in a way I'd never been before. But the tension was pretty terrific because of my homosexual feelings.

There were two or three gay bars in downtown Norfolk. Everybody seemed to know where they were except me. I had to go into every fucking bar in the whole area—and there were probably some two hundred, because it was a Navy town—to find one that was gay. Of course, I had to find one that was sufficiently mixed so that if I met somebody I knew, I could make it look like I'd just stumbled in there by accident.

That's how I got into one-night stands. Those experiences were releasing, but not pleasing. It's the difference between having a carefully concocted fruit punch on a hot day and having a glass of water after crossing the desert. The glass of water is pleasing in a certain way, but it's more a question of survival than of taste or of pleasure.

Occasionally Nick would go out with women he met in Washington: "When I needed a date to take to the captain's house, I couldn't very well ask the sailor I'd met the night before—especially since I didn't even know his name." Yet he remained unable to open his heart to any of the women he dated. In fact, it was a few more years before he was able to open his heart to anyone.

After getting out of the Navy, Nick went to New York City to work in Congressman Allard Lowenstein's campaign for reelection. He had met Lowenstein when the congressman was touring college campuses to enlist students in his Dump Johnson drive, and he had been charmed by his sincerity and warmth. Nick had always been fascinated by politics and attracted to politicians. For as long as he could remember he had talked with his father about the "big issues"—civil rights, war and peace, federal aid to education. The Bollmans were Oregon Republicans, and through one of his father's friends Nick had gotten a job working in Senator Mark Hatfield's campaign for reelection the summer before our senior year in college. He had held that job through November, writing his senior honors thesis on the campaign, and then gotten involved in antiwar activity with Lowenstein.

Nick kept in touch with the congressman while he was in the Navy, and he went right to work for him when he was discharged. When Lowenstein lost, partly because he had been redistricted into a more conservative district (which his supporters viewed as punishment for his break with LBJ and the political establishment of that era), Nick decided to move to California and write a book about that campaign. This time he went west with a political friend, and the two used their contacts to get jobs teaching in a school for emotionally disturbed children. Nick became best friends with another teacher:

John and I hit it off immediately. We took a one-bedroom apartment together because that was all we could afford. He slept in the bedroom. I slept on a couch in the living room. The kitchen was hardly ever used. We were both totally absorbed in our jobs.

The work was very demanding, and we had little time or energy left over, but what we had we shared with each other. We ended up being together continually, working together all day and going out together at night. We'd go to the beach, go swimming in the pool at the apartment house, watch basketball games, or go up to Hollywood and visit friends.

Every once in a while we'd go out together to the singles bars, and we'd pick up a couple of women and bring them back to the apartment. At that point, I wasn't able to have sex with them; I just couldn't. On two or three occasions, I remember, he'd take his date into the bedroom, and all I could think about was what a terrific time they were having in there.

I'd usually tell the woman I was with that I was too tired for sex or something like that. I'm sure they expected to go to bed with me. I guess they wanted to; I was in good shape, very blond—not gorgeous by Southern California standards, but attractive. I really didn't care what they thought; these were just one-night stands. Going out to the bars was a way for me to be with John, so whatever else I had to do was okay. I guess I had really fallen in love with him, though I'm not sure I knew at the time that that is what it was about. I knew it was physical and emotional, but I certainly wouldn't have called it homosexual.

Well, one time we had picked up two airline stewardesses, gone dancing with them, taken them to their respective hotels. Then, somehow, we had both been drawn back home. We got there at almost the same time and started talking when, all of a sudden, he got very quiet and fixed his piercing blue eyes on me. "You know," he said hoarsely, "we were out there on the dance floor and we were each kind of dancing with our dates, but I was really dancing with you."

I managed to say something like "Yeah." It was impossible for me to say more without just leaping on him and smothering him with kisses.

I had never let on about my feelings for him, although it should have been clear that I was in love with him—and that he was in love with me. I don't think there was any question about that. But there had been no signals, not until this point.

Well, there was more talk, and it was all about how much
we loved each other, stuff like "We really have a good time
together" and "I love to help you do this or that." But it was
all kind of skirting the issue. He made no physical advance. I
was not ready to make one. It would have been terrific if we
had been able just to hold each other. But each of us was too
afraid to reach out. We went off to sleep separately.

For the next week or so, the tension between us was enormous. The next step was just so obvious that we both pulled
back—and we did that by striking out at each other. Everything we did led to a fight. One time, after making up, we
decided to go to a movie—*Jules and Jim.* Can you believe
that we picked that movie? Well, I was already crazy, he was
getting crazy, and the movie just set it off.

After the movie, for no reason at all, we started shadow-
boxing with one another in the parking lot, oblivious to the
other people going to their cars. At first we were just throwing mock punches at one another. But at some point he
swung really hard with an open palm and slapped me in the
face. There was such anger and hostility in that slap that I
stopped immediately. I pulled the keys out of my pocket,
threw them at him, and said, "Take the car. I don't care
where the fuck you go. I don't want to be around you!" I ran
off in the direction of the bluffs overlooking the beach in
Santa Monica.

I didn't know what to do. Once I got to the bluffs, I just
stared off into space for what seemed like a long, long time,
wondering what I was going to do next. I was just standing
there, contemplating jumping, when I heard John call my
name.

He had followed me, though he'd obviously stayed some
distance behind me. And as soon as I heard his voice, I
turned around and we ran to each other and held each other
for the longest time. Then we walked back to the apartment
and, without ever really saying anything, went to bed separately again.

I couldn't sleep at all that night. And very early in the
morning I got up and went into his bedroom and sat down
beside him on the bed. He was lying on his stomach, asleep,
or at least pretending to be asleep. When I put my hand on

his shoulder, he stirred a little—the kind of stir you make when you're half asleep and not quite sure what's happening. But I think he was awake and terribly frightened. When I started to massage his shoulder, he got very rigid, pushed me aside, bolted out of bed, and shouted, "I don't want you to touch me ever again!"

I was stunned. I think I just left the house. But that was it. It was over.

He moved out that very day. And when we saw each other at work, we were mean and nasty to each other. Soon he took up with one of the other teachers, a married woman. I remember going to a party at her house and seeing John necking with her in the kitchen. I was really angry because I knew that he was not involved with her for her sake—I was sure he was simply trying to punish me.

I got very drunk and stoned. Then I got into my car and drove off towards Malibu, weaving all over the road. I was in really bad shape. But at some point I grabbed hold of myself, pulled off the road, and fell asleep. The next morning I woke up with a terrible hangover. I was thankful I was still alive.

To get John out of his life, Nick moved back to New York City and took an apartment with an old friend from the Lowenstein campaign. That fall he enrolled in a master's degree program in the History and Philosophy of Education at New York University. Then he went into therapy, complaining that he was a sexually dysfunctional heterosexual.

He stopped therapy after getting involved with a woman who was a regular customer at the health food store that he was managing in order to pay his way through graduate school. This was Jill—"physically attractive, full of spirit, creative, bright, difficult, sensual . . . my ideal of a woman." About a month after they had begun dating, Jill and her ten-month-old daughter, Cori, moved into Nick's apartment. Soon the three of them set up house in Greenwich Village. Nick knew what he wanted—at least he thought he did.

We always talk about what we know and what we don't know, but it's really only at the edge of consciousness that

the important things happen. Consciously I was very much
in love with Jill and in love with the way of life that stretched
out in front of us—a family, a beautiful daughter who was a
delight to be with, a woman who was a person in her own
right and who would insist that we have a co-equal relationship. All of that was terrific. The only problem was that she
wasn't a man.

But that was at the edge of consciousness. It wasn't until
I saw a program on the David Susskind show late in 1973
that I realized I was still being dishonest.

What I was doing was having anonymous homosexual experiences every once in a while, never letting myself acknowledge what they were. Because we were living in
Greenwich Village, there were endless opportunities. I mean,
I couldn't walk from my house to the library at NYU without
passing fifty gay men on the street and being cruised by
forty of them. When I couldn't resist any longer, I'd speak
to someone on the street who stared at me and accept an
invitation to go back to his place. Generally we didn't get any
further than the entry hall. There would be a quick embrace
and that desperate tugging at clothes and my gentle, insistent
pressing down on his shoulders as he worked his way down
my body. And then the blow-job. That was all I would allow
to happen. I didn't do anything myself. There was no giving.
It was all taking. I was in charge. I set the rules. I left behind a trail of bad experiences for other men because, as they
say, I didn't have my shit together.

I was terrified that someone might discover what my name
was. That's the only reason I didn't do it more often. I would
wait until the tension built to the point where I really *had*
to do it. Then it was a question of how much more important it was to do it than not to do it.

I was supremely attracted to men physically. I was also
attracted to women physically, but not with the same intensity, the same longing, the same anticipated satisfaction.
We now know from Masters and Johnson that it is possible
to perform perfectly adequately in a heterosexual relationship and never have a moment of pleasure. I loved Jill, and
we had a good sexual relationship. But even in these desperate encounters with anonymous people, the intensity of the
sexual experience was much greater. That's the real sin of

the homosexual's oppression: that what is perfectly right and natural and exciting has to be sacrificed for what is merely functional and perfunctory.

We had been living together for about a year and a half when I heard that this gay program was going to be on the Susskind show. Jill and I watched it together. My eyes were riveted on the television set. There was nothing else in the entire world but that program. Susskind's guests were David Rothenberg, executive director of the Fortune Society, a group concerned with ex-convicts, and Elaine Noble, the lesbian legislator from Massachusetts, and a couple of others I don't recall. What I saw was a group of people who were warm, human, perfectly successful in their careers, and yet openly gay. This was the first time I had seen all those things together.

After that show, my feelings about my homosexuality began to change. I began to acknowledge that it was part of me. But I didn't want to lose Jill. I loved my daughter very much, and I didn't want to lose her either. I worried for weeks and finally decided to tell Jill I was bisexual. I thought it might possibly be part of Jill's experience that one could be gay and still be natural and normal and do all the other things that people do. That's what the show did for me; it suggested that somehow I could be normal and still have sex with other men. That made me think that maybe Jill had seen the same thing.

When I was ready to tell her, after weeks of internal debate, I sat her down and said, "There is something very important I have to tell you." I must have looked terrible because she immediately got very serious. And I said, "I have had sex with men, and I think I'm bisexual."

And she said, "Isn't everybody?"

That was it. That was her whole response. Until, of course, we talked about what that meant for our relationship.

Just on the face of it, her response was so congenial that it doomed the relationship. I mean, that's what I love about her— she responded honestly and genuinely and sympathetically. If she'd been a real shrew and a manipulator, she would have tried to keep me from feeling comfortable and played on my guilt to keep me in the relationship. But she didn't do that, and from the moment she said "Isn't everybody?" the relationship was over.

After that, I started going from the foyer to the bedroom, and I even began to talk to the people who picked me up, to tell them something about myself. For the first time in my life the men I had sex with were not anonymous. I was still not having affairs in any sense of the word; I still didn't see anyone a second time. But I started relating to them as people and, though not consciously, started to explore the possibilities of romance as well as sex. I'd had sex with men, and I'd been in love with men, but I'd never put the two together.

For a time my fantasy was to have a "special friend" and also to have my primary relationship with Jill and Cori. When the sky fell in, I was still exploring that possibility. I didn't know that there was no chance of that happening until Jeremy told me so.

For Nick, "the sky fell in" in the fall of 1974. Feelings he had always been able to consign to "the edge of consciousness" suddenly forced their way up front.

It was a warm September night in Greenwich Village, and the whole world was out. I had been studying at the NYU library and was walking home slowly. I was feeling really horny and was enjoying being cruised by the gay men on Christopher Street. I was in front of the Riviera Café when I spotted a man, about a block off, by himself, kind of bouncing along in my direction. He was wearing a gray plaid cotton shirt, the sleeves of which had been cut off to expose enormous biceps and the front of which was unbuttoned to show the most beautiful body I had ever laid eyes on: narrow waist, broad shoulders, bulging pecs.

Suddenly most of the energy in the universe was diverted to our eyes fixing on each other. There was a *pow* of electricity. I had quite literally never experienced anything like this before. I stopped right in my tracks, in front of the café, oblivious to the people eating at the sidewalk tables. And I turned around, fully around, and just watched him walk away.

And then—I just couldn't believe what was happening to

me—I started walking in his direction, following him. He glanced back with this impish but puzzled grin on his face. I followed him down Christopher Street and then north on Bleecker Street. And just about as we got to the Horn of Plenty—I think that was the restaurant—I passed him and stopped in front to read the menu.

I know every menu in the Village by heart. That's the way a lot of gay men meet each other. Everyone else is supposed to think they're planning a dinner for Mother and Father who are coming in from Connecticut next weekend or that they're just checking out the menus and making mental notes to themselves. I mean that's what we think they think we're doing. In fact, of course, what we're doing—and what everybody probably knows we're doing—is stopping in front of the reflecting window to wait for the person we've been cruising. Because if that person should happen to stop and look at the same menu, we've already got something in common with them. The fact is that neither person is looking at the menu, that both are looking at the reflection to see if the other is looking at him. And then one says something, which is what happened when Jeremy walked up and started reading the same menu I was reading. I said something stupid like "Hot night." And he said something stupid. Everything important starts trivially.

We started chatting about this, that, and the other thing, strolling in the same direction together for maybe two and a half blocks. Right then he was on his way to dinner and I was due home. So we made a date to meet the following Monday during the day. I was managing an art gallery then, just to pay my way through grad school, and Monday was the day the gallery was closed.

That was the first time in my life I'd made a real date with another man. And the days passed like an eternity. I couldn't stop thinking about him. I couldn't sleep. And I just couldn't share what was happening in my head with Jill. I was racked with guilt every time I looked at her or talked to Cori.

That Monday morning I went over to his place. He had just gotten up and had barely managed to dress. I was nervous. I was thinking, Oh, my God, he's forgotten. He can't possibly be interested in me. I found out later that he'd been involved in gay life for a long time—he came out when he was fifteen—and that he found my uneasiness and naïveté amusing. Anyway, he made some coffee and sat me down in a director's chair next to his. I made polite conversation, the sort of thing one does at a dance, between dances.

Then at one point I stretched out, and my foot touched his. Once again, most of the energy in the universe was diverted to that one little point of contact. It was like God and Adam in Michelangelo's fresco in the Sistine Chapel. He reacted by bolting upright, leaning over, and putting his hand on my knee. That was it. We spent the rest of the day making love, talking about our wildest dreams, and making plans together.

It was the most wonderful and most physically traumatic experience of my life. On that day, and for the next six months, I had diarrhea.

The next morning I called and said that I simply had to see him. The gallery was open, but I took off at lunchtime. We met in Central Park—I'll never forget the bench. Every time I pass it I think of him. It was on that bench that I told him that I loved him and that I was quite certain that I wanted to spend the rest of my life with him. He was a little taken aback by that, but he knew exactly what I was saying.

At some point I said, "Maybe you and Jill and I can live together. Wouldn't that be terrific?"

And he said, "Are you kidding?"

That shattered the illusion. I knew I had to make a choice. I went home that night and told Jill that I had fallen in love with a man and was going to leave.

It was just six months later that Nick participated in his first gay pride march, the one that was my own first march too. When we met at his apartment afterward, we spent almost three hours comparing personal notes, talking about gay politics, and boosting and prodding each other. Then I went back to Cambridge and on to California, while Nick became a figure in New York City politics, gay and straight.

A few weeks after our meeting, he met the executive director of the National Gay Task Force and was invited to go to Washington to seek congressional sponsors for federal gay rights legislation.

Together Nick and Jeremy went to ask Mark Hatfield if he would sponsor a gay rights bill in the Senate. (Hatfield said only that he would do so if other senators would.) Nick wrote me of the visit: "It was a further stage of 'coming out' for me. We all have our own public limbs to crawl out on, and the political branch is mine."

What Nick was most upset about that first afternoon we talked was his relationship with his parents. They had been planning to come to New York that summer to meet Jill. They had not been pleased when informed it would have to be Jeremy. In fact, they were threatening not to come.

Jeremy had said, "I'm not going to be the cause of your not seeing your parents. They won't have to make a choice if I make one, and my choice is not to see them." So I wrote them and said it wasn't my choice and that I didn't agree with it, but that Jeremy would stay out of the way if they came to visit.

So in midsummer they came. They stayed with my brother and his wife in New Jersey. On a Saturday night they came into the city, and I met them somewhere. We went sightseeing and worked our way uptown towards my apartment.

When we were at Lincoln Center, pretty close, I called home to see if Jeremy was there. When he answered, I told him that I was going to go out to dinner with my parents and that he could just relax, they weren't going to come up. Then I got off the phone, turned around, and said to my parents, "Why don't you come up for a drink? Jeremy is just leaving the house, and he's not going to be back for the rest of the evening, so you won't see him." With a clever, manipulative, bald-faced lie, I was intending to get them together. At great, great risk. I didn't know what was going to happen.

So we went up to the apartment, and I unlocked and opened the door, and there was Jeremy lying bare-ass naked on the living room floor.

My mother shrieked, and my father kind of turned around on his heels. I closed the door quickly and said, "Oh, my God, he's here." Impulsively, I opened the door again, stuck my head in, and said, "For Christsake, get dressed!" Then I turned to my parents and said, "Look, he's gone to get dressed. As long as you're here, we may as well have a drink. It will be too embarrassing all around if we leave now."

So they came in. It was very stiff at first, and I made strong, strong drinks for everybody. Jeremy came down, and there were sort of polite hellos. My father was kind of looking off into space, as if he were somewhere else or wishing he were. But after a while things loosened up. Jeremy is a magnetic person. He has a very charming, easy personality. It was hard for them not to like him. Things got very chatty and amiable as people had more to drink and got more relaxed. We ended up going to dinner together, and we had a wonderful time. Jeremy and I didn't talk about being gay, but we lived it; at that point, it was a lot easier to be it than to talk about it.

You know, I believe in being honest and open. I said I don't tell untruths, and I don't manipulate people. But this was an exception. I did that knowingly and intentionally because it seemed the only way I could break through. I just didn't want them to go back to Oregon without having met Jeremy. I knew that if they did, it would have been the end of my relationship with them. I didn't want to lose them, so I used measures that, for me, were extreme.

After the extreme measures, however successful they'd seemed, relations cooled. Nick sent his parents books, articles, and pamphlets about gay politics and gay life. But the replies from his family didn't mention the material, and nothing was ever said about Jeremy. This upset Nick because he believed that if his family really wanted to relate to him, they had to relate to him as he actually was. The next summer, he went to Oregon to give them one more chance to do so.

I was very aggressive about raising the issue. By this time I was involved with the National Gay Task Force and was very clear in my views. I had read everything there was to read. So I gave my family a quick tutorial, and they listened very patiently, but I wasn't sure if I was making progress.

To get out of Salem, where they were living then, we went to San Francisco. And, of course, you can't go to San Francisco without having homosexuality around you constantly. I thought realities might have more impact on them than words, and so I constantly remarked on it.

I didn't take them to the Castro area or to any of the really heavy gay places. But one night, when my father had gotten tickets to take us all to the theater, I led everyone to a restaurant on Polk Street called the Casa de Cristal. When I'd been in San Francisco before, I'd met a man who was the lover of the guy who owned the place. I'd gone there with him, met the owner, and been real impressed.

At dinner with my parents I mentioned—rather casually, I thought—that this was a gay-owned and operated place with a mixed clientele. I was suggesting that people who were openly gay could be perfectly successful professionally. But something in my father had been building up and suddenly he blew his top.

He said, "Why do you always have to tell us it's a gay this or a gay that? What the hell do you think we care?"

I said, "Look . . ." I didn't yet lose my temper. "Look, I have this feeling that if you don't know me as a gay person, you don't know me at all. And I'm trying desperately to save a relationship with you, and you're not being at all cooperative."

He said something back to me, and I started to get angry. Pretty soon my mother was crying, my father and I were shouting at each other at the top of our lungs, and everybody in the restaurant was staring at us. I suggested we get out of there. My father said something nasty about my paying the bill because he wasn't going to give any money to my "gay friends." We shouted at each other all the way out of the door.

Finally I said, "Look, it's just not going to work."

He said, "That's fine with me. Here are the tickets. Take your mother to the show. I'm going back to the hotel."

I said, "That's not right. What do you mean, me take mother? You should take mother. You've got the tickets. I'll take care of myself."

And he said, "No, no, no. You take her."

Well, it was ridiculous. We kept arguing like that about these tickets to some play my father, on his own, had bought. I didn't even know what it was. There we were, arguing back

and forth about who'd take my mother to the show, like typical men, not asking her what she wanted, treating her like a
piece of baggage that had to be delivered to the station.
Somehow my mother calmed us both down and we agreed, in
a gentlemanly but icy way, that we would all go to the theater together.

When we got to the theater, I took one look at the bill-
board and thought to myself, how in the world did he pick
this play for us to see? It was *Diversions and Delights*—Vin-
cent Price doing a one-man show of readings from Oscar
Wilde. My father just sat there and fumed throughout the
entire performance. I had a terrific time watching him get
pummeled with all the stuff I'd been telling him.

In the ways his father failed him, others in positions of authority exceeded his expectations. In the fall of 1976, Nick and Jeremy
were invited to appear on the local *Beverly Sills Show*. Right after
the show was taped, Nick took off for a professional conference in
California. The one thing he didn't do before leaving was to tell
his boss at the Jewish Board of Guardians, a social service agency,
that he and Jeremy would be appearing on TV as a representative gay couple; the man was in the hospital when he left, and
Nick assumed he'd have time to tell him when he got back.
Midway through the conference, Jeremy called to report that the
broadcast had been moved up a week.

Liberationist in his gay politics from the start, Nick had told his
employer he was gay before being hired. At issue was how the
executive director was going to feel about having his chief aide
appear as an openly gay man on TV. When Nick called the hospital from California, he was relieved and pleased to find his boss
supportive. It was with his glowing recommendation that Nick
moved on to his post as executive director of the Task Force on
the New York City Fiscal Crisis.

I was particularly interested in how Nick had fared as an
openly gay professional, and so I asked him a lot about his job
during our interview. He told me that he had earned a good deal
of respect in the social service establishment, but that the people
he dealt with tended to view him more as a politician who happened to be gay than as a gay politician, which is how he thought
of himself.

What is interesting about the potential for becoming a total fraud—and that, I feel, is the greatest danger that faces a public figure—is that being gay gives me a terrific advantage. People know that I'm honest because I acknowledge that I'm gay. They're going to expect me to be honest. And since I've broken one big taboo in the name of honesty, I can break others with what I say, and I can expect people to accept this as eye-opening truth. In a way, I've got an advantage over other people in public life: Because I'm starting out very open, I can continue to be very open.

People who are already intrigued by me will be even more intrigued by my being just a tiny bit outrageous. Not offensively outrageous, but kind of provocative. I think I can get away with saying things that the typical gray-flannel or political-clubhouse straight could never say. Even if he wanted to he couldn't, because it would be too out of context. People wouldn't expect it. Because as a gay person I'm a mystery to most people, I can get away with saying a lot of what I really feel about issues a lot of people haven't thought much about. For example, politicians rarely talk about sexuality or about how people relate to each other, and when they do, they talk only in the most platitudinous ways. And they never really talk honestly about the personal dimensions of politics and government, though these are precisely the things that make the system work.

I think gay officeholders have a special role to play. Anyone can make a judgment about a question as simple as discrimination on the basis of sexual orientation or, as liberationists like to put it in order to encompass all the understanding they've gained, discrimination on the basis of sexual and affectional preference. But there are some extremely complicated issues that lie ahead, and if they are to be dealt with wisely, it is vital that policy makers understand their gay constituents. Gay officeholders can make gay-related issues personal for people who would otherwise find them completely foreign.

I'm talking about issues like the age of consent for sexual conduct, sex education, juvenile prostitution and sexploitation, special gay counseling facilities, the extent to which the gay community should be integrated or segregated in service delivery, affirmative action, and gentrification. These issues are much more subtle than being for or against gay rights, and because they're so new and complicated, it's difficult even for many gay people to understand where they stand on them. How can we expect a straight politician, one for whom gays are only one constituency, to understand the subtleties and the complications? The politician's first job is to educate, and the gay politician's job is to educate both the gay community and the society in which gays have become such a vital presence.

Nick went on to tell me how he had gotten involved in big-time gay politics:

I met Bob Livingston in the summer of 1977. The spring before, he had been appointed to the Human Rights Commission by Abe Beame, largely, I think, as a favor to his mother, Molly Parnis. But it was also an attempt to capture some of the gay vote. Bob became the first openly gay person appointed to public office in New York City, and this gave him the opportunity to do some things he'd never been able to do as a private person. All of a sudden he was a public person, with legitimacy, with a certain credibility with the press, with a platform.

He had grown up as a rich boy, gone to Yale and, I think, Oxford. He was trained to live a life of serious luxury. Yet there was a kind of public-spiritedness instilled in him, maybe by his mother, maybe in reaction to her. Molly Parnis was also involved in politics. She was very close to Lyndon and Lady Bird Johnson. Bob used to go down to the ranch with his mother, and he got to know Lady Bird quite well. He too wanted to do good things with his money. But never to lose it, of course. And never to do anything so seriously radical that he would bring embarrassment to his mother—although that he did when he came out.

When he decided to let the Establishment know he was gay, he gave a party. How else? That was in 1974, just after the founding of the National Gay Task Force, when Howard Brown was still the chairman of its board. Bob invited a lot of people he'd known over the years. He was very close with

Barbara Walters, the Walter Cronkites, the Punch Sulzberg-
ers, John Chancellor.

In a sense it was his coming-out party. Everyone understood that. But officially, it was a benefit for NGTF. So it was
never "Come over and have it confirmed that your old friend
Bob is gay." It was "Give to something that I feel is worthy."
His mother nearly disowned him.

That party marked a real break with his past. He had lived
the life of an Upper East Side queen, though unlike many of
those he didn't have to pretend he had money—he really had
it. And he had a brilliance and a wit, beyond fag wit, beyond
"Mary this, and Mary that. . . ." His was a literary wit.

He never thought of himself as a literary man, but he was
extemely literary. It was his choice of language. He was the
funniest storyteller I've ever heard. As a matter of fact, once
he learned he had cancer, he was going to sit down with
Arthur Bell and tell stories. Arthur was going to transcribe
and publish them. It's too bad that never got done.

Bob made the break when he decided to get involved with
NGTF. And when the opportunity to sit on the Human
Rights Commission as an openly gay person came—and he
made it clear that that was the only way he'd do it—he took it.

It was in March of '77 that he was appointed. And it was in
May and early June that, thanks to Anita Bryant, the legislation that had been passed to protect the rights of homosexuals in Dade County, Florida, was repealed in a referendum.
Shortly after that, because he was probably the most prominent openly gay person in the city, Bob started getting phone
calls from people who said, "We're outraged. We're incensed.
But we're not marchers, not radicals. We want to do what we
can, but there seems nowhere for us to put our energies in
order to make constructive progress."

So Bob called together a few friends: David Rothenberg, a
couple of straight friends, a couple of gay friends. They said,
"Well, we really don't know what we can do, but we know
that there has to be an outlet, an organization, a group which
will involve mainstream professional gay people and concentrate on problems in this city." New York's always been a cultural trend-setter.

They called together about twenty other people. I was in
this second circle of people assembled. We came together in

Bob's apartment and talked about what we could do. I think it was his idea that we should interview candidates for mayor about their positions on gay rights and make known the results. He knew that with his status as a Human Rights commissioner, and his connections, he could probably persuade most of those who were running to meet with a group of gay professionals, people they would have to consider peers.

They called their group NYPAC—the New York Political Action Council. And just as Bob had predicted, they got all of the primary candidates to come visit them, including the eventual winner, Ed Koch.

We were sitting in the living room of Livingston's Upper East Side apartment, which was on the eighteenth floor and had a view which extended all the way down to the World Trade Center. The candidate was sitting in a chair in the middle of the room facing the rest of us—so that he'd know he was on the spot. We sat around him in a semicircle and could look out beyond him through the windows.

Koch was impressive. He was forthright. He was well informed. He promised the world. About the gay rights bill in the City Council he said, "If the mayor wants that bill passed, it will be passed." As you probably know, the bill had been voted down six or seven times since it was first introduced, I think in '70, and we all felt that full-fledged mayoral support was the only thing that would get it passed.

As we were talking, we noted that whole banks of lights were going out on the southern tip of Manhattan. The waves of darkness moved closer and closer until finally we too were engulfed. For a moment everyone just sat there in stunned silence. Then, spontaneously, people began to titter at the fact that here we were, sitting in the dark with Ed Koch, a middle-aged bachelor, talking about gay rights. Someone called out to the candidate, "Hey, Ed, will you tell 'em where you were when the lights went out?"

That broke everyone up. Even the candidate laughed. Bob scurried into his kitchen and got some candles. And Ed led us all down eighteen flights of stairs with a lighted candle in his hand. Very symbolic.

At the end of our interview, Nick told me that he had met another of our classmates through the National Gay Task Force, someone who'd been intrigued by my letter and had asked him about me. According to Nick, this guy was a very successful management consultant who wouldn't dream of taking a risk for something silly. But he was very excited by his discovery—through the Task Force—that there were other gay men who were also successful professionals. He was getting more political. And he just might share his story if he trusted me.

8

PETER FORRESTER

Raw sex wasn't that important in Peter's life anymore—he was looking for a lover. He used that term, as most in the gay male subculture do, to refer to a man with whom to share sexual and emotional intimacy over time, but not necessarily someone to count also as an exclusive sexual partner, a joint economic provider, a constant social companion, or even a roommate. Partly because society has for so long made it difficult for homosexuals, especially male homosexuals, to build and maintain households together—and partly because their natures, life experiences, world views, and aspirations have both inclined and permitted them to experiment with unconventional ways of handling sexual drives and emotional needs—domestic arrangements of the type traditionally favored by heterosexuals are rarely found, or aspired to, among men who call themselves gay. In the past, homosexuals were forced to live their personal lives in ways that ran counter to those cherished in established culture. Now more and more of them choose to do so.

In his yearning for a lover, Peter was most like Ken. Some of the rest of us were involved in long-term relationships: fourteen years in the case of Rusty and me, six for Marty and Ted, two for

Nick and Jeremy. Yet only Marty and I had relationships that could be described as "loverships" that became "partnerships": We lived together with male partners, shared our money, invested jointly, and socialized mainly as members of a couple. Though Nick and Jeremy lived together, they were much less deeply entwined. Yet compared to them, what my other interview subjects were embarked upon were simple, non-living-together loverships: Ben with Mario, his first "sexual lover"; Willkie with a fantasy realized in the form of a guy resembling a Notre Dame basketball player; and Sandy with Ted, a radical therapist and the first man he became involved with after separating from Christina. David Fredrick was moving out of his two-year lovership with Tom. Ken and Peter were the only ones still trying to find lovers: Ken had never had one for more than a few weeks. Peter had enjoyed only one, very romantic, affair.

I liked to think that it was their lack of experience with loverships that led Peter and Ken to believe that they would be able to find a single person who would be able to provide all they wanted for the rest of their lives. All I had seen, experienced, and understood about gay male life and the counterculture inclined me to believe that they would very likely end up with a life in which different individuals fulfilled different needs and wants at different times, i.e., in which their relationships with lovers and partners evolved as they did. Almost by definition, it seemed to me, homosexuals committed to liberation had relationships that were in constant flux, if only because what they had committed themselves to in coming out was self-actualization, and that inevitably produced changes in needs, wants, and expectations that only constantly adapting personal situations—and rarely a single relationship—could accommodate. Save for Ken and Peter, each of my interview subjects and I had fulfilled our evolving needs and desires with a variety of different relationships. Indeed, it was our awareness that self-realization meant growth, and that this required varied experience, that led each of us to maintain relationships that were open in principle, if not always in practice. Our opting for growth and change rather than the security provided by traditional personal arrangements—extended families, spouses, siblings—was another thing that made us countercultural.

For all of his professional success and social respectability, his close ties with his family, and his aspirations for a Mr. Complete-lover, Peter's personal life was countercultural, not only in his acceptance of his homosexuality and his appreciation of gay life, but also in that his best friend was his ex-wife. Claire graduated from Swarthmore the year we all got our degrees from Harvard. She and Peter met when he was in business school, where she was the dean's assistant. Claire had spent six years as the dean's "right-hand man" before beginning to feel that her own major post-grad-uate life experience—that of building a romantic fantasy and then adapting it to friendship as she and Peter came to terms with his homosexuality—gave her expertise that even a lot of academics might learn from.

With Peter's encouragement, Claire enrolled in a graduate school of social work, got her MSW, and became a self-supporting therapist. Along the way, Peter helped her out financially, feeling it was the least he could do in exchange for all she had under-taken with him. She had done more than anyone else, in fact, to help him find himself sexually. And Peter himself had begun to prosper professionally only after he ceased being hamstrung by conflicts about his homosexuality.

There was a time, he felt, when he had wasted endless hours thinking about sex, both trying to control his homosexual desires and being controlled by them. He had spent days on end worry-ing about "being queer" in college, and the understanding thera-pists he'd sought at the Harvard Health Services hadn't been there. He hadn't gone outside the University for help because he hadn't wanted to be a financial burden on his parents. Fears, anx-ieties, obsessions, and depressions had interfered with his work all through business school.

Nothing really changed until Peter met and married Claire. She was the first person (other than the Harvard doctors) whom he'd told about his homosexuality, and she'd been much more skillful in helping him come to grips with it. Claire had been able to listen sympathetically when he told her about the things he'd done in the bathrooms. In fact, it was she who encouraged him to try safer and healthier outlets, urged him to become personal with his sexual partners, and supported him when he began to go to the baths. After helping him get over his fears of rejection and his pickiness, she had watched him progress from his exciting first conversation with another male sexual partner (someone he met in a porno theater) to his first personalized sexual relationships (tricks at the baths with whom he talked after having sex) to his first requited love affair (with a Princeton graduate in much the same mindset and situation as his).

Claire had been "Mrs. Right" in every way but one that neither of them was willing to pass up—shared erotic satisfaction, fulfilled romantic fantasy, lovership. In fact, it was mainly because they felt they would have an easier time finding lovers as singles that Peter and Claire finally divorced.

Running into Nick Bollman, whom he had known and fantasized about in college, and learning that Nick was involved in the National Gay Task Force, was what led Peter into gay politics. This is how the homoerotic appetites whetted and the social opportunities presented by liberationist politicos breed success, even among those who are rather disinclined to involve themselves in politics. For Peter, the political involvement represented by his membership in the Task Force was unprecedented, not only because it was gay, but because it was organizational. Peter had never been one to join political organizations.

By talking about his personal life for the record, Peter was also being a liberationist without knowing it, and he was again when he agreed to help me organize a gay Harvard alumni group. To Peter himself, the idea of an alumni group appealed mainly because it would be such a perfect place to find Mr. Right. In this, again, he was most like Ken.

When I was twelve I started having sexual encounters with some of the neighborhood boys. That didn't present any problems until about two years later, when we got to Chapter Nine in the Baltimore catechism. Then all of a sudden I found out that what I'd been doing was mortal sin. I believed that, and I went through a period of real agony. Everything was terribly undefined and unclear for me. I knew that heterosexual sex was sinful. Homosexual sex was never mentioned. Sometimes I thought that it had to be included, and at other times I thought that, well, it just wasn't.

So for a long time I didn't know whether to confess it or not. And by the time I decided I probably should, I was sixteen and I wasn't doing it as much. I was masturbating a great deal, but I wasn't having sex with anybody else. Periodically I would, and then I'd go to confession and admit to being guilty of "general impurity." I remember that I kept it reasonably vague because I knew somehow that I shouldn't let the priest know what I was really talking about.

I was very aware of being homosexual, but I was quite convinced that it was going to pass at some point. I had read all the proper books, and they'd said that some boys go through this phase and that it would pass.

At that point I was very religious. The phase that did pass was my religious phase, which had lasted from age twelve to age seventeen. During that time I'd felt a lot of guilt and confusion about sex. In December of my senior year of high school I made my last confession. I had decided that I wasn't going to continue going to church—though I did in a kind of *pro forma* way for another two years. But I had lost my faith.

I haven't gotten that faith back yet. I believe that one day I will, but it'll have to be different. Faith then was all tied up with guilt, and I've had enough of that. I think maybe one of the reasons my religiousness faded is because I began to see my sexual feelings not as sinful, but simply as abnormal. That happened when I started reading the psychology books that described homosexuality as a passing phase.

In the public library, 612.6 was the classification for "Sex Education." I read every 612.6 book there was. There was very little on homosexuality, but there was a little bit. There was one book that I found extremely erotic. It was about sexual delinquents, and there was a fair amount of homosexuality described. It was really rather disreputable, and I don't know how the library ever bought it.

Well, when I arrived at Harvard my homosexual phase still hadn't passed. There were all these fantastic-looking men, and that made me even more ambivalent and conflicted about my sexual feelings.

You know, it's funny, but what made me feel the most moral was that I wasn't going to bed with women. You have to keep in mind that, though it's not major and it's very conflicted, I do have a fair amount of sexual feeling for women. I thought that because I wasn't acting on those feelings, I was doing the moral thing—keeping my sexual urges under control.

A lot of that was doublethink, because during that period I

was having sexual experiences with men. Somehow I must have convinced myself that these weren't really sexual—though I have no idea what I thought they were. I think I just knew I had to keep them secret and not think about them too much myself. But—and maybe for that reason—I was still tormented by them.

I had had sex with a guy at home just before coming to Harvard, and when I went for my freshman physical, with a lady doctor, I told her I thought I had syphilis. I thought I had it because I had a pimple on my cock, and I knew I'd have to get it treated. Curiously, all the way through college I had pimples like that, and for four years I constantly had this fear I'd gotten syphilis. I never did. I've never in my life even gotten gonorrhea. But I was in agony about it the whole time.

Well, I told the doctor about the pimple. And I was much too honest: I told her how I thought I had gotten it. So not only did I get a free blood test, I got a free interview with the psychiatrist.

He spent a great deal of time reassuring me that he was not going to kick me out but that I ought to talk to somebody about my homosexual inclinations. And I spent a great deal of time telling him how I was going to work this thing out by myself. After a couple of interviews, I managed to convince him that I didn't have to talk to him anymore.

By that time I was really afraid that they were going to send me home. I was full of regret for having been so honest. Obviously I was asking for some kind of help. I knew I was miserable. It never occurred to me that I didn't have to be. I knew I needed help, but I didn't know who would be able to provide it.

I turned to the tearooms—you know, the public johns—because I didn't want anybody to know my identity, to see my face, to be able to go back to my roommates or my teachers or the deans or the police and tell them about me. I don't know who I was afraid would find out ultimately—probably my parents.

Oddly enough, I came very close to telling them during my sophomore year. I had another syphilis scare, another trip to the health center, and another trip from the first floor to the third floor for a lengthy interview with a Freudian psychiatrist who should have been fired long before I had to deal with him. He told me that if I really wanted to be cured, it would take four years of intensive psychoanalysis that would cost me twenty-five dollars an hour.

So I went back to my mother and told her I was rather perturbed—I didn't explain why and fortunately she didn't ask —and that I wanted to go into psychotherapy. She said she'd try to get me the money if I really needed it, but that she didn't know how my father could manage that financially. I decided that I really didn't have to have therapy that badly.

I came to the conclusion that I was just going to have to keep my homosexuality a secret. I simply could not see myself being gay openly. So all through college I went for sex to Lamont, to Widener, to Burr Hall. I knew all the active johns on the campus. I tried every tearoom I could. I'd sit in a place, and if nobody came along, I'd figure it wasn't hot.

I don't remember how I discovered the tearoom scene in the first place. Obviously nobody had ever told me about it. I guess I just stayed on a little bit in a john one time and somebody came on to me. That's how it works. Two people hang around and hang around, and all of a sudden something happens. People who come in just to use the facilities don't hang around for twenty minutes, so you know that anybody who does is probably interested in the same thing you are.

I always managed to make contact in such a way that my face could never be seen. I was terribly afraid somebody would discover who I was. It never really occurred to me that there could be any personal relationship in homosexual interaction. People would sometimes leave notes suggesting we get together outside the john, but I just ignored those.

That's where the doublethink came in. It wasn't as if I didn't know there were other homosexuals—after all, there were people coming in and out of the johns all day long—but I just couldn't see myself as one of them. I mean I was still dating women and falling in and out of love with them.

I just couldn't imagine presenting myself to the world as homosexual. I couldn't imagine anyone reacting sympathetically—even somebody else I met in a john. Fundamental, I guess, was the feeling that as long as I didn't let anyone know who I was, that homosexual stuff didn't have to become part of me. As long as I could effectively deny it, I could believe it would go away.

You know, it's very hard for me to understand all that now. It's understandable that for six months I could believe I was the only homosexual around and that I had to keep it a very dark secret. But I believed that for twenty years! I just kept praying that my homosexual desires would one day go away.

I met Claire when I was in business school in New York. She was the dean's assistant. After seeing and talking with her a couple of times, I learned that she was at Swarthmore the same time we were at Harvard. We had many interests and experiences in common. Soon I invited her out to a baroque concert. We had a good time together.

A week or two later she invited me to dinner at her place. She made lemon chicken, rice, and salad. I brought a Burgundy. After dinner she gave me my first grass, and when she'd gotten me totally high, she made a pass at me.

I got very uptight and proceeded to take two hours to tell her I was gay. I meant to tell her about *Tea and Sympathy,* but instead I talked on and on about *The Teahouse of the August Moon*—which confused her enormously because, except for the obscure pun on tearoom, *Teahouse of the August Moon* didn't have anything to do with homosexuality. Finally, about two o'clock in the morning, she figured out what I was trying to tell her. And she said, "Well, it doesn't matter. We'll work something out."

She was, after all, the first person aside from the doctors at the Health Center I'd told about my homosexuality. We'd developed a rapport so quickly. I was ready to tell somebody. I just knew that I was going to marry her—sometimes you just know those things—and I thought I should let her know what she was getting into.

I didn't think she'd be freaked out or horrified. She was intelligent and open-minded. She'd worked for a while in a theater company, so I knew she'd been exposed to the world. It's amazing, but just from the way she responded to me I knew that I trusted her and loved her and wanted to marry her. So my inveterate honesty came out, and I told her.

A week later we went to bed for the first time, and I took the fact that it worked to mean that my homosexual phase had finally passed. I mean, clearly, if Peter could go to bed with a woman and actually get it up and actually come, then there was no question about it, he must be straight after all. Just because I had had those homosexual desires for twenty-six years didn't mean that they weren't temporary and wouldn't pass.

Claire was not a whole lot more experienced in these matters than I was, and she bought it too. Remember, this was at a time—and there are people who still believe this today—when they said that if you had enough motivation, you could become straight. I think we both believed that my homosexuality would simply pass and that everything would be wonderful thereafter. It wasn't that I'd do it volitionally exactly, but that once I was living and functioning heterosexually, the homosexuality would wither away—just like the State!

Well, one's ability to ignore the obvious is rather amazing, because I continued to have sex in men's rooms. At the same time, I really did want to get married, and so did she. We went out together for six months, and then her roommate was moving out, so I moved in with her. We'd been playing musical beds, and it was just easier to live in the same apartment.

We lived together like that for another six months. Both of our parents were scandalized. Mine wouldn't allow us to share the same room when we went to visit them. Hers cried and carried on hysterically when she told them we were living together. So there was a lot of pressure on us to get married, and in December we got engaged to be married over the summer.

We were both under a lot of pressure anyway. I was finishing up business school. She was thinking about quitting her job to go to graduate school. I wasn't really sure what I wanted to do with my future, and I began to have doubts whether I really should get married. But by that time, if only because of our parents, the marriage was no longer a negotiable item. It was going to happen when the summer came and I finished school.

I continued doing the tearooms the whole time we were

living together. I spent a lot of time studying in the library, and it was just so available in the library johns. I was still doing it very much on the sly. Though, in my own veiled way, I told Claire, I wasn't as explicit as I might have been because she found the whole tearoom scene so incomprehensible. We had problems from the beginning over that and over other things as well. We were both a good deal more neurotic then than we are today.

Well, for all of our quarreling, Claire continued to be very supportive and very accepting of what she knew about me. She could see that I was still pretty confused, and she encouraged me to go into therapy. I did.

I went to see a psychologist she told me about. He started off by saying, "Tell me about why you're here."

And I said, "Well, you see, I'm homosexual."

Then he said, "Okay." He was waiting for me to continue. And then he said, "So. What's the problem?"

I said, "What do you mean, 'what's the problem?' I just told you what the problem is."

He said, "Well, I don't think you did. You just told me that you're homosexual. What's the problem?"

So I decided I liked him. If he could react that way, he was probably nonjudgmental enough for me to be really open with him. It was through him that I learned to accept my sexuality.

Finding a lover was a harder proposition. A Princeton graduate I met at the baths was my first.

It was one summer weekend after I had returned home from a business trip, and I was feeling quite lonely. I said, "To hell with it. I'll go to the baths." I went to the Club Baths down on First Avenue, right off Houston Street. I knew that baths. I'd been there several times. It was very pleasant, kind of collegiate.

It was a reasonably quiet Sunday afternoon. There were only a few people wandering around. I sat in the steam room for a while; then I went down to the showers and ran into this fellow I thought was really attractive. I wasn't wearing my glasses—I either wear them at the baths and see people clearly or I don't and feel more attractive—but what I could see of this fellow I liked. Anyway, he was a little standoffish, so I went back to the steam room. A few minutes later he came in, and we exchanged a couple of words. Then I left and went upstairs to the dorm. He followed me. We ended up having sex together on one of the mattresses up there.

Before we had said a word to each other I was in love—talk about snap judgments—and so after we had sex, I made sure that we stayed together for a little while and talked. He told me that he had gone to Princeton and was a lawyer. I told him I was a Harvard graduate and a consultant. We seemed to be well matched.

After we talked for a little while, I told him I'd like to see him again. I had never done anything quite like that before, but I felt it was time. I knew this was a man I could trust—and besides, I was madly in love with him.

What was he like?

Well, he was several years older than I. A good-looking man. Blond, six feet tall, one hundred and seventy pounds, nice build, trim, the stereotypical Ivy Leaguer. Or at least the stereotypical Princeton man.

Your type?

Exactly. Though he was in a much fancier economic class than me. He told me that he'd just gotten himself twelve handkerchiefs for twenty dollars, which was a fantastic price at the time. For twelve handkerchiefs I used to pay two-fifty.

Anyway, we went back to our lockers together, and I gave him my card. He told me his phone number. Then he said, "You know, there's really only one hitch that you'd better know about . . ." and he put his wedding ring back on his finger.

Well, by that time Claire and I had gotten divorced, so I couldn't just pull out my ring and say, "Me, too." But I did say, "Who cares. I'm still in love with you."

It turned out that the phone number he'd given me was false, and that he'd given me a false last name, off by one consonant. So he'd protected himself. I'd never have been able to reach him. But he called the very next day and invited me to meet him for dinner at his club the following evening. I must say I was suitably touched to be the object of anybody's snowing to that extent.

After dinner we proceeded to look for a place to make love. I was living on Long Island at the time, so it was too far to go to my house. He, of course, was married, and couldn't very well take me home to his wife. We ended up that night, and once or twice after that, at Claire's apartment.

Claire's apartment? How did that happen?

That was an interesting aspect of my coming out. She was the one who assisted me all the way through. She was the one I confided in. We got divorced because we knew we couldn't stay married—it just wasn't what a marriage should be—but we were still very close. In fact, after I'd met this guy at the baths, I walked out and went to the nearest phone booth and called her up and said, "I want to see you. I want to tell you about the guy I just met."

Anyway, she was away the week after I met Jess, and I had a key to her place. She said I was always welcome to use it. So that's where we went.

That week was the best of my life, I think. We went out together three times. After the first night, Claire was back, and so we went back to the baths to make love. During the second and third week we got into the habit of seeing each other, at least for ice cream or something, about three times a week. We were able to make love together at least once a week.

This guy was married?

Yes, he was married to an investment banker. They were an up-and-coming young couple making a combined salary of ninety thousand dollars a year or more. They had a very active social life. He had belonged to a Princeton dining club and was a member of various men's clubs. She was Junior League, et cetera. His being married was very important to him and to her and to the whole life they were leading. I have no idea how they dealt with his homosexuality.

Had he told her?

Well, it's been over a year since he and I broke up, but up to that point, no. They'd been married for four years by then. I never really asked him much about his marriage. I was always afraid that if I pushed him for information about himself, he'd end the relationship. He was obviously living a very closeted gay life.

So we made it through Christmas. I remember exchanging presents with him on a park bench in Central Park after lunching at his club. By that time I'd decided to move back into the city. I didn't know what would happen with the relationship, but it was going so well that I was optimistic. I'd gotten so that I couldn't stand going to the baths with him; I was renting hotel rooms so that we could make love. I'd rent a room in the city for the night and stay over. He'd come, and we'd go to bed, and then afterwards he'd leave and go home.

I didn't like being left there by myself. It made me feel very alone somehow. I knew that was going to be a problem.

Why couldn't you stand going to the baths?

It was too public. He was obviously conflicted about the whole thing, and the baths just made it worse. After we'd gone to the baths for a while, he became terribly afraid that someone might recognize us, so we decided we wouldn't do that again. If Claire was at home, which she usually was, I'd rent a hotel room.

He was conflicted about the persistence of the relationship?

No, he was unhappy about being gay. I no longer had that conflict. I had accepted it, but he hadn't. He was going to stay married for the sake of his life-style, and he was going to stay firmly locked in the closet.

That made me unhappy. I was becoming restless. I wanted the relationship to grow. I think I could have accepted his being married, but I couldn't accept being part of the duplicity.

I got busy in my job and spent a lot of time preparing to move back into the city. It took a little while, but finally in February I got this apartment. So I called him up and said, "Now we've finally got a place."

In the back of my mind the whole time I was looking for an apartment was this sense that once I'd found one, the relationship would end. I just couldn't help but feel that it would make the relationship too real for him to handle. Yet I could not get an apartment.

I moved back in February, and in March he began to call me less. At the beginning of April I asked him what was going on. He acknowledged that he wanted to end the relationship. I asked him if there was somebody else besides his wife, and he said there was. He'd met this other guy right at the end of February, about the same time I'd moved back to the city.

I told him that whatever happened, I still wanted us to be friends. He said we could continue to have lunch together every now and then. I wanted much more, but I settled for lunch.

It's funny, it was only during those eight weeks we had lunch several times that we talked candidly about his situation. It was as if we couldn't talk when we'd actually been involved. I was scared of shattering the relationship, and he was scared of making himself vulnerable.

Well, I saw him for lunch occasionally. Then I invited him over for dinner, and he accepted. But at the end of the meal he walked out abruptly, saying he'd call. I didn't hear from him for a month.

For a while after that things were pretty good with me. Then one night I had a blowup with somebody I had begun to see. That made me miserable, and of course I began to think about Jess.

The next morning the doorman called and said there was a package for me. I went down and got it. It was a tie that my

Princeton Tiger had left with the doorman, along with a birthday card. My birthday had been six weeks earlier. I'd been mortally hurt when he missed it. I wrote him a two-line thank-you note for the birthday present and nothing more.

That was the end of that one. But I'm ready to try again.

9

COTTIE ADAMS

It's hard to say how common Peter's way of satisfying his homosexual desires was, and is. Of the first eight classmates I interviewed, Willkie was the only other who had turned to sex in public toilets because he was too fearful of being discovered homosexual to look for more pleasant, fulfilling, and responsible ways of meeting other homosexuals. Nick had let himself be picked up on the street until he became comfortable going to gay bars, and he had persisted with this pattern until he found a lover. Ben had turned to the tearoom scene and its outdoor analogues (certain stretches of sidewalk, park, and beach) after learning how to "make out" through the bars and the baths, and now he approached gay low life in a spirit of existential adventure. Ken, Marty, and David had turned first to friends and then to bars. Sandy and I had settled into relationships almost from the start. Willkie had moved on to bars and baths when he gave up tearoom sex and then gotten interested in private sex clubs. Nick and Ken had learned how to use the baths for recreational sex, as had Peter, though, like Ken, Peter now preferred gay social and political events, private parties, and dating to bath experiences and one-night stands—mainly because he felt that the former were much more likely to yield a lover. Each of us had become homosexually active in ways that were different save for one thing: We had all learned to enjoy traditional gay male pastimes in healthy and ethical ways. To the extent that we had done this—Sandy less than the rest—we were liberated gay men.

Being a liberated gay man is something very different from being a male homosexual, which requires only that one be primarily attracted sexually to other males; and from being an active male homosexual, which requires only that one be involved sexually with other males; and even from being a gay man, which requires only that one associate or involve himself with the gay male subculture. The gay male subculture is more than anything else a constellation of attitudes, customs, and institutions having to do with sex. A liberated gay man is one who has rejected conventional prejudices about homosexuality and gay life and learned to view or to enjoy the gay male subculture with countercultural perspective.

More than the particular ways in which we had come to grips with our homosexuality, and more than the particular ways in which we were expressing ourselves homosexually at the time of my trip, it was our rejection of conventional ideas about sexuality that marked me and my interview subjects as liberated gay men. Though in many cases we'd turned to the gay male subculture with ignorance and naïveté, and had immersed ourselves in it out of neediness and obsession, with time, education, and experience we'd learned how to approach sexual promiscuity—which means love of sexual variety—sensibly. For each of us, coming out had meant getting involved in gay male life, and this had meant learning how to enjoy recreational sex. The experience of recreating sexually had taught us to see through a lot of conventional assumptions about what was involved in having sex. All of us had learned how to divorce sex from a lot of the romantic mythology that traditional American mores enshrined it in. We had learned how to appreciate sex for its sheer erotic and sensual delights, how to take it and leave it as sport, how to enjoy it without guilt, conflict, and duplicity. We had become capable of separating it from emotional involvements, personal hassles, and persisting personal, social, and professional responsibilities. This didn't mean that we were incapable of loving in some of our relationships or of combining sex with love in some of our relationships.

It meant that we had learned how to complement our more substantial loving relationships with what some gay men called "varietal sex." Hence it was about unconventional approaches to sex, love, and relationships that we had a lot to teach others by virtue of being liberated gay men.

Indeed, what we most had in common was the perspective we shared on sex, love, and relationships because we were liberated gay men. That perspective was a more powerful bond than our age, sex, graduation year, college, or generation. It provided more grounds for empathy and identification among us than our personal, social, political, and professional aspirations. It was more salient than the class backgrounds from which we had come to Harvard or the social and economic niches that we were in currently.

In fact, if there was anything remarkable about our class backgrounds, it was that so many of us were public high-school graduates, which meant that we probably came from working- or middle-class backgrounds. What made this interesting and significant from the point of view of my research was that the Harvard College class from which I had drawn my interview subjects was composed of 50 percent public high-school graduates and 50 percent preppies, particularly graduates of the elite prep schools in the New England area (Phillips Academy Andover and Phillips Exeter, St. Paul's, Groton, Middlesex, Choate, Brooks, Browne and Nichols, Deerfield, Mount Hermon, Milton, and Belmont Country Day, to name only the most prominent).

For all the effort it made to admit "townies," which began in a post-World War II spirit of democratizing educational opportunity, Harvard—especially the College—was a haven for preppies. Graduates of elite private schools were represented in especially large numbers, not only in each college class and among the alumni, but in the University administration, the people charged with keeping Harvard College the educational heart of the Establishment.

This had been true from the beginning. In the seventeenth century, Harvard was founded and run by people from the "best" New England families, and they admitted generation after generation of their own to be trained as political, financial, moral, and educational leaders—in the family tradition. As America itself became more democratic, as equal opportunity was extended to the middle and working classes, to the ethnic minorities, and finally to women, Harvard itself became more egalitarian. The extent to which the University was a leader in starting, mirroring, and furthering this national trend was debatable, but there was no doubt that Harvard had opened up and broadened its base as the times had changed. And for this, one had to credit the Establishment itself with changing, for the University had opened up with Establishment acquiescence if not approval.

I didn't really know why so few preppies had responded to my call for support in helping Harvard and the Establishment open up when it came to gay people. Only two of the dozen or so classmates who got in touch with me after I came out in the class report were preppies, and they were both guys I had been casually friendly with in college and had seen a couple of times after graduation. One, whom I had spent time with in Europe as well as America, sent me a short note on a Christmas card congratulating me for being so forthright. The other, an Exeter-Harvard-Yale-educated lawyer involved in national Democratic party politics, whom I had not seen since the days when he, like Nick and me, was doing his liberal political thing in the inner city, congratulated me for my idealism but said that he himself didn't see gay rights as a mainstream political issue. To my way of thinking, he had failed to see that the issues being raised by liberated gays were broader—specifically, respect for human diversity, a prerequisite for all liberation, and the regulation of social behavior represented by victimless-crime laws. Indeed, with all of his talk about party politics, he seemed not yet to have recognized that the major political arena in modern America was culture, that the major conduit of influence was the media, and that the most effective political skills and tactics were now intellectual, communicative, and sociopsychological.

The pattern of class differentiation I observed in the responses to my coming-out statement was repeated in the response to my letter to the class asking for interview subjects: None of the four who volunteered to let me interview them were from the prestigious prep schools so heavily represented in the backgrounds of my college classmates, and only five of the seventeen who sent supportive notes were preppies. This is why I was so excited when one of the four volunteers, Paul Detroit, wrote not only that he would be glad to talk with me, but also that he had recently become involved with another classmate who might agree to be interviewed—a classmate who had gone to Andover. This was Cottie Adams, and I arranged to see him as soon as I was back in Cambridge.

In Cottie's story I hoped to find at least a clue to the question of why I had heard from so few preppies. To some extent, this was a corollary to the question of why I had heard from so few of my classmates in general. All told, at the time of my trip, I had heard from 13 self-defined homosexuals, or 1 percent of my 1,180 classmates. Since, following Kinsey, it is estimated that 10 percent of the adult male population is predominantly or exclusively homosexually active, it seemed reasonable to assume that my Harvard College class had its rightful share, which would mean 118. Where were the other 105? Who were they? Why hadn't I heard from them?

As things stood, all I could do was to raise the obvious questions. Was it because fewer of the preppies (or my Harvard classmates in general) were homosexual, or actively homosexual, or involved in the gay male subculture? Or that fewer had developed the countercultural and political perspectives on homosexuality and gay life that made for liberated—meaning identified with and accepting of other—gays? Was it because most of them had adjusted to life as homosexuals so easily that they were unpersuaded that society made it difficult for most people to come to terms with their homosexual feelings? Or was it that most of them felt so guilty and ashamed about their homosexuality that they couldn't see or believe that conventional views and popular prejudices could be blamed for making it difficult for homosexuals to find identity and to enjoy community?

Or did my failure to hear from more preppies (or classmates) mean not that Harvard homosexuals didn't see and accept themselves as members of a mistreated minority group, but that they were reluctant to participate in efforts to improve matters? Did their failure to get in touch suggest that they didn't trust me or that they didn't believe that things could be improved by efforts such as the one I was undertaking? Did this imply that they weren't liberal enough to think that efforts should be made to spare people with homosexual feelings the ignorance, self-hatred, isolation, unpleasantness, ostracism, and danger that so many homosexuals now endure? Or that they didn't see that innocent others involved with homosexuals also suffered because of these?

If nothing else, didn't this indicate that they weren't liberationist-minded enough to recognize that personal and cultural issues like sexuality were realms meriting significant moral, political, and intellectual leadership?

Or was it that they saw and cared but felt that they just couldn't be involved for personal reasons? Were they less willing than other homosexuals to forsake or to risk losing professional status and social approval—mummy and daddy's love, the good opinion of siblings and relatives and friends, the respect of old teachers and neighbors—because they came from exceptionally successful and well-regarded families, had gotten into the best schools, and been well-launched into the Establishment? Or, like so many homosexuals who had come out in the days before liberationist politics, had they simply developed personal, social, professional, and political networks based on compartmentalized lives and become reluctant to upset these arrangements for what seemed like such an idealistic and relatively unimportant cause?

I didn't expect Cottie's story to provide any answers. All I wanted was an inside view of one gay preppy's life that might stimulate others to ask—and to answer—some important questions. About the Establishment. About prep schools, Harvard, and other distinguished institutions of higher learning. And about the awareness, maturity, values, political dispositions, character, and courage with which they are endowing the young they are educating.

I went to Andover because my brother Whit was there. I admired him and wanted to be like him. In those days I really aspired to have a masculine persona, which he certainly had. And yet, although I aspired to have it, I felt defeated about it from the start. So I never tried to enhance it by, for example, playing sports.

I hated sports. In elementary school I was the opposite of the other guys, who just couldn't wait to get out to the field after classes. I wanted to go home right away. I dreaded having to go down to the field, particularly in the fall when we played football. I was afraid of the ball, and I wasn't very good. Baseball wasn't quite so bad as football, because it was spring and I could be an outfielder and look at the trees and stuff.

Every summer from fifth to eighth grades I went to camp. I got very competitive at that age and did very well. I got the highest marks in elementary school and the most points at camp. Even in some athletic things I was good—like swimming, a no-contact sport, and riflery, where I could just sit and shoot at targets. It was mainly the competitive team sports that I loathed.

At Andover I was also very unathletic. In the spring and fall I played what they called "spaz" tennis. A group of us who were among the very best students all played. We were rather "spastic" at tennis, but we brought very high I.Q.'s to the court, or at least so we thought.

My sophomore year was my worst year there. I lived in this miserable little room in the corner on the fourth floor with a lot of athletic kids. I was very frightened of them. At night, after lights out, I would go down and study with friends on the second floor. They didn't have a transom over their door, so we couldn't get caught with the lights on. So I'd be in my pajamas, carrying a pile of books, going downstairs at five minutes before bedtime. And sometimes one or another athletic kid would taunt me: "Oh, you're going down there again. What are you going to do tonight?" I'm sure they thought I was queer.

One time they got me to come into one of their rooms. There were about ten guys sitting around, and they riddled me with questions about my sex life. I was so shy and unable to fend for myself that I just sat there and answered every one of the questions. They asked me if I jerked off or not. I lied and said that I did it very occasionally. In fact I did it every day.

One of the guys said that he wanted to fix me up with this girl, a cousin of his. He said she loved to fuck. I said that it sounded appealing, but that I didn't think I had enough experience to handle it. I actually carried it off pretty well. I probably should have said, "Fuck you, this isn't any of your business."

Andover had this "nego"/"poso" dichotomy. By the time I was a senior, my friends were all negos, which meant that we had a negative attitude, that in some ways we were cynical. We looked down on people who had school spirit, the so-called posos. That classmate of ours from Andover you said told you about his homosexuality on the condition that you keep it absolutely secret—well, I don't know who that might be, but from what little you've said, he sounds like a poso, the well-rounded guy who was not only athletic but also a student leader.

The real negos, the intellectuals who shunned athletics—not all the intellectuals but most of them—were a much smaller group. I remember as a senior actually putting down people who were too athletic, probably out of jealousy. Which is a shame. I wish I'd developed my body at that age. It would have been a great asset later on.

Now when I think about the friends I had back at Andover, I see that I hung around with people I viewed as especially smart mainly to be safe. And I now see that those relationships were pretty awful. They were competitive and full of sarcasm. I had no warm relationships at all in those years. In fact, if someone was warm towards me, I tended to look down on him. You know the Groucho Marx line: I'd never belong to a club that would have somebody like me as a member. That was me.

All the time I was in secondary school it literally never crossed my mind to have sex with anyone. I was very repressed that way. I was not at all close to anybody. I think I was probably incapable of intimacy until after my analysis.

Of course, I was aware that I had sexual feelings about some of my classmates, especially some of the posos, and I hated myself for that. I think that's why I spent so much time putting down the posos; I was fighting my own positive feelings because they were so threatening. I just couldn't accept sexual feelings of any kind.

I didn't know anybody who was actually engaged in homosexual behavior or who was having an affair with another guy. I'm sure that was going on. It just had to be. But I simply wouldn't let myself see it. I was too afraid.

Since I wasn't able to act on the basis of my sexual feelings, I became obsessively voyeuristic. I would spend as much time as I could in the locker room and the showers. I remember being attracted to one guy in particular. He was probably *the* outstanding poso in my class at Andover, and he played the same role in our Harvard class.

I didn't think he was that good looking, but his body was quite a turn-on to me. He was very athletic and was always around the locker room. He was sort of gangly, sort of adolescent. But there was something sexy about the way he moved, something about the totality of him. I remember thinking that his cock was bigger when he was a sophomore than when he was a senior—as if his sexuality was uncontrollable at the earlier age.

I was definitely attracted to him. But I was never friends with him. I thought him stuck-up. He wanted to play the stud a little too much.

It's easier for me to talk about my voyeurism now because I don't do that kind of thing in the same way anymore. Partly because I can do all the watching I want to do by going to porn movies or to the baths, I don't feel my everyday life consumed by voyeurism, as I did back then.

At Andover, as I said, I used to linger in the showers and around the lockers. And I even used to spend time with the lights off in my room, looking out the window to see if I could see anybody getting undressed in the dorm across the way. And I got into more sordid stuff when I went to Europe during spring vacation my junior year. At a hotel in Rome I found a men's room that had a peephole into the next stall. The hole was so small that I really couldn't see anything clearly, but it was terribly exciting anyway. After that, in every hotel we went to, I looked for places where I could spy on men.

In 1963, when I graduated from Andover, my parents gave me a long trip to Europe. They perceived me as being immature and perhaps even antisocial, and they thought maybe a summer on my own in Europe would help me grow up. I knew that I wouldn't enjoy traveling on my own, so I decided to stay in Switzerland and study.

That summer, in Zurich, I hung around men's rooms a certain amount, and I was cruised a couple of times by gay men. When I realized how interested I was, I became very blackly depressed. I really felt horrible. I don't know why—my parents had never said a word about homosexuality—but I grew up feeling that falling in love with a woman was the salvation of life. I was sure that the homosexual feelings I experienced somehow doomed me.

By the time I returned to Harvard to begin freshman year, I felt very trapped. I had no desire to go out with women. I did try it, but I was so tense and nervous and upset that I couldn't even carry on a good conversation.

Some time in the fall I got into a terrible depression and went to the Health Services. I was sent first to a woman doctor, and since I couldn't bear the idea of saying I thought I was homosexual to a woman, I simply broke into tears.

She referred me to a man. I remember being able to see the outline of his cock through his pants the first time I went to see him. I didn't especially like him, but I trusted him to some degree. Psychiatrists, after all, are wonderful listeners. It's gratifying to be able to babble on about anything you want and have a completely attentive listener.

I told him right away I thought I was homosexual, and he asked me whether I'd had any experiences with women. His point was: How could I judge that I was homosexual if I had never had any heterosexual experience? I had not yet had any sexual experience with men—in fact, it was going to be another thirteen years before that actually happened. All I had done was to sit in men's rooms and peer through holes. He said, "Look, you seem to be momentarily depressed, but fears about homosexuality are not at all abnormal. Let's just see how things go." He told me to fight my depression for a while longer and to come back if I continued to feel upset.

Well, I was so miserable that I can't even remember what freshman year was like. It seemed as if my whole existence was in question. I never exerted my will about anything. I simply tried to figure out what everybody else wanted and then to go along with it. I was so self-conscious about my gait I felt at times as if I could hardly walk. And I had this fantasy that I could be the smartest guy in the world. I'd read all of Kant my senior year at Andover, and I used to stumble around Harvard Yard thinking about Kant and trying to figure out how the world worked. I was into some fairly typi-

cal syndromes, but with the added burden of these homosexual obsessions which I thought so horrible that I couldn't
conceive of telling anyone about them.

I felt terribly isolated. I couldn't talk about what was on
my mind to any of my Andover friends or my new roommates. The shrink at the Health Center had sent me off. I was
falling apart, and I didn't know where to turn.

Finally, I went to my brother Whit, who was a senior in
Lowell House. I began by telling him that I thought I should
see a psychiatrist and that I was very afraid of bringing this
up with our parents because they had always made it clear
that they thought therapy silly and self-indulgent. One vacation when I was a senior at Andover, my father had once
come into our living room while I was reading Freud, asked
what I was reading, and groaned loudly when I told him.
Anyway, I finally broke into tears and told Whit I feared I
was homosexual.

Whit thought I was being sort of ridiculous, but he let my
parents know that that was what I was upset about. My
father never mentioned it explicitly, but he sent a letter
saying that he understood I was having problems and knew
that by modern methods these things could be dealt with and
said of course I should go into therapy.

I went back to the shrink at the Health Center and said I
was still upset and that my father agreed that I should seek
treatment. This time we discussed what I wanted and what
might be done. He referred me to a well-known psychoana-
lyst, and so I started going to him.

He was a very imposing man with a deep voice—I think
that deep voice meant a lot to me at that time because my
own voice was soft and, I thought, effeminate. I didn't tell
him that I *was* homosexual, but that I had homosexual fantasies and that I didn't want to be homosexual. I said, "I've
only been attracted to men; I've never been attracted to
women, yet I can't think of myself as being homosexual." I
remember his saying, in his thick Viennese accent, "I think
it is reasonable that you have an analysis."

During that first visit I had the only migraine headache
I've ever had in my life—I was seeing double. He said I was
too anxiety-stricken to start analysis right away. So I saw him

twice a week at first and then, after about a month, started the analysis. Then I saw him four times a week. I worked really hard. It was a big deal for me.

He let me call the shots. He accepted at face value my saying that my homosexuality was neurotic and that I wanted to have a relationship with a woman. He agreed that homosexuality was neurotic. He kept saying that I was not "taking responsibility" for my *real* sexual feelings—in other words, for my feelings for women.

There were, in fact, some such feelings. I could get turned on when I was in an intimate situation with a woman, but it was only on the surface. On the street I never looked at women. And I certainly didn't fantasize about or yearn for them. But I was confused and dishonest enough with myself about my feelings that I was able to convince the psychiatrist that I wasn't really homosexual. Years later, when I went back to see him feeling much more sure of myself and told him the truth, he remarked, "Well, you just didn't *seem* like a homosexual."

I got all kinds of things out of analysis in terms of being able to relate to people. And I understood a lot about my homosexuality and its genesis. But I never did anything of what I'd wanted to do, which was to eradicate my homosexual fantasies and become naturally inclined to have a relationship with a woman.

Even while I was in analysis I was continuing my voyeuristic trips to the public urinals in downtown Boston. I used to describe them to my analyst, saying, "I went on a penis hunt yesterday." I can't tell you how much time I used to spend sitting in public toilets peering through holes and cracks, hoping to see a cock.

At the beginning of my junior year I met Libby. I went with her for three and a half years, on and off. We didn't have sex until my first year in graduate school. And it was difficult. I was always anxious that I wouldn't be able to. It was always a performance. But I did get turned on.

She was a beautiful girl, by far the most beautiful girl I've ever been with. She had powder-blue eyes and looked like the young Liz Taylor—a knockout. I used to feel good just walking down the street with her. Every man on the street would be looking at her, and I'd feel, "Jesus, I'm with this woman." At that time my self-image was much worse than it is now. I mean, I consider myself more attractive than not attractive, but I'm not stunningly attractive. Libby was really stunning.

All this time I was telling myself that I was really hetero-sexual and that I just had to overcome my homosexuality. It was my analyst's idea that if I got into a really good relation-ship with a woman, the homosexual fantasies would fade away or at least assume a very minor position. So I was really trying to set up my whole life by becoming more intense with Libby. I was even trying to control my imagination so that I could have fantasies about her. Occasionally I dreamt about her and there'd be some sexual feelings there. But my really strong interest in men was never even briefly supplanted.

It was when I was in graduate school in New York City that I first began to go to pornographic movies. The first time I went to a gay male film I was almost sick to my stomach I was so afraid. I got robbed on the way to it. That was very symbolic.

I continued to go to men's rooms, of course. The toilets in the Port Authority bus terminal were situated so that you could look right into the urinals from them. I used to go there and sit in a stall and jerk off for hours.

But as gay films got increasingly hard-core—around '69 or '70—I found it much more exciting to go and masturbate in the theaters. That's when I became addicted to pornography of every kind. I used to spend a small fortune on porno-graphic novels and magazines. Now all that pales in com-parison with reality, and it doesn't interest me very much anymore.

Toward the end I decided to tell Libby about my addiction to porn. And I mean addiction: I'd go to Times Square and travel from one movie theater to another and from one porn store to the next for hours, then I'd end up in a toilet in the Port Authority and stay there practically all night looking through the crack.

This went on so persistently that even after I got more comfortable with the idea of sleeping with Libby, I'd some-times be so tired that I couldn't perform. You see, at first I also had tremendous guilt about doing anything heterosexual. It obviously violated feelings I had about the purity of my mother. So at the beginning of my relationship with Libby I had a hard time taking the initiative.

It was Libby's first affair too. I think that's why she tolerated it. It would have been agony for any woman who was more experienced. On the other hand, such a woman might have helped me in a way that Libby, in her inexperience, could not.

Anyway, all that homosexual business ended our relationship. The first time I told her about one of my porn binges she said, "I love you anyway." The second time—we'd had sex in the middle of the afternoon and then I'd gone off to Times Square—she said, "After that, you did that! How could you?"

I didn't treat her very well because I wasn't really in love with her—I was just trying to be. I'd sort of prepare myself to see her and get all worked up and fantasize about her and force myself to think about her. She'd come into the city for a visit. I'd live in the aura of the visit and feel glowing for a few days, and then it would wear off and I'd be obsessed with men again.

I cried myself to sleep for months after we broke up. But at the same time I was terribly relieved. It was a tremendous pressure on me to live up to that relationship, to be able to function sexually with her.

Later, when I'd begun to have sex with men and didn't feel that pressure, I began to develop close relationships with women. I like women. I feel much more comfortable and can share more with women because they're less threatened by my homosexuality. Women seem to be very much less rigid in their perceptions of life. There's a stereotype that they're more open, more receptive, and I think there's some truth to it. They don't have a structure in which they have to fit their perceptions to the same degree that many men do. And the anxiety of perceiving something that does not fit into that structure is not present.

About a month after I broke up with Sharon, another of my girl friends, I came home one night and was listening to music and I said to myself, "I'm going to do it." And I realized that for the first time in my life—I was thirty-one—I was actually going to have sex with a man.

It took me a good while, until the end of that midwinter break, actually to do it. I went to the porn theaters the whole vacation and was tempted several times, but I was incredibly tense. Finally I approached one guy. He was very standoffish, not friendly at all. He wanted me to worship him, and I just wasn't that interested, so I left him.

Before that, of course, in the theaters, I'd had men sit down in the seat next to me and come on to me. I'd always had a negative reaction to that. I'd change my seat, or I'd say, "Look, I really want to sit alone." They'd always go away.

Anyway, one afternoon I went to a theater, saw a guy who looked nice, sat down in the row in front of him, and let my hand dangle over. After exchanging a few looks with him, I reached out and grabbed his cock. He immediately bent over and in a very friendly voice asked if he could come up and join me. I said sure, and so he came up and sat next to me.

After we had fondled each other for a while, he asked me if I wanted to suck his cock. I said, "Well, I've never done that before, and I'm sort of afraid"—very childlike, innocent, you know. Anyway, I accepted his invitation and sucked his cock a little and enjoyed it. And he sucked my cock a little, which I also enjoyed, though I was awfully nervous. And—this is the type of thing that happens every so often in those places—he said, "Do you want to come home with me?" This was the first time I went home with another man.

So we left the theater, and when we got out into the light, I looked at him and thought, "Jesus, this is a normal guy." He was real nice-looking, not a knockout, but very, very appealing: sort of blond, very American-looking, nice smile, tall. We got into his car and went to his place in the Village.

He turned out to be bisexual. There were *Playboys* all over his apartment. And when he found out that I'd also had affairs with women, he was excited because he thought I might be into the two of us getting together with a woman. But I couldn't get into that. I wasn't as interested in women as he was, and certainly not in casual sex with a woman.

We had that child's-play kind of sex. Since my analysis, I'd thought that my homosexual drive was to have a father and to be loved by a man because I'd felt so rejected by my father. But my experience that night was of a very strong desire to give love to another man. That was a revelation that felt quite wonderful. Among other things, it helped me realize that my father had not always been unaffectionate. At times I had refused his attention.

He had to be at work early the next day, and so he drove me home when it was over. I went right to sleep. The next morning I felt really glad about what I'd done. Of course, when I came down with a sore throat, I was sure that I'd contracted gonorrhea. I hadn't. I was really lucky because it was a very positive first experience. It took place on January 30, 1977, almost ten full years after we graduated.

Unfortunately, that very same day I had to go to my parents' house for supper. I remember actually crying on the train because I knew I'd enjoyed the experience tremendously and because I knew it was another step towards the realization that I was really gay. I was crying because I didn't know how I could possibly fit into my family if I was gay. I was quite mixed up. And it was very hard to suppress all that emotion while on the way to see my parents.

They said nothing that suggested they suspected anything, but I'm sure they could sense that I wasn't all right. I just said I was very exhausted, that I'd been to a party and had too much to drink or something like that. I felt very guilty, but I was determined to keep having sex.

Soon I began to go to the baths. That's where I really began to enjoy having sex with men. I met so many different kinds of people there, types of people I wouldn't otherwise run into, types my parents probably never see at all. Going to the baths helped me realize that there had been a certain stultification in my life because of my family background. Between my father's elevated professional position and my mother's social background and my having gone first to one good school and then another, I'd absorbed a lot of expectations that I'd accomplish certain things along certain lines, that I'd be true to the family's class and status, that I'd go with the "right people." In their own peculiar way, the baths helped me see the limits of these expectations.

Paul's done more than anyone else to help me understand a lot of this. Shall I tell you how we met? It was after I'd moved back to Boston and become comfortable going to bars.

I'd been to a concert at Symphony Hall and enjoyed it so much that I decided to do a little barhopping. I went to Darts and then left there and went over to the old Herbie's. That's a leather bar, what some might call an S & M bar. I was drawn to it because I found it more of a catchall bar than the others. Behind the dungarees and the leather costumes there are more different kinds of people than in a bar like The Napoleon, where everybody dresses up. Besides, I'm attracted to masculine-looking guys.

I got there about one o'clock. I saw Paul standing around, and I tried to catch his eye because he appealed to me. He didn't seem to notice, so I wandered into the sort of back room they have there, a men's room that's very active. When I came out, he was standing right outside. I went over near him and stood there for a while and then got to talking to the guy opposite me. We started talking about Harvard—the other guy was in the Med School.

I was attracted to the Med School guy, but Paul was really more my type. He was wearing a marine's fatigue cap and dungarees and a leather jacket. He looked very masculine and kind of dignified. At a certain point he flashed his smile, and I liked his expression. So gradually I tried to include him in the conversation. And I guess something we said made us realize that we'd both been in the same college class.

As Paul and I became very chatty, the other guy drifted off. That was okay. I was thrilled at meeting somebody from my class. I always enjoy running into old classmates. Until proven otherwise, I assume that means we're likely to have something in common. Paul and I were both amused that we had discovered each other in Herbie's. We talked about that, about the happenstance of our never having known each other at Harvard and of our running into each other in this low-life locale, this bar that resembles nothing so much as a motorcycle club. And we found out that we both knew something about art and literature.

But we didn't go home together. He left me at a certain point. He said, "Well, I have to get on with what I came here for." Then he went downstairs.

I was disappointed but not devastated. It had happened so many times by then—either my rejecting somebody sexually

or their rejecting me—that I didn't take the rejection personally. As I'd become promiscuous, I'd become much more sensible about sex.

So I went downstairs myself. I saw Paul on the other side
of the bar, but I didn't come on to him again. I wasn't going
to make a fool of myself. So I stood in a place where I knew
he could see me but where I wasn't facing him. After a few
minutes he came up to me and said, "Call me some time, if
you like. I'll give you my phone number." He had a lot of
confidence. I'd never have been able to do that. Later he told
me that he'd gone home and looked me up in the yearbook.

A few days later I called him. Don answered the phone,
and I said to myself, "Who's that?" It was very awkward.
Then Paul came on the line. I said I was so-and-so, and he
was quiet, and I said I felt awkward calling him up and
asking if he'd like to get together. He said he'd like to, but he
didn't express any great enthusiasm. And finally he said,
"Well, I'm living with someone, and so I'm always careful
about getting involved with someone else." After he told me
a little about his relationship, I felt much better.

So Paul and I met at the Paradise Café—have you been
there yet? It's the first gay bar that's opened up in Cambridge, appropriately enough about halfway between Harvard and M.I.T. We had dinner at a little transformed eating
place just around the corner. Then we went for a walk along
the Charles and talked a lot. Then we went back to the Paradise and talked some more. And then finally, sheepishly, I
asked him home.

We had sex. It seemed pretty good to me. I liked his body,
and I liked his cock. But I was already so into him emotionally that those things didn't make much difference.

I was relieved to find that he also felt a little awkward the
first time, partly, I think, because it wasn't his typical role-
playing scene. He told me later that he'd actually brought
along the usual handcuffs and things that he takes with him
when he's looking for a scene, not knowing what I'd be into
or what I'd want.

That night he left. He said sarcastically, "I'm going to do
something awful. . . . I'm going home. I'm just not used to
spending the night with other people."

Before he left he told me a little about his relationship with Don. He portrayed that as a lifetime commitment—at least as a commitment that had till that point lasted eight years. You project that ahead, and it's a potential lifetime commitment. He described himself and Don as being like an old married couple, and he admitted that he didn't know what to make of his attraction to me. But it seemed obvious that he wasn't looking for a lover.

So I drove him to his car, which was parked near the Paradise, and dropped him off. Then I got really depressed. I thought, another one of these! For all of Paul's candor, I'd gotten my hopes up. There was nothing to do but to go home and sleep it off.

Around noon the next day—I was still in bed—there was a knock at the door. I called out, "Who's that?"

He said, "It's Paul."

So I let him in, and he said he was sorry for waking me but that he didn't know how else to contact me. I'd just moved into the apartment and didn't have a phone yet. And he said, "I'd like us to be friends."

We ended up going out to lunch together. We went to Harvard Square and had a sandwich and then walked back. At the apartment, we kissed each other, but we didn't have sex again. When he left, I felt very good.

A few days later, he sent me what he called an approximation of a sonnet. Shall I read it to you? I have it right here. It's called "The Paradise Café, Harvard-Yale Weekend." It really captures the spirit of the bar, the insides of which look something like the bar at the Hasty Pudding club.

> "The theme's nostalgia, I infer, the name
> itself recycled on the same location
> and further ironized in restoration.
> I order beer and cruise them, frame by frame,
> these college teams entrusting some slim fame
> to frail photography's perpetuation:
> an aura time's reduced to decoration
> at the other end of Cambridge from the Game.
>
> I wait for you, amused to think
> this too's a kind of Harvard date.

I wonder if you're always late
and whether to get another drink
and whither (fare forward, Class of '67!)
this tryst with you in a bar named heaven."

I was very touched. I just couldn't believe that this guy was sending me a poem.

Then I had to go home for Thanksgiving. The night before I left I went to Herbie's and actually ran into Paul. I think I partly hoped to meet him there, but I was surprised anyway. We talked but didn't go home together. He was up to his usual tricks.

After I came back from Thanksgiving, we began to talk on the phone a lot, sometimes for hours at a time. And we went out more and more. We got close rather quickly. A lot of talking will do that.

Pretty soon I had told him about all my experiences with women. He seemed to feel threatened by that. At points he'd say, "Well, it sounds as if all your best experiences were with women. How can I compete with that?"

And I said, "Yes, but those are the *only* relationships I've had. Everything else has been just one-night stands."

I told him about all the ambivalencies I'd had about being gay. I don't think he likes to hear about those, but he understands. He's smart enough to comprehend almost any point of view. He's very smart. He went through Harvard on a Merit Scholarship and was a Harvard National Scholar and Phi Beta Kappa. He comes out of a very ordinary background—his parents didn't even finish high school—but he's made it to the opposite end of the spectrum.

His background—or maybe I should say my background, or the difference between our backgrounds—has been one of the things we've talked about a lot. He's had misgivings. He says he's always gravitated to people with backgrounds more like his own, not to people with backgrounds like mine, and that he finds my background disturbing politically as well as socially. In a joking way, he often uses the phrase, "When the revolution comes. . . ." Well, you know, my family isn't exactly waiting for "the revolution."

✦ ✦ ✦

I realized on my own the need for gay people to exercise political influence. But I certainly was brought to that point by all Paul's talk about gay politics. I was impressed with the intelligence with which he spoke about being gay. He made me think.

Before that I'd thought gay politics meant "gay rally in New York." And I had the attitude that you should keep what you do in your bedroom to yourself. I thought, "Why should people be going to gay marches? There are more important issues." I didn't see why homosexuals should flaunt their sexual propensities in public.

I still don't like too much flaunting, except at the baths, but after I began to see Paul, I realized that a tremendous amount of the problems gays have sustaining relationships has to do with the difficulty of finding social contexts in which they can be natural, of finding models, of finding support for their efforts to develop relationships. It was when I began to feel really sad that we couldn't be more open about our relationship that I realized that there had to be gay people who were flaunting, so people like me wouldn't have to be so frightened about being more visible.

It isn't like sex is something we have a lot of choice about. One of the reasons I've talked so much about my heterosexual experiences is that I feel that I've made a very extended attempt to choose the other alternative, to be what is socially acceptable. And I just couldn't do it. I think it's important for people to know that there are many homosexuals who can't be happy being anything but homosexual.

I don't want to live in an altogether gay community. I want to be part of the world at large. But I'd like to be able to walk down the street feeling free to look at attractive men. I'd like to be able, in an uncontrived way, to be open about my relationship with Paul. If the situation were such that we could live together, for example, I'd like it to be clear that we weren't just roommates who'd found one another through an ad in the paper, but that we were really committed to one another emotionally and sexually. I'd like to be able to have him meet other friends of mine who are straight and be introduced as my lover and not have them feel uncomfortable for the rest of the evening.

As things have turned out, we've been very lucky. One day when Whit was coming over for lunch, Paul had spent the night, and I said, "Why don't you stay and meet my brother?" So we had lunch together, which was very pleasant. And then I began to introduce him to other friends of mine.

We seemed to begin thinking of each other as lovers almost before we knew what was happening, and we've been able to be remarkably natural about that. But I still haven't introduced him to my parents. I'd like to, but I don't know when or how that will ever happen. I've done a lot to declare my independence from my parents, but they're very powerful figures and I don't know if I'll ever be able to be gay when I'm with them.

If I'm the only preppy who's agreed to be in your book, that's probably because most of them come from families like mine—reserved, New England-type families in which people simply don't talk about their personal lives very much.

I have some negative feelings about preppies and about the part of me that is preppy. I think they tend to be very conventional people, people who have difficulty experimenting, people whose identity comes largely from their families and their heritage. They seem to be afraid to do anything that contradicts that. They are often people who believe that happiness lies in continuing to be part of "the family" rather than in striking out in new directions. They already *are* something. Why should they risk that for the sake of the greater good or some higher morality?

I guess I've got some of that in me, but I've always had the feeling that there are lots of things about lineage and tradition that are ridiculous and that I just couldn't accept. I like to think that I don't surround myself with lots of status symbols. I guess I wouldn't be talking to you if I didn't feel that there is something for me out in the world that just isn't there in the family.

The family, for me, has been a kind of closet. Now at least I'm peeping out the door.

10

PAUL DETROIT

Paul, a professor, had the most impressive intellect of all the classmates I interviewed. And he was easily the most thoughtful and articulate when it came to the meaning of gay life and its politics. For almost four hours he lectured eloquently on every topic I put forward, expounding on his own voyage of self-discovery and on the social dynamics he saw at work in the gay male subculture, assessing these in terms of social and political good generally, and talking sensitively and sensibly about his relationships, both the long-standing one with Don and the new one with Cottie.

Though the intellectual attention he gave gay matters was only an avocation—his own academic work was in philosophy—he seemed to have thought about gay life as much as I had, and from the standpoint of his involvement in a sector of the gay male subculture that was much more controversial than any I had experienced personally. Paul had for many years been involved in the "leather set"—the gay insiders' term for what most outsiders refer to as the S&M scene, or sadomasochism. He had been active in the leather scene in Boston during his years as a Harvard graduate student and as an assistant professor at Amherst. He was much less involved in it at the time of my visit, though he still "tricked out" a bit and went for that purpose to "leather bars."

At the time of our interview, Paul's main concern was his career —there was no tenured position available for him at Amherst and he was being forced out into the job market at a time when it was tightening up all around. He was also very wrapped up in his relationships: the eight-year partnership with Don and the new lovership with Cottie.

He was in the process of making a dramatic alteration in his relationship with Don. They'd been drawn to each other the first time they'd met, had begun to live together a few months later, and had stayed living-together lovers until Paul had gotten his job at Amherst. Then Paul had taken an apartment near campus and spent his weekends and vacations with Don. Their relationship had never been monogamous sexually, and they had each had "affairs," but this was the first time that one of them was developing a substantial "secondary relationship."

At Amherst, Paul had been very political, becoming a leader of the gay student group, speaking out in the college newspaper and before the faculty senate, even writing a letter to *The New York Times* using his real name. Now he was reluctant to be so open—in the current job market he just couldn't risk the liability it would hang on him professionally. But he was willing to add to the debate I was trying to raise by speaking candidly about some very controversial subjects. Like me, he saw that the truth showing-and-telling at the heart of liberationist politics was nothing more than that which was also the purpose of scholarly inquiry and the foundation of modern democracy. In fact, if only for the compatible political, academic, and democratic ideals we both cared so much about, Paul was willing to do everything he could do to help me—except reveal his real name.

In high school and early in my college years I dated women off and on. Later I began to do so less and less. It was as if I realized that it wasn't for me, that I wasn't getting particularly close to any of the women, and that I really didn't care.

I knew some terrific women. I dated Radcliffe women almost exclusively, women I met through my classes and whom I liked in some way. But I could never really get to be close friends with any of them—which I now feel is a shame.

I suspect that that was true for a lot of college men in those days. It was difficult to be on friendly terms with women, because such a big deal was made out of relating to the opposite sex. There were all these rituals—you had to ask a girl out on a "date" if you wanted to spend any time with her—and all these regulations, like limited visiting hours for women in the dorms. All they did was to buttress the expectation that every guy interested in a girl was interested ultimately in having sex with her.

Finally, during the break between semesters in my sophomore year, I went to Chicago, which is where my high-school girl friend was going to college, and slept with her for the first time. After that it was as if I didn't have anything to prove anymore. Somehow, having finally slept with a woman, I felt freer to admit to myself that actually I was far more attracted to the guy who lived next door to me in Kirkland House than I had ever been to a woman. This hit me right away. In fact, I wrote my old girl friend a kind of "Dear John" letter almost as soon as I got back to Cambridge.

What I felt for this guy was very romantic. The feeling was familiar; I'd experienced it in high school on occasion. It wasn't a matter of being sexually aroused by him, but of feeling a certain pathos, a deep and inexplicable desire to be really intimate plus the sadness of knowing that that probably wouldn't happen. It's hard not to feel a sense of helplessness in the face of such strong attraction. It's something I still feel frequently when I see someone on the street whom I find incredibly attractive. It comes as a kind of pang.

At some point, much later on in my life, I got to thinking that pretty boys and attractive men are like flowers: There are lots of them in the world, and you can't possibly stop and smell every one of them, let alone pick them. You just have to give in and let those fleeting moments of incredible attraction occur, knowing that they'll pass, and enjoy them.

So that's how I felt about the guy who lived next door. I certainly didn't know what I wanted to do with him. I had a vague notion of wanting some kind of physical contact with him. I suppose I thought that if we touched in the right way, one step would lead to another, and the pang would be satisfied. But I didn't know where those steps would lead us. I wouldn't have known what to do. It would have taken someone who'd already had gay sexual experience to show me what to do. I had an unbelievably vague idea about what men could actually do sexually with one another.

The first year I was in graduate school I lived on Beacon Hill. And being so close to Sporters, I—what shall I say?—I just went wild. I began to explore a lot. And explore is really the right word. At least in my case, it took sleeping with a lot of different people and trying a lot of different things to learn *how* to have sex, how to enjoy it. It certainly wasn't something I'd been taught.

In my exploring I met several other gay men from Harvard, but I never really became close to them. For the most part, I didn't run with other Harvard people or with other graduate students or professionals. I met and slept with a wide range of people from all walks of life.

I wasn't open about my sexuality in the Philosophy Department, but I certainly didn't feel I'd be ruined if word leaked out. By the time I was in graduate school, it was perfectly obvious to me that plenty of people were gay in the University and in academe generally. Still, I kept quiet about my sexuality. What was the motivation to talk about it? One side was work and one side was play.

In a sense, I liked leading a double life. It was like getting away with something, having a little secret all to myself. And if I sound as if I'm making something positive out of what was in fact a bit of oppression, well, I suppose that's what I did.

In the spring of that first year of graduate school, I met Don, the guy I'm still living with. In effect, almost as soon as I came out, I started what has turned out to be a serious, romantic, long-term relationship. I was still interested in exploring sexually, and I continued to have casual sex with other people. But after I met Don, I was no longer looking for a potential lover in such encounters. My casual sex— quickies in the john at Widener, an occasional one-night stand from Sporters—was simply an additional, uncomplicated kind of excitement. I wasn't looking for anything more in it, and I enjoyed it for the immediate, limited sort of thing it was.

I'd met Don at Sporters one night and gone home with him. Some chord was struck, and we started seeing each other regularly. I can't describe what that chord was exactly. I guess I'd say something like "personal chemistry."

I found Don very beautiful. I really like beautiful faces—that's usually the first thing that grabs me about someone—and he appealed very much to me in the bar. It wasn't exactly love at first sight, but there was that "pang" I talked about.

By the way, I don't think there is anything mystical about that. I think in any given case one could figure out all the factors of personality, situation, homoerotic history, timing, looks, and even body language that would explain it. It is nevertheless a very striking effect.

When Don and I got together, we found that we liked being with each other, and so we got together more and more often. I liked the alternative sort of life he provided me with. He lived in Brookline in a little apartment that had been made out of a garage on land that had originally been the garden of a rather grand house. The house was gone, but a small, beat-up greenhouse and parts of the garden remained. There was still a bed of asparagus, for instance, that came up through the grass each spring. I loved going out there on weekends, and during the summer I spent even more time there. We worked in the garden together, and we sunbathed on the roof.

Our relationship didn't ever involve sexual fidelity as a condition. We liked each other and wanted to see a lot of each other. That didn't leave much room for relationships with other people, but there was never really any expectation that we'd necessarily be "faithful." Living on Beacon Hill made it easy for me to continue to go to Sporters for one-night stands. Of course, for a long period after we first met, I simply wasn't interested in other people sexually. But gradually, even as I remained close to Don, I experimented sexually with other people more and more. So did he, though some-

what less than I did. He was older. He had already had his
promiscuous youth.

Eventually what happened is that he and I went our separate ways sexually for the most part, even to the extent of
having affairs with other people. Yet when the sexual part of
our relationship faded, it wasn't as if the relationship had
failed to become what it was supposed to be. Because we'd
never said what it was supposed to be. It was what it was
from day to day, month to month, year to year. Now it's been
eight years. We still have the feeling that there are no con-
tracts; we just see how things go.

We're both pretty considerate of each other. We almost
always have supper together, no matter what we do later in
the evening. Off and on we go out to a movie or the ballet or
to a concert together. If I want to go out alone, or he wants
to go out alone, we do so.

Neither one of us brings other people back to the house
for sex. The house is big enough, but neither of us wants to
inconvenience the other. I don't want to risk waking Don up
late at night or having him run into some stranger in the
kitchen at breakfast. It's just common courtesy. If I've met
someone in the bars who doesn't have a place for us to go,
too bad. Having sex isn't so important to me that I'd disregard
Don's feelings or that I'd keep a place of my own just for that.

We're very respectful of one another and very caring for
one another. My only regret is that we're not very physical
anymore. I'd like to sleep with him more than I do; I mean,
just sleep with him. I think the most beautiful thing of all is
sleeping regularly with someone you love. You can have great
sex with lots of people. But how many people can you really
enjoy sleeping with? I think it has to do with knowing someone long enough and well enough to feel completely trustful
in bed. There's a special way you've learned to fit together.
I'd like to sleep with Don and be more physically affectionate, but he's just not a very physical person. That's his upbringing—his family is not very warm.

I'm not interested in him sexually, and he's not interested
in me sexually any longer. But what we have is still a loving,
gratifying relationship. We have always treated our relationship as a follow-your-nose kind of thing. Neither of us has

ever wanted to tempt fate by making particular promises. I think there's a certain wisdom in that. But obviously, after all this time, we have some kind of commitment to one another, whether or not we've said it in so many words.

I've come to believe that our arrangement is a very workable one. We know an awful lot of gay couples who are approximately our age who either go their own separate ways sexually or bring people back for threesomes or foursomes. The implication of all this is that even if they're still sexually involved with each other, they want more. This seems to be such a common pattern among gay male couples, and one that seems to work out so well, that I suspect it's the couples who still feel bound by the heterosexual tendency to equate sexual monogamy with fidelity who have the most problems with their relationships.

It seems to me that we're talking now about sex not as some kind of expression of deep feeling or involvement but as recreation, sex viewed simply as something that is fun to do with another person, that's a kind of physical therapy. About recreational sex.

Homosexual sex presents the problem of who's going to do what to whom. It's more obvious, let's say, than in the case of heterosexual sex that there's more than one thing to do and more than one way to do it. When you're with the same man over time, this isn't much of a problem because you can experiment with each other, change roles, and do what seems natural and interesting and appealing on any particular occasion. But if we're talking about the kind of one-night stands that are the norm of recreational sex in the gay male subculture, then there is more of a problem. I'd found frequently in such cases that neither I nor my partner had a particularly good time because we went home with the wrong expectations of what we might do. Since we were actually strangers, we couldn't possibly know what the other would like.

I therefore became interested in the practice of wearing signs—keys or handkerchiefs—to tell what I wanted to do sexually, and in seeking out people who also indicated with signs what they wanted to do. This was more or less in the interest of greater efficiency. It was a way to make sure that

I wouldn't go home with someone who liked to fuck when I didn't want to be fucked, to make sure that there wasn't going to be this awkward moment when I'd have to say, "I just don't like this."

And the signing appealed to me not only for its efficiency but also for its security. I mean, it's a solution to sexual insecurity, isn't it? You know what role you're going to play, what the other person is going to be expecting of you. All this, mind you, has to do with recreational sex, not with sex as any kind of deep communication.

Looking for recreational sex of this sort is like looking for a card game. If your game is bridge, you're looking for someone who wants to play bridge, not someone who's interested in poker. It's like a sport: What's at issue is not just which game you're playing, but which position. By the way, the scene I'm describing is often loosely called S&M, but that's misleading. I'm talking about role-playing in general and not necessarily the kinds of experiences involving pain that are usually understood as sadism and masochism.

There are two aspects of signing. One has to do with dominance and submission, with the inclination to be active or passive. Which side you wear the sign on deals with that. You wear keys on a snap that fastens to your belt loop so that the keys hang on your hip. If you wear the keys on your left side, it means you're interested in playing a dominant or active role. If you wear them on your right, then you're interested in a submissive or passive role.

The other aspect of signing has to do with specific sexual scenes—that's done with handkerchiefs, colored bandanas. The various colors refer to various scenes. Navy blue, for instance, is the sign for fucking. If you wear a navy blue handkerchief in your left back pocket, it means you like to take the so-called active role in fucking; if you wear it in the right, that you like the so-called passive role. Lots of people who are fucked are very active, of course, but their role is generally referred to as the passive one. Anyway, that's my understanding of signs. I don't know to what extent, if any, the practice varies across the country.

I started out with a handkerchief and eventually added the keys to underline the significance of the handkerchief. But

I've also worn the keys without a handkerchief, in which case they sign that you're interested in being active or passive in general, in more than one scene.

It's funny. I've noticed that some people are very discreet about their signs, so much so that you can barely see that they have a little bit of a handkerchief peeping up out of their pockets. Perhaps that's because they're embarrassed about being so explicit about their sexual interests. But it seems to me that that defeats the very purpose of signing. If you're very discreet about showing your sign, then you can't be sure if the person you've made a liaison with has actually seen it.

When I decided I was going to go in for signing, in the name of efficiency, I decided to be quite bold about letting my colors show. I should add that I've never really been rigid about what I do sexually, and certainly not in what I've done sexually in the context of my longer-term relationships. The signs are just an expression of preference in the context of purely recreational sex.

As I began to sign myself in the bars and to frequent bars where this practice was prevalent, I discovered that a greater variety of sexual opportunities presented themselves to me than I was originally looking for. I discovered, for instance, that someone who was interested in being fucked might also be interested in being tied up. I'd always been rather disturbed by the idea of sadomasochism. Yet the fact that I found it disturbing also gave rise to a certain fascination. And the more I experimented sexually, the bolder and more adventurous I became.

Since I was signing myself as dominant, I inevitably met people who were signing themselves as submissive and who suggested to me all kinds of things to try: spanking, whipping, bondage, fist-fucking, water sports. At various points and in various circumstances I tried things as they presented themselves to me.

It's clear to me that I wasn't personally obsessed with any of these activities, or even with the role-playing, so much as I was curious. I've read somewhere that Virgil Thomson, the composer, said that cooking is like sex. You should try everything twice, first to see how it's done, and second to see how you like it. I have more or less that attitude towards sex. I got a certain satisfaction not so much from working out fantasies, because my fantasies were markedly undeveloped along those lines, but from doing things that were forbidden and naughty. I used to think, my God, if they knew at Amherst and Harvard what particular perversion I'd gotten involved with over the weekend, what would they think? There was a certain glee in sowing oats that were ever wilder.

It seems to me that the so-called S&M scene, whether we're talking about actual sadomasochism or just role-playing and its various manifestations in general, is not only something that appeals for its efficiency to those who want quick, anonymous, uncomplicated sex, but also something that appeals to people who are, after all, a little jaded. It's something that tends to be for the older set—not people in their twenties who are just coming out and experimenting, but people who have been around a while and who've seen most of what there is to see and who are ready for the more unusual varieties of sexual recreation.

Did you find, on the whole, that your passive partners were psychologically well-adjusted, competent, and successful people? The conventional wisdom is that people into masochism are even sicker than those into sadism. Have the masochists you've met been healthy?

I have no reason to believe they weren't. It certainly was by no means the case that people who enjoyed being submissive sexually were pathological people or people with special problems. It was merely that they got pleasure out of a certain type of sexual role-playing. That was very clear. I never found any correlation between what they liked to do sexually and their education or job or degree of self-esteem. They seemed to be people who just enjoyed playing a passive role sexually.

You said, citing that quote by Virgil Thomson, that you tried things the first time out of curiosity and the second time for experience. Were there any unusual sexual scenes that, the second time around, you found really stimulating, really to your liking?

If anything, being with so many so-called masochists helped me realize how limited I was as a so-called sadist. I just didn't have any sadistic imagination. Occasionally I'd run into someone who presented me with a sort of carte blanche, saying, "Do with me what you will." And I found that compared with theirs, my imagination was really quite meager. I don't think I'm very well suited as a sadist psychologically.

And certain activities I just didn't like. I mean, I've whipped and spanked people a few times, but I could never really bring myself to do it in a wholehearted way. Which meant, therefore, that I wasn't really pleasing them, because they were looking for people who were really into that. The thing I always liked most in this context was fucking—that is, fucking with no concern other than my own pleasure, with someone who liked being in that situation and liked playing the role of merely servicing someone else. But I'm pleased that I've tried all the other things that I have because it's helped me understand my sexual interests.

But aren't there some sadists who have truly pathological drives that they express through the S&M scene, and doesn't this make the whole thing, at least for the masochist, pretty dangerous?

Well, first of all it seems to me that there's danger in any kind of anonymous one-night stand. That's what that terrible movie *Looking for Mr. Goodbar* was about. If you're in the habit of putting yourself in a vulnerable position—let's say, naked and in bed with a perfect stranger—then you have to use your judgment about what kind of people you associate with. In that sense, the danger is less in the S&M and more in the kind of judgment you use in picking people to fool around with.

If you have a lover and you're both into S&M, then presumably you can trust each other, you have worked out just what your limits are, and you know just what you want. Then there isn't any kind of danger, is there?

No doubt some people, especially those into really outlandish scenes, have an inclination to court danger. But usually the idea is to know very clearly ahead of time what's going to happen. After all, word of mouth is very strong in the gay community, and in any gay bar, after you've hung out for a while, you get the word on who's really into what. Needless to say, drugs can be a special problem in this context, because they raise the possibility of losing control over what you're doing.

I've never felt truly sadistic, but I've observed other people who, I feel sure, could be quite dangerous. Yet I think that they're the exceptions rather than the rule among that subset of gay people who go out wearing leather, handkerchiefs, and keys and all that. I want to emphasize that there is a tremendous appeal just for the gear and for the trappings and for the general experimentation with roles. How many people get involved in really weird scenes I don't know, but I suspect that it's a very small number.

As I mentioned earlier, it seems to me that in recent years there's been a kind of S&M chic. An awful lot of people are wearing leather and trying to look macho because, for one reason or another, it's a fashion fad. The image is obviously a supermacho image. In a way it takes what gay men are not supposed to be and goes after it in the most extreme way.

It's exaggerated masculinity. I think that's part of the appeal. I mean, if all your life you've thought of yourself as less than male, by society's definition, then there can be an appeal in playing out that role at its strongest, most obvious, and, in a sense, corniest. You know the joke: "Too butch to be straight!"

I think a lot of the supermacho look one finds among gay men today is also a manifestation of the fact that gay men are more comfortable with the thought that they are, after all, men, and that they can be just as masculine as any other men. In earlier generations of gay men, there was a tendency to act out the societal stereotype of what a homosexual was, to camp it up a lot, to call each other by women's names, and to act caricaturishly feminine. I think that in the wake of gay liberation, all those stereotypes have been belied, and gay men no longer feel that they have to be sissies just because they're homosexual and society associates homosexuality with effeminacy.

Do you think that this whole fascination with supermasculine demeanor reinforces macho behavior and macho attitudes?

No, not necessarily. It does within the role-playing scene itself, of course. That's the point of the role-playing. If you're playing the tough guy, trying to look and act dominant, then obviously you're not going to try to appear kind and loving! You try to play the part. But that doesn't necessarily say anything about what kind of person you are outside the role-playing scene. As a matter of fact, if one listens to the conversation in a leather bar, one soon realizes that, as a group, these men are no more and no less macho or effeminate in their personae than any other gay male group.

So you don't think the growing gay male fascination with traditionally masculine ways has been accompanied by a revival of traditionally macho attitudes about women and about so-called female roles? You don't think it reinforces attitudes and behavior that are antithetical to the goals of feminists and others fighting for sex role liberation?

I would like to think that gay men identify with the feminist movement because they realize that they, like women, are victims of the traditional denigration of attitudes and behavior stereotyped as female. Yet I find that there is a lot of prejudice against women among gay men. There's no getting around that. On the other hand, the argument can be made that when one is aware and integrated enough to play with sex roles, to experiment more with ways traditionally considered male or female, one is more apt to let oneself enjoy nontraditional roles to the extent that one wants to, and to be more open to letting members of each sex express themselves in whichever ways they wish—in as many ways as they wish.

In general, I think that the bad name that sexual role-playing has is unwarranted. I can understand it when people who consider themselves liberationists say that we shouldn't be hung up on roles. Sure, I'm against role-playing —if what that means is that we get stuck in a role that society defines for us, even though that may not be appropriate for us and doesn't do justice to our full human potential. In that sense, I understand people who put down role-playing. But I think that too many of them fail to see that when role-playing is a case of conscious and deliberate choice, its effect can be very liberating, because it helps us to see how much of our lives is a matter of assumed, and therefore changeable, roles.

Isn't sexuality most of the time a kind of role-playing? Where is there some kind of innate sexuality in one's self? You might as well ask, where is the real person in one's self? We do have a sense that there is, in fact, a basic self that is different from the roles we play. But a lot of our daily life is undoubtedly what can be described as role-playing. Don't we talk this way? Don't we say "my role as citizen," "my role as husband," "my role as son"? And don't we call the styles of life, especially the racy styles, "scenes"? It seems to me that role-playing is actually the central fact of social life, that which distinguishes life in society from some hypothetical Rousseauist existence outside of society.

Implicit in all you say is an endorsement of sexual promiscuity.

I think the way so many put down promiscuity has to do with how we're taught to value sexual activity. And whether it's specifically because of our Puritan heritage or more generally the price we've paid to become civilized, clearly our society overvalues sex in an hysterical way. It's all too tied into social institutions—marriage, first of all.

Most people are terribly narrow-minded in their conceptions of sex. Sex can be something as simple as playing cards with someone who enjoys the same game you do, something terribly profound and integrative and expressive of a complete and long-term commitment, and a lot of things in between. But in our society, at least until now, we've taken much too monolithic a view of what sexuality is, and this has loaded people up with all sorts of problems and difficulties and anxieties that have little to do with sex. There ought to be more room for people to have more sexual experience, to get to know the alternatives, to learn what they enjoy. And this shouldn't threaten the deep emotional relationships that people have.

After all, in the long run, sex—sex per se, at its lowest common denominator, sheer sexual activity just for fun—is not really very important. It seems to me that this is something that gay men have managed to learn. Precisely because gay men tend to be more promiscuous sexually than straight people, they have something to teach people about sexuality.

Sex is treated with such a great deal of secrecy that there's a lot we'd never learn if we didn't have varied sexual experience. There are things to do sexually that just don't occur to people. To some extent this has changed in recent years with the proliferation of sex manuals, but there is still a difference between reading about how to do something and actually becoming good at it. The best way to learn about sex isn't to read about it, but to do it, and to do it with different people who know different ways to do it.

We aren't born knowing how to have sex with one another. We have to learn how to have sex. But we're not taught how by any institution in our society. We are taught to read, to do math, to have good manners, but we aren't taught to have sex. We learn it only in the most haphazard and fragmented way. No wonder people have problems with it. I think promiscuity is probably the best way to learn about sex, and that promiscuous people probably have a lot to teach society about sexuality.

I'm not saying that promiscuity is in itself always desirable, but rather that it can be useful. There are times when it isn't desirable. There are times when people need to concentrate on building and maintaining significant relationships. But within the context of a good, well-established relationship, promiscuity need not always be a threat, and it might even be helpful or enriching to the relationship.

How about the promiscuity that involves sex in public places?

You can't separate out that sexual scene from the general context of gay sex in this country. As long as homosexual behavior has to remain hidden, as long as society makes it so difficult for homosexuals to meet and relate to one another and have sex in legitimate places, homosexual sex is going to crop up in inappropriate places. If we could all go to the drive-in with our boyfriends and neck and not worry about it, well, then it might be different. But because we can't, we have little choice but to turn to gay subcultural scenes—some of which exist in public places. So, on the one hand, I can't defend sex in public in a situation where it violates the rights of other people. On the other hand, I can't feel very harsh about that, knowing how little legitimate room there is in our society for gay sex.

It can't be denied that some people then get hung up on this scene. Sex in certain public locales—mostly certain public parks and public toilets—becomes a taste in itself. But that taste is not something bound up with homosexuality per se. It develops out of the particular situation of homosexuality in our society.

Out of the blue a case occurs to me. What about blacks and whites having sex in South Africa? This undoubtedly goes on. I'm sure it's criminally proscribed. Where do they do it? How does it happen? Would it not crop up in shady, peculiar circumstances?

So you think that homosexuals who are into the gay male subculture have something to teach society at large?

Yes. Specifically, they have a broadened perspective on sexuality, and the ways it's related to the institutions of society. They've worked out all kinds of alternative interpersonal relationships. These represent the great range of ways in which people might get along with each other sexually, romantically, and socially. I think that this range ought to be thought of as something that enriches society. Certainly the subcultures created by oppression have negative aspects, but that doesn't mean there aren't positive things that can be drawn from them.

To take an analogous case, as part of the definitions men have imposed on them for a long time, women have been told not only that they're physically weaker than men, but that they're less aggressive psychologically and necessarily more loving, more domestic, better with the kids, and so forth. Well, it's important to let women who don't fit this stereotype be themselves. But maybe others, by playing out so-called feminine roles, have learned certain things that they wouldn't want to leave behind and that are very valuable for society to know about. In rejecting forced adherence to traditional roles, I don't think women want to reject the valuable things they've learned from what they've specialized in, even if that's been the result of oppression.

I think the case of gay people is similar. That latest Masters and Johnson study suggests that gay people satisfy each other sexually better than straight people do. Which isn't very surprising after all: If you're dealing with someone who's the same sex, obviously there's no big mystery about sexual equipment or sexual mechanics. And if gay people are better at sex, maybe they can teach straight people something, particularly in a period in which marriage is having such a rough time and so many straight people are in their own various ways trying to work out alternative arrangements to the traditional ideas of what marriage and family and parenting are all about. Well, gay people have been experimenting with all these things for a long time. Presumably they have something to share with others.

So you think that gay people are different from straight people?

Well, the old response would be, "No, of course not. They're no different." And in essence, no, we're not different. When one gets down to the basics about what kind of people homosexuals are, what kind of lovers they are, what kind of students, what kind of workers, what kind of citizens, I don't think they differ at all.

I do think, however, that gay people have a perspective that's valuable and unique and that shouldn't be lost in the attempt to show that they're just as good as other people. I don't want to be just as good as other people in that sense. I want to preserve what being gay has made me. There are bad aspects of that, no doubt, but there are also good aspects.

I think in particular that gay people, just by being gay, have a critical distance on this society, whether or not they realize it or put it to any use. And critical distance is something it would be valuable for everyone to have, because it's the first step toward changing society, toward improving it.

How will you answer those who contend that you've limited the degree to which you are fulfilled sexually and emotionally because you've assumed such a well-defined role within such a well-defined sex scene?

But I haven't limited myself to a single role or to a single scene. The whole point of my becoming comfortable with playing the macho role was that it helped me not to take all that so seriously. I have a career in academe that isn't any part of a macho role. I have a gratifying, comfortable, long-term partnership with Don that doesn't have anything to do with dominance or submission. And in the last six months I've also been involved in another relationship that transcends sexual role-playing, a situation in which the sex is communicative, where it's what's being said sexually, not what's being done, that matters. It's been very romantic.

I certainly wasn't out looking for romance when I first ran into Cottie. But there was some kind of personal chemistry that drew us together. I was at the old Herbie's, a bar that was about as leather as any in town, wearing my usual gear: faded jeans, boots, my black leather motorcycle jacket, a fatigue cap, and a big heavy snap with lots of keys on my left hip. I was dressed to project a certain image, obviously.

Cottie and I were both standing on the landing between the first and second floors. That's where the men's room was. The men's room at Herbie's was a cruisy place, and, I think, Cottie was waiting for someone to come out. He looked at me, and I looked at him, and I thought he looked very square. He'd just come from a concert and was wearing ordinary dress-up clothes, not gear. He was certainly displaying no signs of any kind.

Anyway, we got to talking, and he told me about himself, and it turned out we'd gone to college together. That put me off right away. When I go out to the leather bars, I'm not interested in getting to know people. I'm after a certain sexual scene, the more efficient and exciting the better. Nevertheless, we had an interesting chat. It turned out we knew a few people in common.

But it was getting late. I only go to bars very late. The idea is not to spend a lot of time in the bar, but to get there for the last hour or forty-five minutes. That's when people really get down to business. I wanted to get on with my business. I didn't want to waste any more time talking to him.

Politely I said, "Good-bye, nice talking to you." Then I went downstairs and cruised around. But the more I thought about it, the more I realized that, for some reason, I did want to see more of him. Not then, of course, but sometime in the future. So I went back up to him and gave him my name and phone number and said, "Call me sometime and let's get together, if you like."

A few days later he called and we made a date for dinner. After dinner we took a walk across the bridge by M.I.T., then went to the Paradise Café, and then back to his place. It didn't work out very well sexually at all. I'd been used to a certain scene, and, for all I knew, even though he hadn't been signing himself when we first met, he might nevertheless have been attracted to the scene my gear implied. It was soon obvious that he wasn't. The whole business turned out to be uncomfortably improvisatory and undirected.

After it was over, I got up, got dressed, and went home. That was my usual way. I've always avoided staying the night with someone after casual sex unless staying is something I really want to do. He seemed disappointed.

The next morning I felt as though there was unfinished business—I had something more to say or to do. So I went over to his place—got him out of bed in fact—and said, "Look. I don't know. We didn't seem to hit it off in bed last night, and I left and all that, but that doesn't mean I'm not interested in you. I think I'd like to see you again. I think there's something possible."

So we started seeing each other, regularly. It turned out to be very good sexually in no time at all, and soon the personal angle was so important that the matter of what we were doing sexually just wasn't that important. The sex became a self-expressive and communicative kind of thing rather than a matter of playing with certain roles.

What was it that you found attractive about him?

In particular, I found his face attractive. He has something of a nineteenth-century romantic poet look—pale skin; dark, curly, unruly hair; dark eyes. And he projects a certain vulnerability that's appealing. It's more projected than real, I've learned. In many ways, I'm more vulnerable than he is.

Did you find that you talked a lot about Harvard—about old classmates and the college years?

To some extent. I think more than anything else we checked out each other's ideas about things, as if testing our common ground, because apart from Harvard, our backgrounds were so different. Certainly we talked about our sexual development and how poorly that was facilitated by life at Harvard. A good deal of our conversation, then and now, does have reference back to our college years. Even though we didn't know each other as undergraduates, didn't take any of the same courses, nevertheless, in a very curious way, there is a common ground there. We speak the same language about a lot of things. I can't quite pin it down.

Same generational experience, same world view . . . ?

Cottie and I are very different intellectually. I'm far more political than he is. I don't mean that I'm now active politically, but that I'm more inclined to look at things from what is broadly a political or social viewpoint. So I wouldn't say we have the same world view by any means. But there's something. It's almost as simple as knowing a generation's jokes or certain catch phrases or certain references to the books and records and cultural events of the period. Maybe that doesn't really mean a whole lot, but it puts us at ease with one another.

Did Cottie present himself as gay?

He presented himself as pretty damned ambivalent—which bothered me. He talked a lot about his sexual experience with women. That was a real turnoff and a source of ambivalence on my part. I don't like being considered less fulfilling or less promising than a woman. I think that many gay men would feel this way.

I'm all for bisexuality in theory. And who knows, maybe it's the way of the future. But my own experience is that heterosexual sex doesn't mean anything to me. I've slept with women, not just my high-school girl friend but a few women later on. And I like women. But I'm not at all interested in them sexually myself.

And when it comes to being part of someone else's bisexuality, in a relationship, I can't help but suspect that given the priorities that our culture sets for us, I'm going to be relegated to second-best. After all, society says it's better to be straight than gay. If someone came up to me and said, "I'm bisexual, and I'd like to see you at the same time that I see a woman," whatever I feel about that theoretically and politically, my understanding of reality would incline me to say, "No thanks." I wouldn't want a relationship in which I didn't feel that I was just as good as the female partner, and given the way our society is, I just don't think I'd be allowed to. I'd want to be just as presentable to family and to friends. And, frankly, I wouldn't be.

Well, Cottie didn't present himself as bisexual. He presented himself as gay, but as having had a great deal of experience with women and feeling that, after all, that was the ideal. That offended me. After all, he was suggesting I just couldn't be as good. And he talked about his homosexuality as a problem he was working on with his psychologist.

I must say that about the time I met him, he was coming around to the idea that he didn't have to think of it as a problem anymore; that even if he were to be bisexual, he didn't have to think of his homosexuality as the bad or the lesser or the naughty side of his sexuality. He was beginning to see it could just be "another" side. I'm glad about that. If he hadn't at least been beginning to think that way, I suspect I'd have been put off right away.

It's not that his feelings weren't understandable. You see, up to that time his homosexual activity had been, in his view, rather sleazy and undesirable. Mostly it had been just quickies—and quickies of the quickest and most mechanical sort —in porno movie houses and the baths. He'd never had a relationship with another man. He'd never felt, about a homosexual, "Here's someone who'll be my friend and who can be presented to other people as my friend." So his image of homosexuality was rather narrow.

I think that our affair appealed to him as something comparable to an affair with a woman—I mean, in the sense that he could begin to integrate it into his life, could introduce me to his friends and family. I was a respectable person, in his eyes, and our relationship wasn't merely a naughty thing to do in secret on the weekends.

Did he view you as someone with whom he could talk about past activities he thought of as sordid and have you assure him that they weren't necessarily sordid and that he wasn't despicable because he enjoyed them?

Yes, I think so. Although he'd already done a lot of that with his shrink. He'd been seeing this psychologist, who I think is on the Harvard faculty, and who's apparently very nonjudgmental. So he didn't need that from me. But I liked listening to him tell me about all that stuff. I was amused and touched by his naïveté. He's actually had a good deal of homosexual experience, but it's been of one narrow kind and within a relatively short span of time. No matter how many people he might have run into, his experience just couldn't compare with mine. I found that somehow touching.

Did you start trying to raise his consciousness?

Oh, in a general way, yes. There are all kinds of ways that people—even homosexuals—unconsciously put down homosexuality, just by virtue of the way they're socialized in this society. And it takes a conscious effort, a kind of consciousness raising, to make someone aware of that. Cottie had never really thought about it. He was inclined to be down on other gay people, which I think is a real sign of that socialization, without realizing why.

I think that when someone new to the gay subculture takes the step of going into a bar or the baths for the first time, he probably sees people he's never, or seldom, been exposed to before: some extremely effeminate people, some leather numbers, perhaps an odd transvestite or genderfuck person. But because he's crossed some kind of magic line and is in there with them, he feels identified with them and finds that very threatening to his self-concept. So he rebels by putting them down, as if to say that he's not really like any of them. It's only after a while, with some thought, that he realizes that he's not necessarily identified with any other gay person beyond also being gay, and that gay people, just like straight people, come in a broad range. Just because he and a transvestite or a would-be Hell's Angel leather queen are in the same bar doesn't mean that there are any other similarities between his life-style and theirs.

The range of people one tends to find in a gay bar: That's an interesting and significant thing about gay life. It gives you exposure to a complete vertical slice of society. If you've been narrowly wrapped up in your own class—upper middle class, middle class, whatever it might be—when you go into the institutions of gay life, you're inevitably going to be exposed to many more different kinds of people than you would ordinarily be otherwise. That's one reason why every gay has the opportunity to develop a critical distance on his or her position in society.

That's a long way of saying that Cottie had been "out" so short a time that he still felt a lot of that need to rebel and to put down other gay people. My attitude—the one I tried to get him to share—is live and let live. I feel I've seen almost everything at this point, and I don't think I'm easily shocked. I don't see why people shouldn't try different things, work out fantasies, play whatever games appeal to them. I mean, people ought to feel free to do what they feel like in the realm of sex—as long as it's consensual and doesn't infringe on the rights of others, of course. Where's the harm?

How about Cottie's famous family background? Did you recognize that instantly?

I didn't have to recognize it. He told me about it almost as soon as we began talking. I think that's one of the ways he compensates for feeling insecure in a cruisy bar situation. He told me a lot about himself right away.

I thought that strange. In that context, looking for a trick in a meat-rack bar, I don't go into such details. That's not the kind of information I'm out to communicate. If anything, his family stuff put me off. I'd never hung around with fancy, wealthy WASPs. Some of my friends in college were fancy, but not quite so fancy as Cottie's family or with so many Harvard connections. His great-uncle was one of the University's most famous presidents. His father was on the Board of Overseers.

You didn't find that attractive?

I found it attractive and unattractive at the same time. I asked myself, "Why now?" When I had the opportunity in college to go after people like that, to explore worlds above me, I didn't. But I find I'm quite fascinated and amused by his upper-class world, though I think it's very limiting. I point out to Cottie, much to his annoyance, all kinds of ways I feel he's blinkered by his class background. There are all kinds of things he ought to know about and just doesn't.

Do you think that his background has made it harder for him to identify himself as gay?

I don't know. That would suggest that his background is so impressive and puts so many pressures on him that he feels he's letting something down if he doesn't follow exactly what's expected of him. He's already had to face one battle along these lines—going into art. No doubt his father would have liked him to become a lawyer or a banker or a Harvard president, something more lucrative and prestigious by Establishment standards. But his family is very cultivated, and they've paid for all of his art training and also for all of his therapy That doesn't suggest that his life is the great act of rebellion he sometimes makes it out to be.

I don't think there's necessarily a direct correlation between family social niche and difficulty in dealing with homosexuality. There are people from average and low-class backgrounds who have great difficulty coming out. Everybody has to deal with family pride. I suppose that the lower your family status is, the less you have to lose. And the upper class is perhaps more visible than the lower classes. Still, I think that personal factors and circumstances affect any given individual's struggle with homosexuality more than social class. I think, frankly, that Cottie is rather immature, that he stayed a child for a long time, and that that's why he's had so much difficulty with his sexuality.

So you see his putting down homosexuality and other gay people more as a function of the fact that he's just come out than that he has all that lineage to live up to and all those social and economic opportunities to safeguard?

Well, it's a little bit of both. I want to say that he's gotten over putting down gay people just because they're gay. But he still puts down people who don't talk as nicely as he. And he still has a tendency to judge people as stupid or unintelligent by the way they look. That's a bizarre notion to me.

Cottie went to Andover. They spent a lot of time there comparing I.Q.'s and test scores, which recognize only one kind of intelligence, of course. My experience was very different. In my high school, only a few of us had high I.Q.'s, and while we no doubt enjoyed a feeling of superiority on that count, we didn't talk about it. There were too many other and more conspicuous ways in which people were ranked, and we had to respect and to cope with these as well.

I'm always putting Cottie down for being so judgmental. I've tried to show him that there's a narrowness that comes from never having gotten a perspective on his own class. He's no more or less a product of his own class and circumstances than anyone else is. The difference is that some people—especially those for whom it's an advantage—can step away from their class long enough to get some perspective on it and to see what part of their class background they like and what part they're better off abandoning. Cottie's class is so high that he's seldom found it advantageous to step away from it. I think he's beginning to do this for the first time as he gets into the gay world.

I think that's rather important. Class is really the dirty secret in American life. People pretend it isn't there. But it is. I've spent a good deal of time in England, and I was horrified at how strong the class factor still is there. Maybe for that reason I'm extra sensitive to it here. And maybe for that reason I jump all over Cottie about it every now and then.

How does Don feel about Cottie?

Well, I think he feels somewhat threatened. I'm still not sure how I feel myself. I met Cottie at a transitional point in my professional life, when I was feeling particularly unsettled and vulnerable. I just have to wait and see what happens. That's also Cottie's attitude. And I suspect it's Don's. In any event, a six-month lover measured against a nine-year partner—after all, I've had affairs before—is not an occasion for immediate alarm.

I feel a certain degree of conflict. At this point I feel very strongly for both of them, though in different ways. I feel a great deal of ambivalence about a lot of the things that Cottie stands for. At the same time, he opens up a different world for me, a world I haven't previously chosen to explore much even when I've had the opportunity. And this gives me a certain perspective on my relationship with Don.

Are you being open about the whole thing with Don and with Cottie?

Pretty much. I edit a little bit when I talk to each of them. But the fact is that they're both there. Don knows I've been seeing Cottie a couple of times a week for six months, and no matter what I say, that says something. Meanwhile, Cottie knows that I have certain loyalties to Don and that, after all, I live with him.

Do you tell Don when you're going out to see Cottie?

Oh sure, that's simple politeness. If I'm going to be away the full night, I say so. In general, I try to let Don know my plans ahead of time so that he can make his own plans accordingly. And I'm not the only one in a new relationship. Don's been seeing someone recently too. It's not as intense as with Cottie and me, but it's there.

Do you talk to each other about how your feelings are evolving?

A little. We don't go into that in great detail. I think I'd probably like to talk about it more, but Don isn't interested in hearing about it or in talking with me about his feelings for other people. But there's no big secrecy going on or any animosity.

Do you have any qualms about saying so many controversial things for the record?

Occasionally, as we've been talking, I've asked myself, would I really want that in print? But I've also asked myself —and I decided to do this before you came over today—why not just go all the way and tell it the way it really is. There's not that much I'm ashamed of. If I'm not ashamed of what I do, then why not talk about it? Besides, it seems to me that that's the whole point: We're made to feel ashamed of too many things unnecessarily.

We all do things we're ashamed of, mind you. But if we're talking about general attitudes toward sexual activity and relationships, well, I'm not ashamed of mine. My God, this *is* 1979. A great many people know about these kinds of things. Why shouldn't they be associated with Harvard? They're *at* Harvard. Harvard is not a world apart.

But would you feel comfortable, for instance, if you knew that your old thesis adviser, who can still influence the course of your career, knew who you were when he read the book?

Well, it may seem overly bold of me to say so, but I don't worry much about that. In any case, he shouldn't be evaluating my worth as a scholar and a teacher on the basis of my sex life. He's supposed to evaluate me intellectually, not morally.

The fact is, I have enormous respect for the man who supervised my thesis. He's a brilliant man, and he's a man who's always willing to learn. He was one of the few who really learned some things during the years of student revolt.

Do you think many people at Harvard will be as open to what you have to say as you think your thesis adviser will be?

I don't know. I can think of people in the Philosophy Department who would be horrified and who would mark me forever if they guessed who I was—not so much for what I've done, but for blabbing about it.

I think this is an important point. At Amherst I was involved in a campaign, which was eventually successful, to get a statement forbidding discrimination on the basis of sexual orientation on the official records. The initial response was to the effect: "Look, we're not going to discriminate. We don't really care about what people do in their personal lives. But let's not talk about gay life, let's not single out that group in the bylaws. It's bad publicity for the school."

Okay, it could be bad publicity. But I just didn't feel it was good enough for the administrators to say, "Amherst has never been antigay. For Christ's sake, look at old professor So-and-so, everybody knows he was gay." The point is that everybody didn't know he was gay. And if we in the campus gay group didn't know he was gay, then not enough people knew. What we wanted was not that homosexuality be tolerated as something that's okay as long as it's in its place—that is, its hiding place, the closet—but that it have an open place, that it have its say, that it find its own overt expression. So I don't have much patience with people at Harvard who might say, "Of course, there have always been plenty of homosexuals in academe. One knows who they are, and they know that people know. But at least they have the decency and the manners not to go around proclaiming it."

In a sense, if I don't proclaim it, I'm participating in the oppression of it. It's analogous to saying that Blacks are okay as long as they don't act Black, so to speak, as long as they straighten their hair and wear Brooks Brothers suits. It's acquiescing in an image that isn't you. It's accepting someone else's view of what you are, even when you know that that view is terribly ignorant, misguided, and benighted. People who do that are oppressed.

I sympathize personally with people who for one reason or another feel that they have to be discreet and can only be gay secretly. I don't think that homosexuals should come out unless they feel like it and are in circumstances that make it feasible. I'm not condemning closeted gays. But I am saying that if everyone stays completely closeted, if no one speaks out, we're not going to make any progress. Those who feel they can't speak out ought at least to recognize how those who do help everyone else.

Do you have feelings of loyalty to Harvard?

Yes, in a sense. Loyalty has a very old-fashioned ring to it. I do have a certain love for the place. But that doesn't cover up what seem to be real flaws at Harvard. Chief among them, in this context, is the oppression of gay people.

I'd really like to know what it's like to be openly gay at Harvard today. If there are anywhere near as many problems for gay people as there were in my own day, I'd say something is seriously wrong with Harvard. And I mean Harvard per se, not simply Harvard as part of the whole society.

I don't know if loyalty is the right word. While I see shortcomings here and there, I am very happy with the education that I got at Harvard. I feel grateful for having had it. And I feel that in dealing seriously with a topic of some importance to me, like this, I'm doing justice to that education. I'm following my education through rather than disregarding it or making a spiteful gesture against it.

In the last few years, whenever I've gotten requests from fund raisers at Harvard, I've sent off letters telling them that I won't contribute a penny until they let me know what Harvard is doing officially to assure nondiscrimination on the basis of sexual orientation for faculty, students, and staff. I've never gotten anything but the most mealy-mouthed responses in return. That doesn't strike me as a hopeful sign.

One of the arguments that was made by opponents of an official nondiscrimination clause at Amherst was that it would brand Amherst as especially sympathetic to gays—that if Amherst did it alone, Amherst alone would be put in a bad position. Now if Williams would also do it, if Harvard would do it, if Yale would . . . Amherst would have no objection. They didn't object to what we wanted. They just didn't want to stick their neck out alone.

Well, if Harvard can't do it, who can? That's why I think it so important that Harvard put something in print and quit beating around the bush. I don't care how chummy things are with the gay students' groups or how easy gay life may be. I'd like to see Harvard take the initiative of officially prohibiting discrimination on the basis of sexual orientation. I'd like to see it acknowledge that society has a lot to learn from gays. Other colleges and universities might find it easier to do this if Harvard takes the lead.

Afterword

We have found our voices. We have found our selves. We have found our voices because we have found ourselves.

Who are we? Whom do we represent?

Broadly speaking, we stand forth as homosexual members of that generation of Americans who came of age after World War II. We had our elementary and secondary school years in the fifties and early sixties, when there seemed no limit to what America could accomplish. We went to college and usually graduate school believing that we could make the American dream ours, and everybody else's. Not least because we grew up in such affluent, peaceful times, we were unusually well-educated, idealistic, ambitious, and self-confident.

Partly because we were exposed to so much, and partly because we were so equipped, permitted, and driven to make sense of all we saw, most of us did a lot of reassessing of traditional views and values. For some it was realization of just what "The Bomb" meant for the prospects of human survival that made us think so much about what we hoped to achieve and how we wanted to live. For others, it was immersing ourselves in foreign cultures, spending time in ghettos, working with the mentally ill, listening to the complaints of Blacks, and seeing insensitivity to political and social diversity in Cold War foreign policy: phobia, containment, and Vietnam. Slowly but surely, most of us came to believe that we could do a lot for our country by challenging what we saw as popular myths that made life unnecessarily difficult for proponents of unpopular beliefs, members of minority subcultures, and individuals with nonconforming life-styles. Our aim was to make America mightier, stronger, richer, and more humane by helping it be truer to its founding ideals of liberty and respect for social diversity, more adaptively pluralistic, and more sophisticated psychologically.

We believed most of all in human potential. Having been raised in a culture leavened by liberalism and enlightened by psychology, we were sure that every person had some contribution to make and that each individual could make life better for other individuals simply by treating them right in day-to-day life. This meant, at a minimum, empathizing with varied life experiences, understanding human complexity, and accepting nontraditional modes of self-expression and social interaction.

When we encountered unfamiliar behavior, especially if there seemed to be strong negative prejudices about it, our inclination was to be open-minded. We worked to understand our personal anxieties, to learn from experience, and to move beyond what we thought of as conventional, middle-class, and bourgeois biases. Ignorant generalizations, simple-minded condemnations, unwarranted snobbery, and unreasonable ostracism and punishment: these we abhorred. Compared to our parents and grandparents, we were both optimistic about human nature and sanguine about social evolution. We believed that human beings should be allowed to be whatever they were naturally and wanted to be, as long as they showed the same respect for others and were nonviolent. Everything not obviously antisocial we considered part of the natural, reasonable, evolving social order.

It was this understanding of the universe and its unfolding that the first chroniclers of our generation's mores called "new consciousness." Because we tended to approach behavior that most found foreign with the spirit of open-mindedness called for by new consciousness, and also because we usually came up with opinions that ran counter to conventional beliefs and enjoyed activities that were deviant by prevailing standards, we were called a counterculture—indeed, "the" counterculture. In fact, of course, there have always been individuals who have thirsted for self-actualization and social betterment as we did and explored taboo terrains with countercultural perspectives. Historically, these have been intellectually adventurous and self-reflective people, found particularly among pioneers of every sort and in religious life, educational institutions, media, the arts, and the upper classes. The difference was that we were a mass of young people from many different backgrounds eager to spread ourselves throughout society and let everyone know what we were doing—not least because we were convinced that others could learn and grow as we had.

By sharing our new consciousness with others, i.e., by "raising consciousness," we hoped to endow our country with a "new morality." The more historically minded of us saw this new morality as an adaptation of traditional American ideals to contemporary realities. Some people called our new morality secular humanism, but for most of us it was humanism based on new and sophisticated understandings of religion.

We promoted our new morality in a variety of ways. Many of us thought it most important to extend it internationally, seeing the war in Vietnam as the most dramatic evidence that traditional American ideals were being betrayed. Others made our major focuses of concern hunger, poverty, exploitation, deprivation of rights, materialism, development, and the plundering and pollution of the natural environment. Most of us thought Richard Nixon's behavior during the war and after Watergate the greatest sign that there was a need for new morality at the highest levels. Many of us became so disillusioned with the Establishment that we felt it necessary to withdraw in order to build afresh. Some of us hoped to do this through action—by learning to live off the land, getting involved in small towns, joining grassroots political groups, committing ourselves to public-service professionalism, and lending our support to "new politics." Others set out to improve the quality of life in more personal ways—by trying to understand our feelings and to act naturally, being nice to everyone we dealt with, thinking a lot about everything we did and said, expressing ourselves artistically, exploring our senses, experimenting with altered states of consciousness, unraveling the mysteries of metaphysics, assaying other cultures and unfamiliar religions, and understanding the processes of human development, particularly how to attain self-awareness and sensitivity and how to enjoy naturalness and intimacy. Only a tiny, misguided segment of our generation advocated, engaged in, or approved of revolutionary violence.

Those of us with a special interest in human relationships worked hard to make ourselves good in them. Indeed, it was not only because we had come to believe that being comfortable with ourselves was the only existentially sensible way to live, but because we thought it important to be fair, honest, and intimate in our relationships that most of us worked to be centered, fulfilled, and self-sufficient as individuals. So we engaged in more introspection, spent endless hours working things out with lovers and partners, read psychology, went into various kinds of therapy, and joined together in rap groups to figure out what our needs, wants, and problems were.

All of this made us receptive to the ideas espoused by the most prominent politically minded members of the counterculture, who called themselves liberationists and assumed a commanding presence in the New Left. They told us that by banding together with those whose problems and interests seemed most like our own, we could come to grips with our selves, lend a hand to those we were most suited to aid, and help society at large see how popular prejudices were limiting human potential and creating unnecessary pain. Led by liberationist leaders, we banded together with other countercultural members of our generation in "the Movement," then made that movement as pluralistic as the new society we hoped to build by coalescing as Blacks, Latinos, Native Americans, women, disabled people, Asian Americans, and the elderly. It was as members of these groups that we developed awareness of our races, sexes, looks, and age, and promoted understanding of racism, sexism, "looksism," and ageism. Those of us who separated out as homosexuals called ourselves liberated lesbians and gay men as we developed countercultural and liberationist outlooks on our sexuality and our subcultures. We believed it our special mission to comprehend and to teach others not only about homophobia— the irrational fear and loathing of homosexuals—but about sexual liberation.

More specifically, then, what we foregoing sons of Harvard represent are a new breed of male homosexual. We speak in behalf of liberated and liberationist-minded gay and bisexual men. For our countercultural and political ambitions have led us into intensive explorations of homosexual feelings, sexuality, sex roles, gender, and the gay male subculture. Indeed, we are working to endow traditional gay male customs and institutions, which are not always engaged in healthily and responsibly, with the new morality so championed by our generation.

For a good many years, most of us accepted what traditional moralities said about homosexuality. We believed our homosexual feelings wrong and sick. We thought it sinful and perverse to engage in homosexual acts. We did everything we could to ignore, repress, and replace our homosexual longings. We viewed sexual promiscuity as a sick and sinful substitute for substantial relationships.

This made us less happy, healthy, ethical, and productive than we might otherwise have been, and we were not the only ones to suffer. We spent endless hours feeling alien, odd, inferior, bored, trapped, and hopeless. We wasted time and energy struggling to be heterosexual, pretending to be asexual, and presenting ourselves to others as straight. Some of us added hypocrisy to our dishonesty by making fun of "fags" and "queers" while secretly savoring homosexual fantasies and covertly engaging in homosexual behavior. Others of us were so hung up by ignorance, guilt, delusion, neurosis, and obsession that we had unnecessary conflicts with our parents and unwarranted fallings-out with friends. We dated, romanced, lived with, and even married women without being candid about our deepest sexual yearnings, our secret homosexual activities, or our conflicts about them. We had sex at inopportune times and in inappropriate places. We mistreated sexual partners, lovers, and life partners. We were profoundly untrue to ourselves while admiring elders who spoke glowingly of character and integrity, and touting openness and honesty about feelings as virtuous extensions of these.

Each of us had our eyes opened in different ways and at different times—after discovering and reading something positive about gay life; after realizing the foolishness of some common belief about homosexuality; after seeing or meeting acknowledged homosexuals who belied all the stereotypes and refused to project them on us; after having a series of experiences in the gay male subculture, or enjoying an extended homosexual relationship, and learning from personal experience that these involved much that was good. The milestones in our journeys of self-discovery were turning points in our processes of coming out. For us liberation meant learning how to admit to ourselves that we were homosexual; to think highly of other acknowledged gays; to enjoy the homoerotic dimensions of our life experiences; to approach in enlightened ways customs and institutions characteristic of the gay male subculture; to accept our sexual preferences as perfectly natural; to let nongay intimates know what we really felt; to find more time and energy to devote to our jobs, families, nongay friends, communities, and country; to discover some sense in traditional ways and some truth in conventional wisdoms; and to give homosexuality a natural, appropriate, and enriching place not only in our personal and social lives, but also in our professional and political pursuits.

It is this last that sets us apart most dramatically from older generations of homosexuals, though more and more of these, like growing numbers of younger homosexuals, are following our lead. For there have always been individuals with strong homosexual feelings who have let traditional moralities and unflattering stereotypes keep them repressed, conflicted, guilty, and self-hating. This is what has made homosexuals suicidal, socially irresponsible, destructive in their relationships, distorted in their attitudes, values, and demeanor, and less productive than they might be. But there have also always been individuals—countercultural long before the sixties and seventies—who have accepted their homosexual feelings without great difficulty and found ways of diverting or expressing their homosexuality without experiencing or producing unnecessary problems. Indeed, what most makes us a new breed of gay men is less our liberation than our desire to let others know about it. It is our conviction that by being open and outspoken about our homosexuality, we can contribute to a reduction in suffering, the enhancement of social harmony, the pursuit of knowledge, the progress of sexual and sex-role liberation, and the advance of both humanism and productivity.

In short, what most distinguishes those of us who appear in this book, and the many other liberated gay men who could and would share similar stories, is our sense of liberationist politics and its grounding philosophy—essentially, the belief that accurate information, powerfully presented, will result in more sensible laws and more enlightened living. Gay liberationists want every-one to know the truth: We homosexuals are as competent, reli-able, and responsible as nonhomosexuals in the familial, fraternal, civic, and occupational parts of our lives, which are very much like everyone else's. In increasing degrees and growing numbers, we are also healthy, ethical, and successful in the homosexual parts of our lives. Yet we have learned to approach sex, sex roles, intimacy, love, and relationships in very nontraditional ways, and this sets us apart as gay men.

Acknowledgments

Writing this book has been a labor of love because it has involved working with so many who are important to me. From each of my Harvard classmates—those who appear in the preceding pages and those who have lent strength and support behind the scenes—I've learned much not only about Harvard, homosexuality, gay life, and the counterculture, but also about myself. Rusty has done more than anyone else to help me understand all of these, and for this—as well as for his helpful critical perspective on several drafts of this book—I want to express my deep love and gratitude explicitly.

For aid with practical matters these last few years I have no one to thank more than the Grant family. In addition to sharing valuable perspective, Howard Grant has helped me appreciate not only his extraordinary esthetic sensibility, but also the challenging world of parenting. With her careful editing of two versions of my manuscript, his wife Judy steered me back to basic English and stirred me to weigh my idealism against her reality. Jessica and Colby Grant, vivid personifications of that reality, reassure me that our culture is evolving in ways I think healthy.

I have learned, too, from the lives and the perspectives offered by friends who have read chapters of this book. These include old friends—Rob Straus, Sherry Foti, Barbara Milton, John Brockman, Dick Ferguson, Richard Baltzell, Pam Reiser, Patty Straus, Jim Landis, Zeph Stewart, my mother, my brother Jeff, and my sister-in-law Terry, a writer herself. Also new friends—Jeri Mersky, Jonathan Galassi, Lisby Mayer, and Helena Worthen. I want to thank Sylvia Turner, B. J. McNeil, and Dolores Henricksen for their typing.

This book is the third product of my unusual collaboration with Toby Johnson. The first is my *Politics of Homosexuality*, primarily a history of the gay and lesbian liberation movements. The second is his *Myth of the Great Secret*, an explication of the countercultural perspective on existence responsible for the ideas and lifestyles championed by so many liberationists. For *Sons of Harvard*, Toby served not only as listener, believer, editor, and partner in planning and investment, but also as original transcriber of the transcript material and cheerleader for the tentative first drafts of the manuscript. He is continuing his part of our work in a second book, now titled *Finding Spiritual Meaning in the Sexual Underworld*. My next book will be my own report on the study of male prostitution, pornography, and sexploitation that Toby and I have been working on for the last two years under the auspices of the federal government.